Inside
Organizational
Communication

LONGMAN SERIES IN PUBLIC COMMUNICATION

Series Editor: **Ray Eldon Hiebert**

Inside
Organizational
Communication

The International
Association of Business
Communicators

Edited by
Carol Reuss, Ph.D. and **Donn E. Silvis, ABC**

Longman
New York & London

INSIDE ORGANIZATIONAL COMMUNICATION

Longman Inc., 19 West 44th Street, New York. N. Y. 10036
Associated companies, branches, and representatives throughout the world.

Developmental Editor: Gordon T.R. Anderson
Editorial and Design Supervisor: Diane Perlmuth
Interior and Cover Design: Antler & Baldwin, Inc.
Manufacturing and Production Supervisor: Maria Chiarino
Composition: Book Composition Services, Inc.
Printing and Binding: The Maple Press

Library of Congress Cataloging in Publication Data

International Association of Business Communicators.
  Inside organizational communication.

  (Longman public communication series)
  Bibliography: p.
  Includes index.
  1. Communication in organizations—United States.
  I. Reuss, Carol. II. Silvis, Donn E. III. Title.
  IV. Series.
  HD30.36.U5I57 1980   658.4′5   80-23426
  ISBN 0-582-28235-7
  ISBN 0-582-28234-9 (pbk.)

MANUFACTURED IN THE UNITED STATES OF AMERICA
9 8 7 6 5 4 3 2 1

A000004771821

Acknowledgments

Inside Organizational Communication is an example of what dedicated people can accomplish when they work together to do something for their profession. They represent the 8,000-plus members of the International Association of Business Communicators.

A great amount of the credit must go, of course, to the twenty-one contributors who devoted time, talent and energy to produce the text. The book's editors—Carol Reuss, Ph.D., of the School of Journalism at the University of North Carolina, and Donn E. Silvis, ABC, director of corporate communications at Avco Financial Services, Newport Beach, California—edited manuscripts, supervised editorial details, and held the sometimes fragile threads together. Wilma Mathews, senior public relations specialist at Western Electric, New York, deserves plaudits as the IABC elected officer who organized the team that produced this book in little more than one year. Irene Piraino, IABC research director, juggled administrative details to make this book a manageable package for the publisher and a service to readers.

We wish to thank the following people and organizations for their kind permission to use illustrative material in this book:

The figures on pages 19 and 27 and the illustrations on pages 83, 190 and 268 are reprinted with the permission of the *Journal of Organizational Communication*. The illustrations on pages 83 and 268 were drawn by Curt Hopkins.

The illustration on page 31 is from the *Donnelley Directory Record*, 78/4, p. 10. Reprinted with permission.

The illustration on page 51 is reprinted with the permission of Digital Equipment Corporation.

The employee survey guide on page 58 is from *Communications & Management* September/October 1979, "Cafeteria Communication: A

v

Survey Menu." Reprinted by permission of Towers, Perrin, Forster & Crosby, Inc.

The figures on pages 68, 70 and 72 are copyright 1980 by Jim Haynes. Used with permission.

The upper illustration on page 97 is from *Long Distance Management*, #2, 1980. Reprinted by permission of AT&T Long Distance Lines.

The lower illustration on page 97 is courtesy, *Amoco Torch*, Standard Oil Company (Indiana).

The illustration on the left on page 100 is reprinted by permission of Resources for Education and Management, Inc. Decatur, Georgia.

The illustration on the right on page 100 is from *Food to Grow on: Nutrition from Newborn Through Teens*, © 1979 by Tupperware Home Parties, a Division of Dart Industries, Inc. Reprinted by permission.

The illustration on the left on page 112 is from *ArcoSpark*, November 16, 1979. Reprinted with the permission of Atlantic Richfield Co.

The illustration on the right on page 112 is reprinted with the permission of Ingalls Memorial Hospital, Harvey, Illinois.

The illustration on page 117 is from *International Scene*, July/August 1979. Reprinted with the permission of Diamond Shamrock Corp.

The illustrations on pages 127, 128, 130, 131, 132, 133, 134, 135, 137, 139, 140, 141 and 143 are reprinted with the permission of Nebraska Educational Television Network. The illustration on page 127 is from *Choice*, November 1976, pp. 6 and 7. Image of "The Buffalo Hunt" by Charles Wimar, courtesy of Washington University Gallery of Art, St. Louis. The illustration on the right on page 130 is from *Choice*, June 1978, p. 7. The illustration on the right on page 131 is from *Choice*, August 1976, p. 1. The illustration on the right on page 133 is from *Choice*, October 1977. The illustration on page 134 is from *Choice*, September 1975, pp. 2 and 3. The illustration on the left on page 137 is from *Choice*, November 1978, p. 3. The illustrations on page 139 are from *Choice*, August 1978, p. 1, and May 1976, p. 8. The illustration on the left on page 140 is from *Choice*, January 1976, p. 1.

The upper left illustration on page 151 and the illustration on page 161 are reprinted with the permission of Herman Miller, Inc. On page 161, the illustrations are from *Herman Miller Scanlon News, Jobs, People, Corporate News, Dates* and *Ads*.

The lower left illustration on page 151 is reprinted with the permission of Marathon Oil Company.

The illustration on the right on page 151 is reprinted with the permission of Toronto Dominion Bank.

The bulletin boards on page 158 were designed by Janet Bianchi and coordinated by Laurie Himmelman Alire, both of Varian Associates, Inc. Reprinted with the permission of Varian Associates.

The illustration on page 163 is reprinted with the permission of Boston Edison Co.

The illustration on page 173 is reprinted with the permission of Dennis L. Crow, photographer.

The illustration on page 174 is reprinted with the permission of Duffie White, photographer.

The illustration on page 205 is reprinted with permission—The Toronto Star.

The illustration on the left on page 210 is reprinted with the permission of Blue Bell.

The illustration on the right on page 210 is reprinted with the permission of the United States Chamber of Commerce.

The illustration on page 213 is reprinted with the permission of Bemis Co., Inc.

The illustration on page 217 is reprinted with the permission of Phelps Memorial Hospital.

The illustration on page 224 is reprinted with the permission of Panhandle Eastern System.

The illustration on page 270 is reprinted with the permission of Rainier Bancorporation.

The illustration on page 279 is reprinted with the permission of Weyerhaeuser Company.

And we thank the following organizations for their permission to reprint:

Excerpt on pages 41 and 42 reprinted from *Inside Newsday*, Newsday, the Long Island Newspaper.

Excerpt on pages 57 and 59 reprinted by permission of Xerox Corporation.

Five suggested goals for an employee orientation program on page 204, suggested elements for an ideal annual report on pages 211 and 212,

Contents

Preface

Organizational communication is somewhat akin to the actress who, after spending years in stock, finally lands a Broadway part. She is acclaimed as a surprising new talent, an "overnight" sensation—although she was developing and polishing her talent for years.

Organizational communication has existed for four hundred years. Yet today, almost overnight, communicators are recognized as prime problem solvers, and communication is regarded as a necessity for *all* organizations—large or small, profit or nonprofit, private or public.

Only recently have communicators gained visibility and stature in their organizations. And the trend is not likely to be reversed. Like the actress who quietly played stock for years before her "discovery," communicators were ready to assume major roles in their organizations once communication moved from the status of luxury to that of necessity.

"Communication must be continuous and it must look ahead . . . good communication must be a day-after-day fact of corporate life," says Leslie Warner, former chairman and chief executive officer of General Telephone and Electronics. And James P. Low, president of the American Society of Association Executives, puts it this way: "Communication is an essential fact of life for associations and other nonprofit organizations which depend upon volunteers for their very survival."

Organizational management style has slowly evolved from the "tell 'em as little as possible but be firm about it" approach to one of genuine respect for an ever-changing, multifaceted audience—an audience that seeks information, not commands. The contemporary communicator is prodding organizations to ask themselves, Are we talking *with* people rather than *to* them? Are we candid? Are we listening? Do we look for opportunities to communicate rather than for reasons to keep quiet?

The "house organ," that chatty little paean to baby photos and bowling scores, has, for the most part, been scuttled. It has been replaced by bold and creative publications—newspapers and newsletters and magazines—that rank with the best in writing and design. Today's organizational publications deal with real issues and relate those issues to real people. These publications are supplemented—and, in some cases, replaced—by a wide range of media: bulletin boards and telephone hotlines, video cassettes and films, displays and group meetings, paycheck stuffers, handbooks, manuals, brochures, feedback programs, slide/tape shows, and much more. All are tailored to meet the communication needs of specific audiences.

As the need to communicate becomes increasingly apparent, more and more jobs have been created—jobs that demand sophisticated skills with commensurately high salaries. Organizational communication, in short, has become a profession requiring a knowledge of journalism and communication, the social sciences, business and economics, and organizational dynamics.

A survey by the International Association of Business Communicators found that fully one-third of those queried were in newly created jobs. At the same time, the survey found that communicators now earn, on the average, more than $20,000 a year. Salaries of $50,000 and more are increasingly commonplace as organizational communication becomes a career in its own right rather than a steppingstone to a more lucrative slot.

But the field still can serve as a steppingstone of sorts—communicators, too, must know about their organizations. That knowledge can pay off handsomely. Paul Lyet, chairman and chief executive officer of Sperry Corporation, started out as a communicator. So did Jean G. Cormier, president of CN's Hotels and Tower of Canadian National. Both still consider themselves communicators. Mardie McKimm has moved steadily up the ladder since 1972 when she joined Kraftco. Today she is senior vice president, public affairs, and is on the board of directors of both DuPont and Woolworth, among other companies.

The authors of this book have established careers for themselves in this business. They are respected as leaders in this paradoxical young profession with a long history. The authors, in conjunction with the International Association of Business Communicators, regard this book as a way to return something to their profession and the people who work in it. The book represents their commitment—and IABC's—to the future of the profession and the education of future communicators.

We hope that *Inside Organizational Communication* will serve both as a text for students and as a resource for practitioners.

John N. Bailey, ABC
Executive Director
International Association of Business Communicators

Inside
Organizational
Communication

PART I

ORGANIZATIONAL COMMUNICATION

It's so easy for people to quit listening to what is being said and to begin listening for what might be said. In business and other organizations, discovery of the gap between these two poles of information has created a radical albeit slow to evolve change in the philosophy of organizational communication, directed to everyone with whom the organization can be involved. To recognize, identify and address these audiences is the primary challenge of the contemporary communicator. The chapters in this section examine the challenge more closely and offer a base from which the organizational communicator can operate.

CHAPTER 1

Communication in Contemporary Organizations

ROY G. FOLTZ, ABC, APR

PARKINSON'S LAW: The vacuum created by a failure to communicate will quickly be filled with rumor, misrepresentation, drivel, and poison.

Organizations are people, not boxes on a chart. So there's just no way an organization can operate without communication. The organization will die when the communication nerve cells are paralyzed or don't develop. Yet there is probably no other function about which so much discussion has produced so little real understanding. This is a critical issue because the effective use of communication in an organization can mean the ultimate success or failure of that organization.

Organizational communication is *the* vital link in the chain of events comprising the process of managing a business. It is the single factor that makes an organization viable, successful, effective, enduring. More than any other element, the communications of an organization project the "personality" of that organization to its internal and external audiences.

Definition

What does *organizational communication* mean? It means different things to different people. In fact, there are probably as many different definitions of the term as there are practitioners in the field. But the definition used here is simply this: organizational communication is the *exchange* of information, ideas and feelings down, up and across organizational lines. Or, in a word, *exchange*. It says it all.

5

Organizational communication isn't and wasn't always defined that way. There are those who think of communication hardware only when they hear the term. Others confine the meaning to the transmission of information. Others equate communication and media. But these meanings are only parts of the whole. All must be utilized effectively to promote the *exchange* process and set the tone for communication in an organization. Although many of the examples cited in this chapter refer to employees and work situations, the principles apply equally to all organizations.

As I see it, organizational communication has two primary responsibilities: (1) to support organizational objectives, policies and programs; and (2) to meet audience (employee, member) needs. The two responsibilities can be viewed as contradictory or mutually exclusive, but doing both jobs well or closing the gap between the two becomes the real and constant challenge to organizational communication and organizational communicators.

The key to gaining support for organizational objectives, policies and programs is to serve the organization's internal audience: to know what information they want and the media they prefer. Even though these needs might never be met completely, people who feel they "belong" and are important to organizational success will be much more likely to support their organization than those who say that "management hardly tells us anything and they couldn't care less about what we think."

The Audience

In recent years, technological advancements and the availability of mass media have had an impact on people's perceptions. The social environment has contributed to increased demands for candor in organizations. Overall levels of education and income have risen. The work-force profile is changing: more young people, women and minorities are part of the work force. It is virtually impossible now—and will be even more difficult in the future—to lump employees into a single group having the same interests and similar information wants and needs.

There is also a growing recognition of the multidimensional nature of audiences. Employees, for example, are also voters, stockholders, consumers, community residents, and so forth. They have always had more dimensions than most communication with them would seem to indicate. Certainly there is an awareness that they come from different environments and have different backgrounds and different points of view. Historically, though, employees were viewed as owing gratitude and loyalty to a firm simply because it provided them with a job and took good care of them. And with respect to communication, the party line was pretty much "just tell 'em what they need to know." It was expected that the organization's philosophy was also the philosophy of employees. This is no longer true. Employees often are every bit as skeptical as the general public on controversial issues facing their organization.

An example: Employees in a privately owned utility—whose management firmly believes that "nuclear energy is the only way to go ... our employees know this and support this"—don't go along with that position. One employee says, "I'm loyal to a point. But there are too many negatives to be considered when it comes to nuclear energy. I just won't buy the company line that says it's absolutely safe." Another employee adds, "I don't know why the company is closing down these little hydro plants. They run cheap and clean. I really don't know why the company would even *want* to get into something as controversial as nuclear at this point."

If this company wants support from its employees on the nuclear energy question, the company must meet employees' informational needs. It should also reexamine its overall approach to the issue. The company needs to exert considerable effort—be it frequency of message, reasons for its positions, or type of media—to transform disbelievers and doubters into supporters.

The internal audience is not the only one with specific informational needs about an organization. There is a rising acknowledgment that the organization must also paint a clear picture of itself and its views to its many diversified "outside" audiences—the general public, customers and potential customers, suppliers, government officials, stockholders, local community residents—and must listen to their views and comments. Coupled with this acknowledgment is the recognition that the exchange works best when low-ranking as well as high-ranking employees become involved in the communication process. In fact, the lower their rank, the greater their credibility. But employees must understand the organization's mission, objectives and plans, as this quote from an annual report to stockholders suggests:

Well motivated and skilled employees are essential in meeting our company objectives. Of critical importance to the ability of employees to fully contribute to the future of the enterprise is the degree to which they are kept informed and enabled to understand the increasingly complex issues with which the business is confronted and how various company functions interrelate in dealing with them.

The implication for organizational communication is clear: find the best way to bring an understanding of these complicated issues to increasingly diverse audiences, both inside and outside the organization.

Support from the Top

Now that we have defined organizational communication and examined audiences, how does the professional communicator cope with it all? How can the pieces of the puzzle be fitted into a down-to-earth, meaningful, practical, affordable program of organizational communication? There's no easy, universal answer. But perhaps the most important requisite is support from the top.

Organizational communication is a responsibility of line management, and as the top manager, the chief executive officer (CEO) should support and become involved with the objective setting process for communication. In many organizations, this has been recognized in just the past five to ten years. And there are still a large number of organizations where it isn't recognized at all. In 1978 the International Association of Business Communicators and Towers, Perrin, Forster & Crosby jointly surveyed CEOs for their views on the role of communication and its many functions. The survey showed that more and more chief executives are taking their communication responsibilities to heart. Here are some comments from these CEOs:

"Any employee communication program that is successful should be administered by the chief executive. The program won't work if the CEO isn't committed to it."

"The communication department is a tool, but the responsibility for communicating is one we all share."

"Our job, and mine at the corporate level, is to motivate and support operating managers to communicate. We can help upgrade their communication skills and show that communicating is important, but we have to do it by showing and encouraging, not by edict."

Sometimes, the CEO is out ahead of the communication professionals. An example: In a large manufacturing company, the head of the communication department decided that there would have to be severe cutbacks in his budget for organizational communication. Shortly after this decision, the CEO asked about progress on stepped-up communication activity. When told of the planned cutback, the CEO said, "It can't be. Internal communication is one of my top priorities."

Policies and Objectives

The ideal first step in putting together a communication program is developing an overall policy to set the tone for the program. Mapping it out can be a form of organizational psychoanalysis because much management time and thought are required. Organizations, like people, differ widely. So, the primary task in developing a policy is to define the organization's unique character and top management's communication philosophy. Ensuing programs will also differ according to beliefs about why communication is important, what should be communicated, who should do the communicating, and what media should be used. Here are three points that might be included in an overall communication policy:

1. Better communication will encourage employees to make a greater contribution to organizational goals simply because employees will have a clearer understanding of the goals and what they mean to employees' well-being.
2. More effective downward communication will stimulate increased ideas from employees, who will be encouraged to pass ideas upward without fear or concern that they will be considered dumb, stupid or beside the point.
3. Better communication will help secure wider support for the organization's stand on important national and local issues. And employees will be better prepared to explain the organization's position in contact with friends, neighbors and government officials.

After a formal policy has been written, clear and specific objectives should be articulated. The same procedures also apply to other situations; they are not limited to communication with employees. Here are some examples of specific communication objectives, most of which can be measured:

1. Establish a formal program of regular communication with all employees.
2. Establish one regular channel of downward printed communication to all employees to inform them about all aspects of issues pertinent to the company and industry. Distribute at least once a week.
3. Issue a publication that will permit more in-depth coverage of internal and external issues. Distribute to all employees on a bimonthly or quarterly basis.
4. Issue a special management publication that will address the special needs of managers.
5. Emphasize subjects that relate to corporate objectives. The subjects will include competition, government regulation, marketing plans, productivity, pay and benefits.
6. Hold regular meetings between management and employees. Encourage questions from and discussions with employees on problems, opportunities and how employees fit into the big picture.
7. Give employees an annual state of the business review—of corporate as well as local matters.
8. Encourage supervisors to meet regularly with employees to discuss issues, problems and opportunities. (Ideally, specific communication responsibilities should be written into supervisory position descriptions.)
9. Communicate information about the organization to employees no later than information is distributed to outside news media.
10. Install methods and procedures that encourage employees to ask questions, such as telephone hotlines and "Speakup."
11. Conduct surveys every other year to evaluate the effectiveness of the communication program and determine audience needs and interests.
12. Reexamine these objectives annually to be sure they are in line with organizational objectives.

Audience Needs and Interests

No set of communication objectives can really be complete without knowing audience needs and interests. Employee understanding, support and commitment must be earned. And getting that understanding, support and commitment from employees will come easier if the employees' needs and interests are addressed regularly.

Survey after survey shows that employees have very specific infor-

mation needs. Personnel policies (especially regarding pay and benefits), current operations, future plans, products and services usually
surface near the top of every list. It's easy to find out what employees are
interested in knowing. Just ask them. Here are some typical comments:

> "We've been hearing of record orders for fourteen consecutive
> quarters, and at the same time we hear of layoffs. How do we recon-
> cile this?"

> "Wages and salaries here are a deep, dark secret."

> "I'd like to see them publish costs of scrap and repair, or pinpoint
> the areas causing it—for us."

> "We ought to lay all our cards on the table. Why can't management
> show employees in which direction they're going? We need a bet-
> ter understanding of what the goals and objectives are. How are we
> going to get there if nobody knows where we're at?"

> "Why don't we know further ahead what day around a holiday we
> will get off—or if we'll get off. It makes it pretty hard to make plans
> with the family."

And employees have definite ideas on how they would like to receive
this information:

> "I would welcome more meetings with high-level management
> telling about specific plans for the present and future."

> "That new video equipment is OK, but those interviews with the
> president have got to go. . . . Canned questions and canned
> answers. . . . And how are you supposed to ask any questions?"

They'll tell you when you're doing a good job, too:

> "The company's safety magazine is just excellent. It's the only
> magazine my whole family reads."

> "There will always be some problems, but [this survey] is one of
> the best things about this company. They really want to know what
> people think, and try to make improvements."

The upward dimension of communication means more than simply giving employees a chance to say what subjects or issues they would like to
hear about. It also means openly seeking employee opinions and giving
employees the opportunity to comment on or question anything related
to the organization and their own jobs. *People want to know that they're*

important and that the work they do is valuable. And they believe that the people who do the work are the ones most likely to know how to improve those operations.

> "I don't care so much that they didn't put through my suggestion, but at least they could have told me why. In fact, *why* things are done the way they are is something we never hear."

> "Nothing in our communications suggests that the employee might have useful ideas about management policies. It's possible that we might not merely want to hear more, but that we might even have something to say."

Without employee input there is a good chance the message will miss its mark completely. Take this case: The top management of a large multinational company was about to launch an economic education program for employees. The company thought the main problem on employees' minds was the export of jobs overseas. When employees were asked what *they* were concerned about, job export wasn't the problem at all. Someone actually said, "You have to be near where the markets are."

These employees had something to say. Luckily, management was listening. Their employees' big concern was when the layoff ax would hit their locations, because the employees had heard of a major layoff in one of the company's big divisions. They did not know (because no one had told them) that the layoff happened because of a technological breakthrough affecting the manufacturing process in that one division. No other layoffs were in the offing anywhere in the company. What would have been the result if the company had embarked on a communication program to justify the existence of overseas operations? Achieving *common* goals can best be accomplished by addressing *common* interests and concerns.

The Employee Publication

Although subsequent chapters describe employee publications, they deserve mention here. After all, the employee publication was once considered to be the sum total of communication in many organizations. And, sad to say, it still is in some.

The publication was most often referred to as the "house organ." Many were often little more than propaganda mills whose main objective (probably not formally stated) was to tell employees only what they needed to know and give them a heavy dose of the "three Bs"—births, bowling scores, and babble.

The "house's" attitude has changed—and so has the look of the employee publication. The old house organ is playing a different tune, supplying different information. The old predictability is gone, and styles and formats of publications are as varied as the organizations they represent.

Least predictable is the content of the publication. In the last ten years or so, there has been a steadily growing acceptance of the idea that the employee publication—probably still the cornerstone of a well-balanced communication program—should tackle tough issues such as alcoholism and drug addiction, "burned-out" employees, pay and benefits, new product developments, new marketing strategies, possible acquisitions or mergers, Equal Employment Opportunity and other government regulations, consumer movements, competition, layoffs. If the information supplied by the organization is unsatisfactory in quality, amount or timeliness, employees will find out what they want to know from other sources: the grapevine, the union, the local newspaper, radio or TV. Then the chances are good that incomplete, distorted messages are being sent and acted on.

Other "Downward" Media

Beyond the employee publication are a number of other print media used to communicate downward. There are letters, booklets, bulletin boards, posters, payroll inserts, handbooks. And more and more, the computer is being used as a downward communication tool; many organizations now use computerized total compensation statements to give employees personalized reports of their pay and benefits. Beyond the host of printed materials are a variety of audiovisual materials; but for maximum impact, neither should attempt to go it alone. Some commonly used audiovisual media are overhead transparencies, slide presentations with live or taped narration, filmstrips, movies, videotape, closed-circuit television.

At this point, there tends to be an imbalance between an abundance of excellent hardware and a scarcity of effective software. We have really just begun to utilize the power of television in organizational communication. We can expect further rapid changes in video hardware capabilities in the near future. Satellites and other advancements in tele-communication technology make it feasible to reach people both near and far. In the not too distant future, two-way picture and sound trans-mission will permit an exchange of ideas and information, not only among different levels in the organization, but among different opera-tions and locations as well.

Informal Media

Informal communicating goes on all the time. The informal chan-nels must exist to provide the avenues of exchange in an organization. In *Communicating at the Top,* George de Mare said: "The first and by far the most common level of communicating is that which goes on below the conscious control of social mechanisms and channels. Perhaps 70 percent of the communication in an organization occurs at this informal, unorganized level." In the past, many organizations were unwilling to recognize or use informal channels. Now, more and more informal com-munication channels are being used to help meet formal organizational communication objectives.

Organizations do not get results, people do, as Dr. V. Dallas Merell suggests in *Huddling.* Merell describes a huddle as "a temporary, inti-mate, work-oriented encounter between two or more people. A huddle is the source of considerable information, the locus of significant decisions, the setting for power transactions, the place where many responsibilities get defined and the impetus for motivating people to get things done. . . . Huddles are a critical aspect of any organization. They are to the infor-mal organization what business meetings are to the official, formal or-ganization."

It might not have been defined as an "informal channel," but twenty-five years ago a half-hour stroll through the plant by a chief executive or senior vice president *was* employee communication in many organizations. Though the difficulty of doing this today is well appreciated, employees keep saying that this kind of face-to-face interac-tion is the best way to communicate. Here are some employee comments on the subject:

"I'd like to see top management get out and talk to people. I don't think they give a damn."

"Chuck has the best operation here. He'll come right down and talk to us about what's going on. There are not too many (other VPs) who will do that."

An employee's desire to come into contact with management is seldom at odds with what management says it *wants* to be doing. Here is a CEO comment:

> "I do believe that communicating cannot be done unless you actually go out and talk to people. I believe that it's important for me to be out there visiting people on the line doing their jobs."

In any discussion of informal communication media, the importance an organization places on developing, maintaining and nurturing strong and open exchanges between supervisors and subordinates cannot be overemphasized. Over and over and over again employees say that they prefer to get information about the organization from their supervisors. And communication research shows that this relationship is the element that most strongly affects such attitudes as job satisfaction, group cohesiveness and morale. One top executive summed it up like this: "First-line supervisors are the window on this organization. An employee who sees good things through that window sees a better organization than someone who sees bad things."

More and more organizations are recognizing the need to develop effective supervisors and are training them in communication skills— speaking, writing, listening—because, as one steelworker observed, "Supervisors with sandpaper personalities just don't belong in today's workplace."

Upward Media

Informal, face-to-face exchanges are valuable, but perhaps the "window on the company" is more of a two-way mirror. The opportunity to communicate upward—to know that one's suggestions and comments are being heard—is the other half of organizational communication exchange, and whatever can be done to facilitate this exchange— specifically, the upward flow—should be done. Informal, face-to-face exchange is by no means the only way to get feedback or an upward flow of communication moving. Techniques used to spur it are advisory councils, ombudsmen, speak-up programs, attitude or climate surveys and communication audits.

A cautionary note about upward communication: listening implies action. It is not enough to provide the channels and listen attentively. The goodwill derived from such exchanges will quickly turn to disappointment, and later to resentment and bitterness, if nothing is done to follow up on comments, suggestions or complaints.

Summary

Organizational communication has come a long way. If nothing else, we are seeing a more businesslike, disciplined approach to communication activity than ever before. Articulating management *objectives* and getting at *audience* needs and interests are preceding *message* preparation and *media* selection. In fact, both message preparation and media selection are easier when communicators know where they're going.

The effectiveness of communication programs will increase as they facilitate the *exchange* of information, ideas and feelings among people from all levels of the organizations. And the importance of communication in organizations will continue to grow as it becomes apparent that communication activity has a real impact on overall organizational results. In truth, management itself *is* communication.

Roy G. Foltz, **ABC, APR,** is a vice president and director of Towers, Perrin, Forster & Crosby in New York. He is 1981–82 president of the International Association of Business Communicators and is accredited by IABC and the Public Relations Society of America.

CHAPTER 2

Communicators in Contemporary Organizations

ROGER M. D'APRIX, ABC

If organizations are going to deal with the loss of confidence and mistrust demonstrated by poll after poll throughout the last decade, they must begin to develop new insights into the process of organizational communication. Survey data accumulated in the United States by Opinion Research Corporation over the past twenty-five years show that most institutional managements do not understand this process. Or if they do understand it, they have not taken the pains to do anything about it.

Writing in the *Harvard Business Review*, Michael Cooper and other ORC researchers described some clearly documented demands of the work force for self-expression, self-fulfillment, and personal growth:

> The changes reported here are ubiquitous, pervasive and nontransient; any reversal is unlikely in the foreseeable future. The goal for management is to be aware of and prepared for new and surfacing employee needs, before it is forced to take reactive, ignorant, and resistive postures. . . .
>
> What is undeniably required, however, is that corporations recognize the new realities within which they must function. The crucial issues then become the degree to which management can successfully identify, anticipate, and address these changing values as they surface, or before they surface, in their own organizations. But, make no mistake about it, changing employee values are no myth. They will be the realities that companies must face in the 1980s.

The ORC researchers have put their fingers squarely on the key issue for effective organizational communication with employees. If management is going to address employees' communication needs, it must first under-

stand those needs and the values that shape them. Then it must understand which issues the employee audience should be informed about
and communicate accordingly.

The Reactive Communicator

Organizational communication typically operates almost exactly the opposite way from that suggested by informed research. Using the model of
the journalist, the reporter of news, the organizational communicator and
his or her management often merely *react* to events inside and outside
the organization. When the organization is not sophisticated or not large
enough to have a professional communication staff, management simply
does its best to keep people informed of events. In many cases, management takes the position that the process will take care of itself and that
people will be informed "on a need-to-know basis" while performing
their jobs.

The predictable result is communication anarchy. To understand
why, look at the journalistic communication process in an organization
(fig. 2.1). It is almost exclusively a *reactive* process. A particular event
takes place within or outside the organization and is witnessed and re-
counted by the members of the organization. Depending on its significance, the event is retold through the informal channels of the
organization—the famous grapevine that exists wherever two or more
people gather to work. Depending again on significance and on how
enlightened the organization is, the event may or may not be related
through formal channels. Often there is a difference in the formalized
version. It is either more or less candid than the informal version, more
or less informative and more or less accurate depending on many variables, not the least of which are management's commitment to communication and its stake in the particular message. Ideally, there is little
dissonance between the formal and the informal versions. In practice,
the dissonance can be considerable.

Whether the audience gets the message from formal channels in the
organization or from the grapevine, the audience is still compelled to
interpret the event according to its individual and collective experiences. When communication is reactive—either from formal or informal
channels—people are required to perceive the event and then put it into
some kind of perspective for themselves. The fundamental question is,
What does this mean to *me?*

FIGURE 2.1 Reactive model

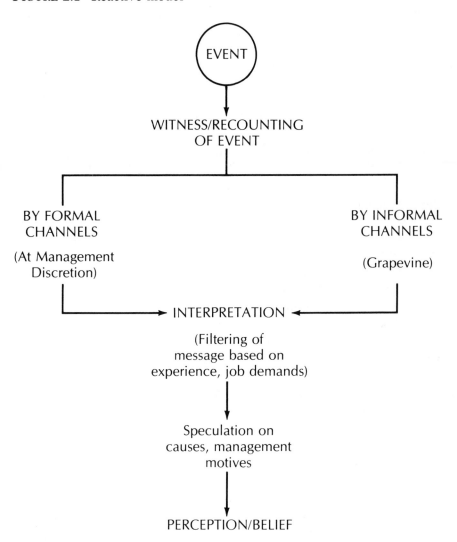

Reactive communication in the journalistic manner of merely reporting events is risky in any organization because it focuses mainly on *what* happened. It leaves the audience to speculate on the cause and significance of the event and to deduce motives from the event. A major government contract is lost, says a company's announcement to the local news media. Employees read or hear the brief report about their company's bad luck and, naturally, they begin to speculate on why it happened and what it is likely to mean to them. They begin guessing about the government's motives for choosing a competitive contractor and about their management's likely reaction, based on what they have come to expect from management in such circumstances and what they know or have heard.

In reactive communication situations, the audience is overloaded with raw information—news, rumors and opinions—that they have great difficulty piecing together and that leaves them confused and bewildered. When organizational communication is merely reactive, the audience is left to speculate. Their inevitable conclusion is that organizational life is chaotic, unplanned, and unmanaged. The alarming fact is that management does not take responsibility for communication; it simply lets it happen as it will.

Compounding all this is the organizational communicator's identity crisis. Because management often does not understand precisely why it hired such people—except for some vague pieties about "the need to communicate with our people"—communicators in organizations are often left to their own devices. Without proper direction and with no direct link to the final process of producing the organization's product or service, they begin to search for a suitable model for their efforts. Unluckily, the logical role model they seize on is that of public journalist, the reactive communicator. So often I have heard the wish expressed that the employee communication professional really ought to be free to perform his or her job in the same way that the press is free to do its job in the society at large. That is utter nonsense, but it remains the secret hope of many misguided people in this business.

The problem is not management's penchant for deceit or a desire to cover up. It is a rightful concern about what raw, unprocessed information does to or for an employee audience, something that is difficult, if not impossible, to predict. This is also the reason why so many managements are nervous about the mere reportage of organizational news without putting that news in some kind of perspective for the audience. Management likes news to have a beginning, a middle, and some probable and predictable outcome before it is ready to say much about it. It also wants to present its actions and performance in some kind of favorable light. That's not an unusual human desire.

The role of doing otherwise should not logically fall to communication people who draw their salaries from the organization. That altogether proper role belongs historically and correctly to the public press. In fact, the organizational communicator who models his or her work on the public media is doomed to a career of frustration and loneliness.

The opposite extreme, of course, has been even more typical of corporate communication. The old-time house organ "where never is heard a discouraging word and the skies are not cloudy all day" is fully as unsatisfactory as the ludicrous hope that organizational communicators should be hired as investigative reporters in their own establishments. In both instances, the role models are wrong and the results are likely to be disastrous.

A Too-Often-Heard Story

Let us look at a mythical company called United Industries. United made its name in the oil business. In the '60s it nervously acquired three other large organizations to protect its base. With the onset of the energy crisis in the early '70s, it began to take more than a passing interest in its nonpetroleum companies—a television and motion picture production outfit, a chemical company, and a manufacturer of air conditioners.

When United finally built a management organization to direct the activities of its conglomerate operations, it set up its corporate headquarters in neutral territory, San Diego. A vice president in charge of corporate communication was appointed to ensure that the world understood exactly who United was and its role in the business world. Huge sums of money were pumped into television advertising and paid-space think pieces in the nation's leading magazines and newspapers.

In 1971 the new vice president decided something had to be done about the company's creaking house organ, a monthly called *Folks United*. When there was only the relatively small oil business located mainly in the Southwest, *Folks United* was able to do a reasonable job of reporting the bond drives, engagements, birthdays, new hires, activities of the United Recreation Association, employees' hobbies, and the like. But as United grew significantly, the publication became sillier and sillier—especially to the employees of Hollywood Productions Unlimited, who would sit around and mock the names and activities of their fellow employees from the oil fields. When *Folks United* arrived in the mail, it was the occasion for lots of merriment and what they called the continuing saga of Willie Joe and John Bob. It wasn't much better at Koolking Air Conditioning, whose production people each month sent their stack of copies—unread—to the shipping department to be used as packing material.

Bart Damon was hired as employee communication manager. He was instructed "to bring this publication into the twentieth century" and to build an appropriate communication program for all of United so that its internal efforts would be as sophisticated as its external efforts. Damon's first move was to assemble a staff. He began by hiring the business editor of one of southern California's major newspapers. Next, he recruited an outstanding freelance writer. His third hire was an audiovisual manager from Hollywood Productions Unlimited. The rest of the staff consisted of the former staff of *Folks United* and the communication people who had previously been at Jiffy Chemical Products and Koolking Air Conditioning.

The early days of Bart Damon's regime were very exciting as the new staff eagerly planned their publications and programs and turned them from concept to reality. *Folks United* became a weekly tabloid, *United Industries News*. It was to be the showpiece of the effort to keep all United's people informed of news affecting them and their work. Dick Larkspur, a former newsman, was named editor and given free rein to report the news. Former New York freelancer Gabe Newcomb was assigned to produce a management magazine that reflected the strategy and priorities of United management for all United managers.

After six months, the honeymoon came to an abrupt end. Larkspur had produced a series on the disruption suffered by families of United employees who had been transferred from the Southwest to the West Coast to the East Coast, and in some cases to the Middle East and back. It was a frank story, spiced with bitter complaints and heartrending stories of uprooted families. There was little of the stiff-upper-lip philosophy that corporate families are supposed to espouse, and marketing vice president Sheldon Horowitz was furious when the first of the series appeared. He called Larkspur, sputtering about whether he thought he was Woodward or Bernstein. Horowitz demanded that Larkspur kill the series and hung up before a dispirited Larkspur had a chance to reply.

Through a series of skillful negotiations, Damon was able to keep the series from an untimely and abrupt death. But this was only the beginning of a gradual polarization of United management, on the one hand, and United communication people, on the other. It was fueled regularly by haggling over stories and communication proposals, and even by the last-minute killing of a whole issue of one publication.

Poor Damon is caught in the middle of this continuing conflict between his staff, who constantly confront him with their views that United people have a need and a right to know what is going on, and his management's accusations that "these people have no understanding of the sensitivities of this business." His plight is compounded by his sympathy with his staff's beliefs and his journalistic training—both of which tell him that United management is too conservative and too worried about reactions that will never materialize.

On top of this, Bart Damon, thirty-one years old, a Vietnam veteran and a product of the campus upheaval of the class of '69, confides to friends that he is not pleased about working for United, but the money is excellent and he lives well. Damon's peers in the communication profession rate *United Industries News* as one of the top company publications. In professional competitions, it continually walks off with prizes for candor and excellence.

So what's the problem? It's one that isn't spoken of much outside the gatherings of people who make their living from organizational communication. But it's really classic. The United communication staff is "doing its own thing" in the organization—writing the kinds of things they care about, quietly jabbing and prodding management and producing publications and programs that are professionally satisfying. Because the programs are usually of reasonable quality and because management does not honestly know how to get hold of the reins, the communication staff can do pretty much what they like. The one exception is management's right to review content, and this it does with relish.

The question that does not get raised, let alone answered, is, What is all this activity doing for United and for United Industries people? The classic answer from the communication people is a soft-shoe dance. "Well, you know there is really no objective way you can measure the effect of communication. . . ."

Is there an alternative to this scenario? Until recently, most communicators thought it was simply to serve their employers as hired guns, grinding out copy they didn't really believe and finding the right sugar coating for the "truths" management wanted people to swallow. It's a depressing alternative, and it's no surpise that the people who opted for it became disenchanted and cynical. It's also no surprise that the Bart Damons of the world are trying to walk a different road. But the role of self-appointed purveyor of the truth is a thankless and often arrogant one.

The alternative is for the communicator to lead the way in making

communication in his or her organization *proactive*. Communicators can
no longer afford the waiting game in which they expect management to
define the communication task and then provide the money and psychic
support to do the job. When management ignores the communication
function, or emasculates it because the senior staff cannot figure out how
to work effectively with this alien breed, the predictable result is that the
professional communicators sulk, sink into despair, or "give them what
they want." The result of all three reactions is that the organization is the
loser.

The Proactive Communicator

The solution lies in what any intelligent staff member must do in any
organization. It requires communication people to think through the
organization's needs, assess their own potential ability to help address
those needs, propose an intelligent and carefully developed plan, and
then execute it as professionally as they can. No self-indulgence can be
tolerated, no bitterness, no lamenting about not being understood or
appreciated.

Proactive communication requires the communication professional
to see himself or herself in a different role from that of the working
journalist. Though it is probably one of the more distasteful words in our
vocabulary, the proper word for describing proactive communicators is
"propagandist," which conjures up visions of twisting the truth and the
reality of our lives into lies that only serve special-interest groups. That
is the commonly accepted notion of propaganda dating from the 1920s
and '30s and the penchant of totalitarian leaders to lie to the people they
have oppressed.

Business and organizational communicators often carry this burden
whether they pose as independent journalists or company spokespersons. Our various audiences invariably filter our messages, words and
claims through their belief that we are paid to say these things. The truth
is that we *are*. But the truth also is that the most believable propaganda is
the truth. Ergo, good communicators rely on truth rather than lies to
influence opinions and attitudes. More to the point, ethical communicators will not lie for anyone, because that is prostitution.

All of this requires that people who cast their lot with organizations
as organizational communicators had better be pretty smart and have
well-formed consciences. If not, they are frequently in danger of com-

promising however much integrity they have, a situation that requires sober and continuing personal reflection.

Organizations will always propagandize, just as all of us individually propagandize about ourselves. We contrive noble explanations for our actions. We try to put ourselves and our behavior in the most acceptable light possible. That is human nature if we are to live with ourselves. So it is with organizations as well.

Since that kind of behavior is both inevitable and vital to the well-being and even the survival of the organization, the real question becomes, How can any management and its communication staff propagandize as decently, truthfully and effectively as possible? The communicator's responsibility is complex. It is to the well-being of the organization first, to the audience second, and third, to society at large. In some cases these priorities can shift.

The proactive communication process is based on the assumption that organizations spend much of their time and energy trying to meet objectives they have set for themselves. In accomplishing those objectives, they invariably are required to identify, confront and solve problems, which they rank by priority.

The dynamics of the situation are the raw material of real organizational communication. They raise the life-and-death issues that determine whether the organization succeeds or fails, the issues that those who have a vested interest in the organization care about. This is true whether we are speaking about employees (and, of course, the intensity of *their* interest depends on their perceived stake in the business), shareholders, customers or the public at large.

Good organizational communication focuses on the issues that are important to the organization. Everything else is secondary and peripheral. Therefore, the effective organizational communicator must first identify the issues and then speak to them. That is the essence of the job. Further, the organizational communicator must speak to them when they first begin to shine on the horizon, not *after* they have become like blazing comets in the organization's night sky. The organizational communicator must work with management to foreshadow change, to prepare the audience for that change, and to allow them to accommodate change. Otherwise, the organization's various audiences are left with the belief that no one understands or is acting on the problems that stand as obstacles to the organization's success. When they believe that, they do the natural thing and lose heart in the organization.

In today's world, the work organization carries an increasingly heavy burden. With the increased mobility of the worker, with the decline of the community as a support system for the individual, and with the breakdown of the nuclear family, it is logical that the individual places more hope for personal fulfullment in work. It is not too much of an exaggeration to say that many of us look to the workplace to provide meaning in our lives as well as a sense of hope.

For this reason, organizational communicators are very much in the meaning and hope business. They must understand and communicate issues in the organization so that the employee audience in particular has the feeling that the work environment is being managed in everyone's best interests. If communicators report the news, if they produce slick media, if they stimulate effective face-to-face communication, they do so only to achieve the larger goal of proactive communication of issues as soon as they emerge as issues.

How does an organizational communicator do that? The answer lies in planning and analysis.

For both the veteran and the neophyte communicator, such planning can be bewildering. The problem is that no one has taught them how to do it; they have been expected simply to report events and issues reactively. By definition, proactive communication requires the communicator to get much closer to management. It also requires that management be more open with the communicator, more trusting with information, and more willing to seek advice on how best to communicate issues in the early stage of their evolution.

Proactive communication (fig. 2.2) begins with an assessment of the organization by the communicator. What are its goals and priorities? What are the values and dreams of its management? How is it seen by employees, by customers, by shareholders? What is its relationship with the various bodies it must interact with? How does its management treat its employees? How does it regard their values, their human needs? Is there mutual respect or enmity?

The sources the communicator can and should use to address these questions are legion. A good starting point is the organization's long-range plan, assuming that it has one. Another good source is the annual operating plan. In these two documents are generally listed management's goals and aspirations and the risks along the way. They are a gold mine of information for any communicator who understands how to sift through them and identify the major issues that emerge.

Another invaluable source is the organization's leadership. One of the simplest and most direct ways to find the issues important to an

FIGURE 2.2 Proactive model

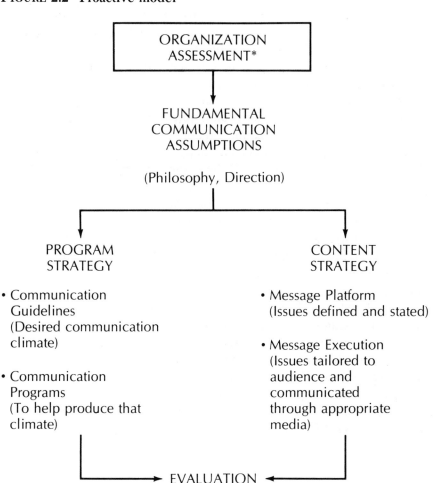

ORGANIZATION
ASSESSMENT*

FUNDAMENTAL
COMMUNICATION
ASSUMPTIONS

(Philosophy, Direction)

PROGRAM
STRATEGY

- Communication
Guidelines
(Desired communication
climate)

- Communication
Programs
(To help produce that
climate)

CONTENT
STRATEGY

- Message Platform
(Issues defined and stated)

- Message Execution
(Issues tailored to
audience and
communicated
through appropriate
media)

EVALUATION

* Probable sources for assessment include: long-range plan, operating plan, executive interviews, personal observations, employee surveys, third-party analysis.

organization is to ask senior management to define its major concerns for the foreseeable future. Their answers generally make a good list of immediate objectives and attendant risks and likely shortfalls. Employee attitude surveys are also extremely useful. They can tell what the various employee work forces in the organization are individually and collectively pleased about, upset about, or questioning.

A final source for the organization assessment is third-party analyses. Read the standard security analyst's reports on how the organization is faring. Examine assessments from the public press when they are done by informed and responsible reporters. These can be excellent checks on management performance because they are done by knowledgeable sources with no ax to grind.

Most important is the communicator's own sense of the organization and how it behaves. Not enough communicators trust their own perceptions in assessing the organization's reality. They tend either to buy the party line or, more often, to become hopeless skeptics and even cynics where their own organizations are concerned. Neither of these postures works.

When the communicator has completed the organization assessment (in truth that assessment is never really done because the organization keeps changing), the next step is to establish a set of fundamental assumptions about communication in the organization and to propose what effective communication can accomplish in the organization, based on the assessment and the communication priorities of its management. It is crucial that these be understood and stated. Otherwise management can well be assuming one set of outcomes from the communication effort and the communicator another. This is the place to get rid of unrealistic or impossible views of what communication alone can accomplish in and for the organization. If these assumptions are not stated and agreed upon, program and content priorities can become a matter of considerable disagreement and haggling. Serious questions can surface later about effectiveness and what has or has not been accomplished.

Programs and Content Planning

Once the fundamental assumptions are articulated by the communicator and approved by the senior executive of the organization, it is possible, and indeed essential, to begin developing both the program and content strategies. These are parallel tasks in the sense that it is impossible to focus exclusively on program and then exclusively on content. Logically, in the process of formulating the organization assessment and in developing the fundamental assumptions about communication in the organization, communicators will uncover issues and think about how to discuss them in convincing terms. They will also inevitably think about programs.

Once the organization assessment is complete and the fundamental assumptions have been agreed upon, the next step is to develop communication guidelines for everyone in the organization to live by. These guidelines should articulate the role and responsibility of management in the communication process for the simple reason that management is normally the author of issues and plans in response to the tasks and obstacles the organization faces. The guidelines should spell out where communication responsibility lies and how that responsibility should be carried out. They should be pronounced from the top of the organization and endorsed at every key level.

The next step is to develop effective communication programs. Or, where such programs already exist, to be certain they are appropriate to the needs of the organization's various audiences.

Next comes content strategy. Here the task is to articulate the issues that are critical to the well-being of the organization and to the people who depend on it and support it, as well as those issues that are likely to be seized on by its opponents. In today's organizational world, it might be such matters as eroding productivity, affirmative action policy, overseas competition, the impact of inflation, or dozens of other issues unique to a particular organization. The task is to reduce these matters to message objectives or themes that will drive the content of the organization's communication programs—a message platform, so to speak, that will define the communication needs and concerns of the organization.

How the message objectives are to be communicated is the next stage of the proactive communication model. It is here that communicators worry about the needs and interests of the particular audience or audiences that must be reached—whether employees, shareholders, customers, the community, or perhaps government regulatory bodies at the local, state or federal level. This process, of course, requires communicators to determine which issues are important to which constituency and to tailor messages and media accordingly.

The final step in the proactive model is evaluation, a difficult process that does not normally yield a lot of objective data. Nevertheless, it is imperative that communicators use every technique they can afford to measure effectiveness—public opinion surveys, employee attitude surveys, readership surveys, interviews, practically any means communicators can devise to determine that the message is getting through.

Look for These Advantages

There are many advantages of proactive communication. First, this disciplined approach to communication directs the effort of the communication staff toward organization issues and priorities. In no time it is clear to management that the communicators are no longer working "the other side of the street"; they are concerned about the matters that have the attention of senior management. The inevitable result is that the communicators get greater attention, acceptance and support from management.

Second, this process has the advantage of helping the communicator understand better that the job is not journalism or publishing per se. It is organizational communication; journalistic or publication skills are critical, but really incidental to the tasks at hand.

Third, proactive communication influences the process and content of communication so that professional communicators are not merely pursuing subjects and issues that excite them, or producing only the kinds of media that are fun to work on—such as slick four-color magazines or newspapers or television tapes they find professionally intriguing but that may have little value to the organization or its constituencies.

Finally, because the process requires careful evaluation and an analysis of issues, it helps to ensure that communication is an honest process matched to both management and audience needs. Issues are not merely top down; they also become bottom up as the communicator attempts to determine the concerns and information needs of the audience as well as the organization.

There are some significant advantages for management in the proactive approach to communication. Communication becomes a planned process rather than an afterthought or an attempt merely to explain what went wrong or why something was done. The reactions of various constituencies are anticipated and addressed as the policy or program is being implemented. In short, communication is a *planned* part of the process. Another advantage is that management is continually reminded of its communication responsibilities in the formulation and execution of the communication plan. There is a definition of management's communication role, and the role is thus formalized and institutionalized as part of the organization's culture. Finally, not only does it *appear* that the organization is a rational universe; to the extent that proactive planning

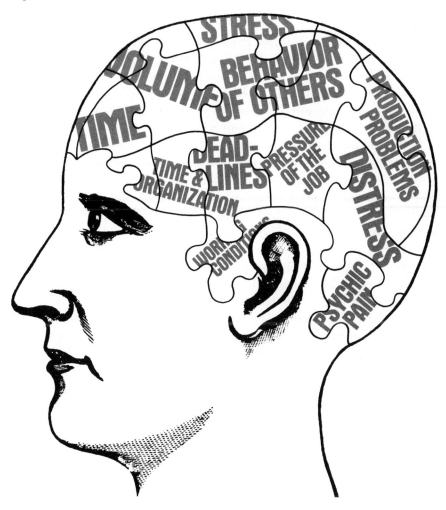

Proactive communication lightens the audience's burden by focusing on *why* things have happened or are happening.

and communication are carried on, but the organization *becomes* more rational and methodical in its behavior.

Perhaps most important, proactive communication lightens the audience's burden. It focuses on *why* things have been done or are happening, not merely that they have happened, which is the case in reactive communication. The audience is left less to its own devices in speculating on the cause or significance of events. It is not required to deduce management motivation from the event.

Proactive communication cannot presume that such speculation or deduction will never take place. But if management has a good track record of truthful and responsible action, audience distrust and doubt will be far less widespread and less damaging. To the contrary, if the track record is of deceitful and irresponsible action, the remedial action will be painful and take some years to accomplish.

Proactive communication is never totally an either-or proposition vis-à-vis reactive communication. The communicator cannot get totally out of the reactive mode because there are always surprises, disasters and unexpected responses to policies or issues. The communicator has to have his or her antenna high in the air and be *prepared* to react, to modify a communication plan as necessary.

Is this process somehow unfair to the audience? Manipulative? Wouldn't it be better if the communicator merely reported events and let the audience make its own interpretations? No, because people invariably ask, What does such and such an event *mean* to me? How does it affect my life? Those are the questions they want addressed honestly and candidly. Even if the news is bad, it is better than no news or news that merely reports events without commenting on their significance. The key, obviously, is honesty and candor. Without them, the audience *is* in danger of short-term manipulation. But actions are always scrutinized by audiences to see if they match the words. If they do not, the words are soon ignored as lies.

Roger M. D'Aprix, ABC, is manager of employee communication at Xerox Corporation's Business Systems Group, Rochester, New York. He is accredited by the International Association of Business Communicators and was named an IABC Fellow in 1978.

CHAPTER 3

Assessing and Meeting Audience Needs

THOMAS C. HUNTER

The extent to which organizational communicators must be sensitive to the expectations, interests, needs and values of their audiences is enormous. It exceeds whatever degree of sensitivity is required in practically any other form of structured communication.

For the most part, audiences of "public" media bring a fairly objective and unemotional set of needs and interests to such communication vehicles. Radio listeners, television viewers, and readers of newspapers and magazines primarily seek information or entertainment. Rarely do they have any special-interest ties beyond that.

Editors of a consumer publication, for example, assuredly must know what their readers want and how they want it "packaged." Beyond providing their readers with what they want, however, the editors hardly need be concerned that their work indicates the publisher cares about the readers; is personally concerned about the readers' problems; or feels the readers, as individuals, are important. Organizational communicators, on the other hand, must reflect those concerns, subtly or overtly, on behalf of their publishers—the organizations for which they work. This is true whether the communicator is an employee, a freelancer or an agency representative.

If a commercial broadcast station or a commercial publication is not in tune with and responsive to what a portion of its audience expects to receive from it, that audience segment simply can, and usually will, turn to alternate sources of information or entertainment. That certainly is not without its harmful consequences to the media involved, most notably in reduced revenues if the number of defectors is significant. But the issues and effects involved are rather clear-cut and impersonal. The understanding of them does not call for too great a degree of sensitivity.

The needs and expectations audiences bring to organizations in which they have a stake are highly subjective and complex. These needs are often emotional and psychological, as with the employee whose sense of self-esteem and personal worth can be affected positively or negatively by the regard in which the employer holds the person and, to a large degree, by how employee communication reflects that regard.

The relationships between an organization and its varied audiences, and the organization's responsiveness to audience interests and needs, are critical to effective communication. Those relationships are born of the special levels of involvement that exist between employers and employees, companies and shareholders, companies and customers, nonprofit organizations and volunteers, health-care facilities and patients, associations and members, service organizations and clients, and on and on.

Based on staff time, production costs and the scope of activities, few, if any, organizations can or should attempt programs that cater to every communication interest or expectation of each individual with whom they are involved. That surely would create an unmanageable myriad of communication vehicles; conceivably, one for each person. Still, the communicator should seek to find out as much as possible about each person in a given audience.

When asked to explain the key to his ability to produce consistently successful commercials, Chuck Blore of Chuck Blore and Don Richman, Inc. of Hollywood, explained, "We go for a one-to-one with our audience [in order to] understand and touch their basic drives, needs for security, affection." Blore says, "What we do is take 30,000 people, who have 30,000 sets of worries, 30,000 sets of moralities, 30,000 sets of problems and attitudes, and find something that will reach out and touch all of them."

The same task awaits the organizational communicator who expects to be successful; he or she must make every effort to know the audience—with all its needs, expectations, interests and values. The communicator might not always be able to respond. The fact of not responding should be a decision made by choice, however, after knowing and considering all the factors involved. It never should be a "non-choice" resulting from a lack of awareness of an audience's expectations.

Sometimes, awareness of audience interests can come about unexpectedly. When one company introduced a "Letters" section in its corporate magazine, it anticipated a high response from its active employees, to whom the magazine's editorial content was oriented. The first year, however, retired employees, who represented less than 2 percent of the magazine's total circulation, accounted for more than 22 percent of the letters to the editor. Obviously, they were a special-interest audience eager to communicate with the company for which they had worked and anxious that the company keep communication channels open to them. From the content and tone of the retirees' letters, it was clear they had strong positive feelings about the company.

Faced with the high response from the retirees, the editors of the magazine considered the possibility of developing a separate newsletter for retirees. There were a number of reasons to do so, aside from the fact that retirees obviously were a receptive audience. Retirees often feel they are cut off from the company and no longer needed. A special communication vehicle, offered out of a sense of corporate responsibility, would help assuage such uneasy feelings. Also, a special publication could supply information to help retirees be effective voices for the company in their contacts with others in their communities.

After weighing these and other considerations involved—including staff time and costs—the editors decided instead to alter slightly the content and slant of the articles in the employee magazine. They did so in a way that reinforced the good feelings existing among the retirees but without jeopardizing reader interest among active employees.

Lack of Awareness Leads to Negative Communication

To attempt to communicate without a deep awareness of an audience's interests and attitudes and everything else that goes into its makeup is to attempt to communicate without a clear sense of direction. The chance for communication to be fully effective under such circumstances is merely that—a chance. The outcome can be worse than not communicating at all. Recipients of misdirected organizational communication can easily conclude, "They not only don't know what corner I'm coming out of, they don't even care."

Consider the effects when organizational communication conveys an evident lack of caring. Employees may begin to approach their work with far less enthusiasm—and a corresponding decrease in their performance and effectiveness. They may seek employment elsewhere. Customers or clients may take their business to competitors who value them and show it. Prospective customers may choose not to get involved with the organization. Shareholders may transfer their investment dollars to companies responsive to their particular needs and interests. Volunteers or donors may seek more appreciative organizations to which to lend support. People may begin to regard the organization as an insensitive and unattractive neighbor, one the community can easily do without. These consequences should not each be treated as an isolated case, for one can quickly trigger the others, contaminating all the relations with which an organization may be concerned: employee, customer, community, financial and even government relations.

An employee who senses a lack of concern on the part of the employer, for instance, can lose concern about producing a quality product. As a result, customers soon discover they are purchasing defective products or products that are of poorer quality than before. If this lowering of worker performance and product quality is widespread, the company can encounter a sales decline of such severity that the financial community no longer regards the firm as an attractive investment. A rash of consumer complaints can lead to escalating demands for stronger consumer protection laws. Meanwhile, there can be a growing awareness among the general public that the company apparently is not concerned about the quality of the products it manufactures. This, in turn, can lead to serious questions about the company's sense of responsibility regarding other aspects of its operations—for instance, the effects its manufacturing processes have on the environment. The example is extreme, but the point is valid.

Harry Mullikin, president and chief executive officer of Western International Hotels, once put it this way: "The hotel business operates on saying 'Yes.' Our decisions are made on the basis of 'What does the guest want?' " In other words, what are the guest's expectations and attitudes?

"The essential question," Mullikin elaborated, "is, 'What can be done within the framework of a business in which success is based on satisfying the guest?' The next most important consideration after the guest is, 'What does the hotel employee want?' How can we design a hotel and lay things out so that employees can do their jobs better and more comfortably? Because, if the employee is happier, the guest gets better service, and that then lets us make money to take care of the shareholders. If the guests are dissatisfied and the employees are disgruntled in a hotel in which the shareholders might have $30 million invested, we're soon going to have an empty building."

Demographics: The Basics for Understanding an Audience

To answer the questions Mullikin raised, the communicator eventually must come to grips with attitudes. Before assessing and dealing with the attitudes of an audience, however, there should be an awareness of its basic makeup—the demographics of that audience. In the case of hotel guests, for instance, are there more men than women? Are they usually vacationers or business people? Do they usually travel singly or with their families? Is the average stay a night or a week? In the case of an international hotel, of what nationalities are the guests?

In general, each group has some needs and interests the others do not. They will guide the communicator in choosing the media to use to convey various messages and what the content and tone of the communication should be. Many communication decisions can be refined by matching demographics against the results of attitudinal surveys. The findings of one extensive research effort indicated that newspaper readers under the age of thirty have a lower attention span and are more visual and less verbal than other readers. The research also concluded that readers are turned off by newspapers that are hard to handle: contain blurred pictures; and use stilted, formal or pretentious language. It showed, too, that many readers dislike "jumps" and continued articles.

Assuming that general findings automatically apply to particular audiences can be a serious mistake, though. All readers under thirty are not necessarily more visually than verbally oriented—nor, as implied, is everyone over thirty less visually oriented. Also, the study cited above pertains to readers of commercial newspapers. Had it focused on employee newspapers, the findings might have been somewhat different. So communicators should keep up with general attitude trends, but they should not follow them blindly in developing programs for specific audiences. General findings can give strong indications of attitudes that probably exist among comparable audiences, but before addressing them, the communicator should determine, as accurately as possible, whether or not they apply.

Basic demographics that are important for developing and directing effective communication programs are relatively easy to obtain. Ready sources include personnel records; customer, client and guest lists; patient records in health-care facilities; and student records in educational institutions.

The ease of access to as much information as is available has created a communication problem of its own: invasion of privacy. In cases where it might be a concern, communicators should use extreme care in addressing an audience so that no portion of its members will have reason to feel that others know more about them than they are entitled to know—which is as it should be. Where confidentiality is a concern in obtaining demographic information and other statistics, persons with proper access to such records should be the ones to uncover the non-confidential information helpful for tailoring effective communication.

Demographics often are highly important in achieving communication goals—and avoiding communication errors—whether aimed at internal or external audiences. An example: A salesperson suggested that his company's employee magazine devote a portion of each issue to publishing product specifications the sales force could pull out and leave behind when calling on customers. Sales personnel, however, accounted for less than 1,000 of a total circulation of more than 15,000. To have followed the suggestion of using the employee magazine for sales information clearly would have meant including material of little interest or value to the majority of readers. In another instance, a state chapter of a professional association located in a state with two telephone area codes listed the president's number in the chapter newsletter without listing the area code. The editor was not oriented toward the people who needed the area code. Likely interpretation? Some members' status was secondary to that of others'.

A national organization started a series of articles in its quarterly magazine, profiling its operations at locations throughout the country—one in each issue. When readers began to ask when the magazine was going to get around to them, the editors did some simple calculations and realized that it would take more than twenty years to cover all eighty-six locations. Although the audience population at a featured location was pleased when it received the coverage and attention, those at scores of others felt overlooked—and obviously would continue to feel so until the editors could get around to them—years later.

This case is an example of why demographics are important, not only in developing communications but also in monitoring its implementation. A rule of thumb is to maintain in any form of communication a content balance based on the makeup of the audience. Production workers should be able to feel they are receiving treatment equal to that for office workers: men the same treatment as women, field personnel the same as headquarters personnel, and so on, according to the makeup of the audience. Periodic monitoring of the makeup of an audience will alert the communicator to any changes that might occur and indicate, when appropriate, the need for a revision of priorities.

Address the Audience from Its Frame of Reference

A major shortcoming in organizational communication is the result of managements that insist on addressing audiences—employees, in particular—in terms of what management thinks their attitudes and interests should be, rather than what they actually are. Communications about employee benefits and economic issues are two prime examples. The following, which appeared in an employee newsletter, is an extreme illustration, but archaic as it is, messages similar to it do surface now and then.

Every payday you are handed a check for so many dollars and cents. You've earned it; you know you've worked hard for it. It looks pretty good. Do you ever think about the other paycheck? Your company has several extras for you. These may be medical and life insurance, pension plans, parking lots, vacations, holidays, and sick leaves. Even coffee breaks are fringe benefits. But maybe you would rather see these extras put into cash that you can hold in your hot little hand. Let's pretend you decide to do this. You asked your company to cancel all your benefits and add all the money to your paycheck. You feel so much richer. But this feeling doesn't last long. You arrive at the company parking lot and are stopped. You're told that this is one of those fringe benefits you've given up. So you have to find another place to park, which costs you money and a long walk to get to work. You really need that cup of coffee at your break. Sorry about that, but no benefits. Remember? You suddenly feel a little sick. Better not do that; you can't get sick now. You gave up all the company insurance. And you didn't take out any on your own because it was so much higher for an individual than under a group plan. You're really in a fine mess. You go home at the end of a frustrating day and spend a restless night wondering how you could have been so stupid. You wake up with a migraine headache but no paid sick days. So, off you go with the feeling that life is getting very complicated. You remember that feeling of security you used to have. It came from the thought of that pension or profit-sharing plan that was almost like compulsory savings. You didn't ever manage money too well, but the company was taking care of it for you.

Guess you'd better make some changes and make them fast.

Now, aren't you glad we were just pretending? It was a little scary, even though you knew it wasn't true. But it did make you realize those little extras aren't so little after all.

It is hard to imagine anyone considering an article of that nature even thought about employee attitudes regarding benefits and the ways in which they are communicated, much less attempted to ascertain what those attitudes might be. Employees hardly ever consider a parking lot a benefit. When told that it is, they most likely will react with feelings ranging from ridicule to resentment.

Consider other serious ramifications of such an article when matched against the following attitudes people have voiced:

An advertising executive reacted to the addition of each new benefit his agency offered by describing it as "just another fishhook in my back to tear away that much more flesh if I ever get up the nerve to leave." A staff consultant described benefit packages as corporate "bondage systems" that keep employees anchored to jobs they don't care for. A regional sales manager reacted to her employer's describing as a benefit the money it put into pension plans with: "Baloney. That's a straight-out employment cost for them." A secretary said about her payroll savings plan, under which the company matched dollar-for-dollar the funds employees deposited through payroll deductions: "Terrific. Now all I have to do is go out and get a part-time job so that I can afford to sign up for it."

To publish the above article for employees holding these viewpoints is not only useless, it creates an adverse reaction. It does not matter whether these employee viewpoints are *right* or *wrong;* that's the way they at present perceive things. Nor can an organization effectively communicate about benefits as "extras" when employees regard them as rights to which they are entitled. What possibly could have been the advantage to the Illinois company that apparently decided to set the record straight and, in its annual report to employees, made it clear that while employees "earned" $65 million in wages in 1978, they "were paid" $16 million in benefits?

Obviously, there must be communication about employee benefits. They are part of the package that encourages workers to join an organization and stay with it, no matter what employees attitudes are and even though internal rather than external rewards are receiving higher priorities in the search for job satisfaction. Organizations, however, should never communicate about benefits in a paternalistic tone. People resent that. How much better, in view of the diversity of employee attitudes, to handle such communication the way *Newsday*, the Long Island daily newpaper, dealt with a benefits story in *Inside Newsday*. First, it described substantive benefits—not parking lots and coffee breaks. Second, it was a first-person account by staffer Michael Unger, not a management piece saying, in effect, "Let me tell you what we've done for you lately."

A heart attack, open heart surgery and complications after surgery were terrifying enough for me and my family last year, but they would have been financially catastrophic were it not for *Newsday*'s sick pay benefits and medical and hospital insurance. Without them, my illness would have left us heavily in debt. More importantly, knowing I had such coverage with *Newsday* was a big relief, a load off my mind, while I was seriously ill. And these vital fringe benefits enabled me to concentrate on getting well without having to worry about huge hospital and medical bills mounting up or how my family would get by from day to day.

I received my salary during the six months I was out of work, part of it directly from *Newsday* and part of it from *Newsday*'s insurance carrier, Equitable Life. And the medical and hospital bills were almost totally paid through Equitable, while my wife's separate coverage picked up most of the remainder.

My total hospital and medical bills amounted to about $50,000 between February and June, 1979, and they continue to come in for postoperative care that includes participation in a cardiac rehabilitation program. Obviously, with costs like that, *Newsday*'s fringe benefits become absolute necessities.

Luckily for me, my wife, Amy, handled all of my medical and hospital bills as well as the disability insurance benefits, for which claims had to be filed periodically. But neither Amy nor I could have done it without the concerned and continuing help of *Newsday*'s Employee Relations Department. So, here's a special thank-you note to *Newsday*'s terrific Rembert Brown, Barbara Zielinski and Sue Hickey in Dan Mannix's department, and to Pat Stewart of Editorial who made sure my paychecks were mailed to my home.

When the hospital costs really started mounting up, the *Newsday* Blue Cross coverage was excellent. For example, the bill for the shortest of my four separate hospital stays last year at St. Francis Hospital in Roslyn—two weeks for the open heart surgery—was for a little more than $14,600. Of that amount, just $70.50 was not paid by Blue Cross. Equitable paid the medical claims with dispatch after Rembert Brown helped my wife file those insurance claims and other more complicated forms. He and Sue and Barbara in Employee Relations made my wife's task much easier. They and Pat Stewart in Editorial really went out of their way to help on a personal basis.

And in a large and growing company like *Newsday*, it's nice to know that can happen.

The two employee benefits articles speak for themselves. The second one is an example to follow when employee attitudes about a subject are not known: make a supposition as to the most negative attitudes that could exist among an audience and consider them when deciding how best to communicate.

It is especially difficult to anticipate all the attitudes that exist among an audience when dealing with international communication. Lack of awareness of subtle cultural and political differences and sensitivities makes it almost impossible for a communicator in one country to relate totally to audience interests in other countries. Some organizations hire entire staffs of local communicators in other countries, people who naturally understand and empathize with the interests and attitudes of their audiences. Few organizations can afford such staffs, however.

Riss Victor, associate editor of the Credit Union National Association's *Everybody's Money*, with editorial offices in Madison, Wisconsin, found a workable solution when it became evident that many of the articles in *EM* didn't apply to its Canadian readers. First, *EM* had contracted with Canadian freelance writers for occasional articles. However, this was not satisfactory. It seemed that unless every article was researched and written across the border, the magazine wouldn't meet the concerns of Canadian readers. Budget constraints and desire to maintain editorial control of content kept CUNA from establishing a full-time staff in Canada, so the editor contacted Canadian consultant Don Stewart, who suggested that, instead of originating articles, he would like a shot at "Canadianizing" the U.S. material. He examined some back issues and pointed out information that could make the articles more pertinent to Canadians. Stewart noted that "Canadians are somewhat nationalistic and resent U.S. 'arrogance,' particularly when there is an apparent insensitivity to Canadian feelings. Our Prime Minister, Pierre Trudeau, put it this way, 'Being neighbors to the USA is somewhat like being a mouse in bed with an elephant; the elephant's every move, however well-intentioned, is a serious risk to life.' "

The editors of *EM* agreed to let Stewart remove the irritants that annoy Canadian readers. Now they send him galleys of the U.S. articles, and he checks information with Canadian sources and does whatever rewriting is necessary. Sometimes Stewart simply changes *state* to *province;* sometimes articles require research and rewriting or editing to give them a Canadian flavor—or "flavour."

The Importance of Personal Contacts

Lack of personal contact with audiences severely restricts a communicator's ability to relate to them. The give and take that a one-on-one situation affords is especially effective in getting at deep-rooted attitudes, concerns and interests.

Opportunities for informal sensing of attitudes and interests are countless—for example, by really listening to casual comments in the office and plant, during lunch, in car pools, when visiting clients, and on so many other occasions. Frank W. Considine, president and chief executive officer of National Can Corporation, has remarked that whenever he visits a plant, he sits down at a table and talks to the supervisors. Communicators should be doing the same thing constantly in their areas of activity—always keeping their antennae out to discover what is on people's minds and to ascertain how receptive people are to what is being communicated and the ways in which it is being communicated. As helpful as formal surveys are, face-to-face encounters offer a far greater opportunity for probing and opening up new areas of thought.

When Western International Hotels opened the Century Plaza in Los Angeles, employee attitudes were unbelievably good. According to President Harry Mullikin, management had gone to great extremes to ensure that. "It was so good," Mullikin says, "we wanted to be sure we wouldn't lose it." So, during the first summer it was open, the hotel took one of the hotel management students it hires each year and assigned him to survey employees to find out what they did and didn't like, what bothered them or didn't bother them.

After hundreds of interviews, management learned that a major source of discontent was due entirely to a lack of communication. The hotel had no parking lot, so, before it opened, Western International arranged, for the convenience of the employees, to lease parking space from a company right behind it. The company charged the Century Plaza $10 a space a month, a charge that the hotel passed along to its employees. It never explained to the employees what the arrangement was, however. As a result, the survey revealed, the employees' number-one complaint was, "Why should the hotel make $10 a month by charging us for parking? That's not fair." The hotel management immediately explained the arrangement to its employees—and from then on included the explanation in its orientation program for new employees. Once these steps were taken, the complaint disappeared.

"One of the biggest mistakes management makes," Mullikin says, "is to assume that people know the full story. We had done something we thought was nice for the employees, and we assumed they'd know it. But they didn't."

The extent to which an audience's impressions conform to the facts is not the issue. What an individual *perceives* as reality *is* reality to that person—and it is that with which communicators must be concerned when they are addressing their audiences.

Thomas C. Hunter is director of public relations for Union Camp Corporation, Wayne, New Jersey, and is editor of its corporate employee magazine.

PART **II**

GETTING STARTED: Analyzing and Organizing the Work

Planning is essential to individual elements of organizational communication as well as to the total communication program. But how does one begin to plan? This section looks at the primary steps in planning for communication. Fact gathering—assessing the audience and auditing the existing communication practices—is followed by staffing the department and organizing the organization's communication program. These basic steps—assessing, auditing, and organizing and staffing—are essential in any organizational communication program.

CHAPTER 4

Auditing Communication Practices

MYRON EMANUEL, ABC

"How am I doing?" is the number-one question asked by communicators, far outnumbering the five Ws and an *H*. And the answer is sought in a variety of ways: surveys, both formal and informal, homemade or professional; letters and phone calls; corridor and cloakroom conversation; "gut feelings"; and astrological charts.

Most of these methods are pretty good. After all, an intelligent person usually can tell whether he or she is on target or off the mark. We don't need a formal survey to tell us that an article or a videotape was well received; an informal telephone survey can do this effectively. Why, then, this sudden and fairly widespread interest in communication "audits?"

An Old and Common-Sense Activity

The communication audit is really a new name for an old and common-sense communication activity. Communicators have always tried to assess the effectiveness of their programs, or to examine the relevance of what they were trying to say with what senior management wanted them to say, or to make sure what they were saying was being heard by those they were trying to reach. If they didn't do these things, and on a regular basis, either of two bad things happened: they found themselves looking for a new job or, worse, they discovered they were working for an organization that did not care about communicating or did not want to communicate.

Today, there is little danger of an organization not wanting to communicate. In fact, all the evidence points the other way. Communication budgets are up. Staffs are being increased. Senior management is far more involved in communication than ever before. And communication programs and communicators are being scrutinized far more critically because they are now being seen as essential contributors to the profit-and-loss statements. This is the reason for the widespread interest in the communication audit. It makes good business sense and takes its place alongside other organizational reviews: the financial audit, the benefits review, strategic planning, market research and manpower needs analysis.

A Complex and Time-Consuming Process

Despite the pervasive need for communication audits and a long history of attempts to carry them out, the true communication audit has been rarely attempted until recently. One reason is that it is a very complex and time-consuming process. Another is that it involves skills and techniques not always found in the communication process or among those who direct the process. These require considerable knowledge of business and business terminology, easy access to top management, intimate knowledge of organizational goals and philosophy (including those on the hidden agenda). Then it requires expertise in conducting surveys—preparing bias-free questions, administering surveys, leading focus-group discussions, reading and analyzing computer printouts to identify significant patterns and trends among the responses. Then all this must be reduced to an action plan for the long and short term.

Still another reason for the fairly limited use of communication audits is the confusion many people have in distinguishing them from other surveys and audits. In its essence, a communication audit is a comprehensive and thorough study of communication philosophy, concepts, structure, flow and practice within an organization—small or large, profit or nonprofit, private or public. A communication audit should be able to uncover information blockages, organizational hindrances to effective communication, and lost opportunities. It can expose misunderstandings, help gauge media effectiveness, and provide an evaluation of ongoing programs. It may be broad in scope or limited. It may be used to measure the effectiveness of communication throughout a large organization or in a single division or location. Like any audit, its value is increased if it is used regularly. A periodic checkup is good for people, finances and communication programs.

SURVEY

Communication survey for U.S. Area employees of Digital Equipment Corporation   February 1980

37. Do you regard this type of group meeting as useful?
   □ a. Yes
   □ b. No
   □ c. Sometimes

38. Do you feel a need for a centralized system by which you could send in questions about the company, for answer in writing by an appropriate manager?
   □ a. Strong need
   □ b. Occasional need
   □ c. No need

39. Do you have a need for a similar system for sending in suggestions?
   □ a. Strong need
   □ b. Occasional need
   □ c. No need

The answers to questions in this section are needed so that we can analyze survey results by categories such as age, function, wage class, etc. Answers will not be used to identify you.
□ If you are not an employee in the U.S. Area organization, please check the box above and skip to question 49.

40. In which of the following age groups do you fall?
   □ a. 25 or under
   □ b. 26 to 35
   □ c. 36 to 45
   □ d. 46 to 55

46. Which of the following classifications best describes your job?
   □ a. Office/clerical
   □ b. Technical
   □ c. Exempt (other than managers)
   □ d. Manager

47. Out of what type of facility do you work? (If several offices are at your location, which one are you a part of?)
   □ a. Regional office
   □ b. District office

The following question, dealing with your opinions about the company, will give us a sense of how employees perceive the company. Answers will help us to identify areas where more communication may be needed.

49. In each of the following categories, how would you rate Digital on a scale of 1 to 6, based on your experience in the company? Please place the appropriate number on the line provided:
   1 = Excellent
   2 = Good
   3 = Fair
   4 = Poor
   5 = Very poor
   6 = Don't know/can't rate

   ____ a. Recognition of employees for their achievements at work
   ____ b. Responsiveness to employee ideas and suggestions
   ____ c. Feedback on performance (performance appraisals)
   ____ d. Orienting new employees to the company
   ____ e. Quality of employee benefits
   ____ f. Quality of products and services
   ____ g. Pay or salary rates
   ____ h. Providing you with career opportunities
   ____ i. Work environment (office space) that promotes productivity
   ____ j. Training and development opportunities

50. Would you like to make any further comments relative to communication at

What It Isn't

A communication audit is *not* an attitude survey, which is the tool that an organization uses to examine employee feelings about the work atmosphere, working conditions, pay and benefits, and so on. Questions about communication may appear in an attitude survey, but they constitute only a relatively small number and are rarely specific to the kind of information a communicator needs.

It is *not* an opinion poll, which also has a place in the organizational arsenal of research tools. Opinion polls, apart from their political context, generally focus on specific subjects: for example, cafeteria vs. vending machines, flextime vs. regular hours, feelings about overtime or a third shift.

It is *not* a readership survey, which tells you what audiences think of a publication. For example, it cannot tell you whether you should issue the publication at all, or what value it is rendering the organization, or where it ranks as an information source among other competing media, such as the grapevine or the outside press.

It is *not* an issues awareness survey, which tries to gauge employee knowledge of organizational activities and plans. Among the things investigated here are employee *knowledge* of their benefit plans and how they work, or their awareness of specific government legislation or regulation affecting the organization and its future.

It is *not* an economic information or awareness survey, which is designed to probe employees' knowledge of, and attitude toward, the economy and how it affects their organization and their jobs. The purpose here is to help strengthen positive attitudes, address negative ones, fill in information gaps, and win employee understanding for organizational goals and activities, particularly where they concern productivity, business direction, governmental regulations and political activities.

It Is "Zero-Base" Communication

A standard approach to a communication audit is analogous to the zero-base budgeting process. In effect, you start your study from ground zero, as if you have no program, no communication vehicles, no goals, no staff, no budget. The focus, pure and simple, is on communication of all kinds. But the results of such a study explore all aspects of the organization:

- Organizational goals and philosophy.
- The audience's perception of these goals and objectives.
- The climate for communication.
- The structure of organizational communication, formal and informal.
- The nature and information needs of the various audiences (e.g., management groups, including specific breakdowns for professional, first-level supervision, middle management, sales, etc.; hourly employees and their various groupings; non exempt; plant; office; field). If the study involves external audiences, you should identify their specific characteristics and information needs, whether they be shareholders, members of the financial community, opinion leaders, neighbors, media professionals or private interest groups.
  - How the communication organization can best meet these audiences' information needs and expectations.
  - Where to locate the communication function within the organizational structure so that it can do the most good.

The goal of an audit is to determine which of the organization's philosophy and goals need communication supports. It should identify the audience or audiences for these messages and determine their information needs and wants, then establish an organization and pipeline to make sure these messages and information can move freely, efficiently and swiftly in both directions.

When to Audit

Communication audits should be carried out

- When organizations are aware that their programs lack credibility, are inefficient or ineffective, but find it difficult to uncover or resolve specific problems.
- When there is a need to evaluate a new communication policy or practice. Whether the policy or practice has been announced, initiated, or merely planned or conceived, an audit—ideally by an outsider who has been exposed to various business and communication assignments—can often help avoid pitfalls and make improvements.
- When there is a need to develop or restructure the communication function within the organization.
- When there is a need to develop communication guidelines or budgets.
- When there is a major change in the direction or structure of the communication function.
- When organizations merge or acquire new properties. A careful evaluation of the ongoing communication practices of the firms involved may show that different techniques will be required in each to allay employee fears and suspicions and to develop a positive, cooperative spirit.
- When new personnel practices or changes in the organization are being implemented.
- When there is labor unrest. Often the problems that lead to dissatisfaction among employees are the direct result of poor communication.
- When there are economic crises such as layoffs or cost-reduction programs. Employees are sometimes told *when* this is happening, but seldom *why*. Knowing the degree of their understanding of management's motives for the cut can provide a basis for explaining it—perhaps even soliciting help in the form of cost-saving ideas and suggestions for improvement. Further, an audit can tell you

whether the vehicles and staff you have in place are adequate to the job facing you.

Conducting the Communication Audit

There are a number of ways to approach the communication audit. One that we use at Towers, Perrin, Forster & Crosby incorporates a three-tier probe:

1. Intensive interviews with senior management
2. A comprehensive probe—often a survey—of the employee audience
3. A critical review and evaluation of employee communication practice, structure and materials

The result should be a clear picture of what senior management wants to say to employees; what employees want to hear and know; and how effectively the communication organization is meeting these needs. This research effort should produce material to create an action plan—short-term and long-term—for a communication program to meet these needs. It should indicate how the communication organization should be structured, what media you need, what you should be saying to audience or audiences, and how to manage an upward communication program.

Executive Interviews

Step one should be a series of one-on-one, intensive discussions with the senior officers of the organization. When we conduct these interviews, we always include the CEO, the chief operating officer, all the other senior officers (executive vice presidents, senior vice presidents, division presidents, etc.), and *anyone* else who is in a position to make and enforce corporate policy. The questions we ask are direct and blunt. We probe organizational goals, problems, challenges. We ask for candid assessments of the communication process, organization, effectiveness. We never discuss media, personalities or methods. What we are after is the personality of the organization as reflected in senior management, their concerns, and the key messages management wants to send out to win employee understanding and support. Our assumption is that there is no existing communication program, that we are starting from scratch.

Without question, this aspect of the audit should be conducted by an outside organization. It would be difficult—if not impossible—for an employee (and a subordinate employee at that) of the organization to extract the kind of information needed. Much of the information gleaned in these interviews is incorporated in the next step—in business organizations, the employee survey; in other organizations, the audience probe.

The Audience Probe

The next step is to go to the employees to find out what they know about the organization, what they don't know, and what they "know" that is wrong; how they receive their news and information and how they prefer to receive it; what they think of the information (is it credible, pertinent, timely, understandable?); how they evaluate the various media; which subjects are of greatest interest to them and which turn them off. Other topics brought up in the executive interviews often provoke additional questions that should be asked.

There are many ways to conduct such a survey:

Telephone interviews. Generally these are unsatisfactory for such an investigation.

Individual interviews. These are ideal but prohibitively expensive in terms of time and money.

Printed "check off" questionnaires. These are the most cost effective and provide a statistical benchmark against which you can measure future progress. But questionnaires have a number of drawbacks. Many people claim they're bored by such surveys because they're oversurveyed. Further, the responses you get are specific to the question you ask; if you don't ask the pertinent question, you can't get the pertinent answer. In other words, questionnaires leave little room for uncovering the unexpected or unmasking a serious concern that may be unknown to you. Unless questionnaires of this type are administered on site to everyone, or are returned by everyone in your sample, your response rate may be less than adequate. If it's a mail survey, you're at the mercy of the postal service or of employee indifference, distractions or forgetfulness.

The "Communi-card" * card-sort survey. In essence, it's another way of doing the statistical survey, but the technique seems to fascinate participants and helps overcome the boredom factor. Par-

---

* A servicemark of Towers, Perrin, Forster & Crosby.

ticipants are given a "deck" of cards with statements printed on them. The cards become the "answers" and responses.

Focus-group discussions. These are almost as good as individual interviews. The essential factor here is an experienced "neutral" group leader who is able to assure participants of confidentiality, keep the discussion on track, and be firm about keeping nonstop talkers in check. A drawback to this method is a lack of statistical data. Your information is subjective in nature—what the people said or what the group decided. One way to overcome some of this is to select the participants by a sampling method that reflects closely the employee population.

A combination of the statistical survey and the focus-group discussion. This approach offers the best balance of cost effectiveness, appeal, valid statistical data, flexibility, and in-depth probing. This technique was one that Sperry Corporation found useful and informative. Employees from throughout the organization assembled in conference rooms in groups of twenty at their work sites. Because of a modified random sampling technique, a very small sample of the total employee population was sufficient for the study. Each group consisted of peers—supervisors in their own groups, hourly people in their groups, managers in theirs. The first 45 minutes of the allotted hour was devoted to the "Communi-card" card-sort survey, which provided the statistical base required for the benchmark. The remaining 15 minutes was a candid discussion, which often brought out points not covered in the formal survey and provided insight into geographic and divisional differences and special concerns. It brought to the surface many rumors and so-called "facts" that the ensuing communication program could address.

The result of the survey or investigation should give you a report of how employees or members view the communication environment in your organization, what they want and need, how well your messages and those of top management have been received, and how well or poorly employees' and members' messages and questions move up the line.

The Critique

The final research step is to examine the organizational structure and communication vehicles, formal and informal, to see how well they are meeting the organization's expectations and employees' and members' needs. Publications, bulletin boards, memos, slide and video presentations, and the like are examined for content, appearance, frequency, pertinence, credibility and readability. Meetings of various kinds are examined. The grapevine and other informal communication networks are scrutinized.

The product of all this research effort is a mountainous and mind-boggling collection of interview notes, computer printouts, group discussion notes or tapes, publication critiques and evaluations. From this, a coherent picture of the communication process in your organization should develop

- What messages does management want to send?
- What messages does management think it has sent?
- Through what media did the messages travel?
- How fast or slowly did these messages flow through the communication pipeline, and with what degree of accuracy or distortion?
- Where are the blockages? How selective are the blockages—total? only some messages?
- How did employees or members understand the messages?
- What do they want to know?
- What do they feel they need to know?
- Is what management wants to say of any interest to them?
- Is what they want to hear of any interest to management?
- If there is a gap here, how wide and deep is it?

A thorough analysis of the research should give you the data and authority to create a set of communication policies and guidelines responsive to management's expectations and employees' or members' needs. For example, after a major nationwide survey of Xerox Corporation employees (through focus-group discussions), Joseph A. Varilla, the company's director of corporate communications, developed the following statement. Because corporate top management was involved early and heavily in the survey by way of lengthy executive interviews, they endorsed these policy guidelines in toto and made sure that the policy statement carried their names:

1. Responsibility for the success of the Xerox communications program is vested in all Xerox managers.
2. Communications leadership in any Xerox organization is the responsibility of that organization's senior management.
3. Each manager is responsible to his or her manager and to his or her people for communication of information on the state of the busi-

A Guide to Employee Surveys

	ATTITUDE SURVEYS	COMMUNICATIONS AUDITS	AWARENESS SURVEYS	READERSHIP SURVEYS
	Also known as "organizational climate" or "environment" surveys, "employee relations" or "human relations" audits or surveys; can measure feelings about a wide range of subjects, or zero in on just one topic— benefits, for example.	Focus exclusively on what an organization (or any part of an organization) is doing to communicate with a given audience; may also include a review of all media being used.	Assess employee knowledge and attitudes regarding specific issues; "economic awareness" survey measures understanding of the firm's business; "health awareness" survey (C&M, July/August 1979) determines understanding of national health insurance, health care cost containment.	Simplest survey type; unlike Communications Audit, cannot provide broad-based communications information.
SOME REASONS WHY...	– To assess employee understanding and/or acceptance of personnel policies and practices – To assess training needs – To measure morale and identify causes of employee discontent – To provide management with an objective overview of organizational characteristics – To check on supervisory effectiveness – To identify specific problems in individual demographic groups – To establish benchmarks – To measure progress against previously established benchmarks	– To find out how well communications programs are working – To diagnose current or potential communications problems or missed opportunities – To evaluate a new communications policy or practice – To assess the relationship of communications to other organizational operations on corporate and local levels – To help develop communications budgets – To develop or restructure the communications function within an organization – To provide background for developing formal communications policies and plans	– To identify areas of special employee concern – To assess current levels of knowledge on a specific issue – To pinpoint gaps in knowledge – To gauge attitudes toward a specific issue as input for a possible communications program – To evaluate the effectiveness of a current communications program	– To find out if readers are receiving publications regularly – To evaluate the impact of content on readers – To assess readers' perceptions of the quality of publications – To get reactions to or ideas about a possible new publication – To develop a list of topics that would interest readers – To provide background for developing an annual plan and budget for publications
SOME TIMES WHEN...	– Major reorganization – Merger or acquisition – New management team – Business downturn (layoffs, cost reduction programs, plant shutdowns) – External events (unfavorable publicity, lawsuit) cause concern – Upcoming union negotiations		– Issue spotlighted by current events (e.g., oil company prices) – Knowledgeable spokespersons on issue needed by management – Policy shifts (organizational or national) affect the firm	– Flagging interest in existing publications – Planned changes in publications – Development of publication budgets – Circulation of "underground" publications
SOME THINGS TO EXPLORE...	– Physical working conditions – Basic job satisfaction – Personnel policies and practices – Pay and benefits – Working relationships with others – Attitudes toward management – Communications	– Management's communications philosophy – Messages being sent – Messages being received – How messages are being received— accurately? favorably? uniformly? – Sources of information— real and preferred – Quality and effectiveness of current media	– Economic facts of the business – Productivity – The organization's role in a national or local issue/event – Pay and benefits – Personnel policies and practices	– Content – Readability – Distribution – Graphics – Frequency – Format
SOME POSSIBLE PARTICIPANTS...	– Senior executives, divisional managers, middle managers, professional employees, salaried employees, sales and field personnel, first-line supervisors, foremen, rank-and-file employees.			– Anyone who receives the publication(s); survey should be administered so that nonreaders also have input

ness, the tasks and goals of the organization, and the progress of the work organization's programs.

4. Each manager owes it to his or her employees to pass their concerns and questions upward and to press for timely and responsive answers, if answers are not immediately available.

5. Each manager is responsible to his or her people for candid communication on the individual's performance and career aspirations and for resolving misunderstandings of Xerox policy and its application.

6. Employees' self-esteem, as well as the quality of work life, can only be protected through continuing inter-personal and inter-group communication between them and their manager.

7. It is the responsibility of the senior manager of each Xerox operating unit to maintain an appropriate employee communications media program for the organization.

8. In their communications with their people, all managers have an obligation to be forthright and timely in discussing objectives, results, problems, difficulties and opportunities.

Each organization, of course, must develop its own policy guidelines based on its own philosophy, personality and needs.

Communication Plans

Two communication plans generally evolve from an audit: a long-range plan, tied rather closely to the organization's long-range business plan; and a short-term plan, tied to the organization's current fiscal-year plan but also incorporating and addressing the employees' or members' information needs and desires uncovered during the audit.

The long-range communication plan, of necessity, has to be general because it conforms to the organization's strategic goals. For example, an insurance company may establish as one of its long-range goals an earnings growth rate of 9 percent annually, compounded. Further, it may decide that half this growth will be achieved internally—through work efficiencies, more and better equipment, reassignment of key personnel and groups, and so on. The other half will be achieved through acquisition. The long-term communication plan must flow from this, and the communication organization must be ready to prepare the employees for major shifts in personnel and work assignments, new methods and procedures, cost cutting, and even layoffs. It must keep quiet about negotiations concerning acquisitions (for obvious legal and financial reasons) but have all the information ready to release if and when an acquisition is announced.

The short-range communication plan is very detailed. It flows from the specific findings of the audit and lists the subjects to be covered, the specific audience for each of these messages, the communication methods that will be used to cover these topics and audiences, the way feedback will be obtained, and the personnel and budget required to carry out these assignments.

The budget is always the last element to be developed, which is as it should be. The reasons are these:

- The organization has determined that there was a need for a communication audit.
- The audit was done, with heavy involvement of senior management—through extensive interviews with them. Further, their views and questions were carried forward into the employee survey.
- Communication guidelines and policies were hammered out to conform to organizational philosophy and policy and these were approved by top management.
- Communication plans, long- and short-term, were developed and approved by top management.

Therefore, the budget to support the operation is almost a by-product of all these steps. In fact, if management buys the new communication program, it almost automatically buys the budget. That, among all the other benefits, is one of the great dividends of the communication audit.

Communication audits help establish benchmarks and indicate directions the communicator should follow. They should be done every two years because organizations change. The communicator should reexamine audit results and proposals stemming from them quarterly to monitor operations against goals.

Why Outside Consultants?

The use of outside consultants often is a touchy subject with organizational communicators. A substantial number feel that calling in a consultant is an admission of failure or weakness—besides, "We don't have the budget for it" or, "Our firm doesn't believe in outside consultants."

These comments are ridiculous. Any medium-to-large firm depends on consultants, often of many different kinds. Legal departments always have outside legal counsel, often on retainer. Finance departments retain outside auditors and accounting firms. Most firms have outside actuaries. Benefits departments almost invariably use outside consultants to establish or alter benefit plans and design and prepare employee annual benefits statements. Compensation departments use consultants for a variety of purposes. Production, marketing and engineering departments are deeply involved with consultants. And they *all* have the "budget" for it. If you have no budget for a communication consulting service, obviously you are doing a perfect job, or you are not aware of what help is available to you, or your management doesn't think communication is worth more than they are now paying.

How would you go about selecting a consulting firm? Dick Coffin, a vice president of TPF&C, makes these suggestions: Look at the field, check reputations, talk to friends, check professional organizations like the Association of Consulting Management Engineers (ACME). Get a list of the four or five most likely candidates. Send them a request for a proposal, defining the nature and scope of the assignment and what is expected of the consultant. Ask direct questions about fees and timing and request written proposals. Then meet with the candidates to test their understanding of your problem and your organization or industry. Are they interested? Have they done their homework carefully? Ask if they are selling you canned solutions or programs. These rarely work well even though the world is full of consultants trying to make your problems fit their solutions. Beware of consultants who have the solution to your problem at the first meeting.

Two tests of a good consulting firm are its client list and repeat business. Get references and follow up on them. Ask if they have ever been sued by a client. In larger firms, ask about the ratio of consultants to support staff (e.g., research people, administrative assistants, creative directors). Some run very thin.

Ask about costs. Confirm verbally the quotes in the consultant's proposal. If supplier costs are involved, check on markups. Ask that the consultants include their perception of expected results of a project in the proposal.

Myron Emanuel, ABC, is a principal and director of business communications programs for Towers, Perrin, Forster & Crosby, a New York-based management consulting firm. He is accredited by the International Association of Business Communicators and was named a Fellow of IABC in 1975.

CHAPTER 5

Organizing and Budgeting Techniques

JIM HAYNES, APR

Everything an organization *does* or does *not* do communicates something about it. Since organizations are made up of people, everything any person within the organization does or doesn't do communicates something about the organization as well.

An organization's reputation, or "identification," is based on its actions, operations, public policies and statements, products, services and financial results. Equally important is the way the organization and its representatives are *perceived*—the way the buildings look, the telephones are answered, the organization's print materials look, the logo and the letterhead . . . *everything* communicates something about it. Because everything and everyone related to an organization are parts of the communication effort, communication is a team effort. Successful, effective communication is achieved only by planned, coordinated, professionally executed efforts.

Planning for Success

To organize all the elements essential to successful communication, the professional communicator should carefully assess the organization's needs; analyze goals and audiences; carefully apply specific, targeted media and messages; and then present the entire program in a written communication plan. Only when communication assists the organization in achieving specific objectives is the communication function recognized by top management as a successful, essential part of the organization. In preparing the communication plan, it is appropriate and essential for the communicator to begin with a clear understanding of top management's goals for the entire organization.

Once you understand organizational objectives and begin developing communication objectives that will help the organization's management accomplish its objectives, it is a good idea to meet with vice presidents, middle-management personnel, and department heads. This step is important because a communication program must have widespread support to be workable. By incorporating suggestions from throughout the organization, and by serving as communication consultant to those people and helping them with specific problems, you will be paving the road to the success of your communication program.

As you prepare communication objectives, remember that progress toward a goal must be measurable; otherwise, objectives are worthless. Having immeasurable objectives puts you in the same situation as runners in a race without a finish line. All too often, communication "objectives" are wishes rather than goals, since there is no provision for determining when the "objective" is accomplished (see chapter 4).

Consider the possibility of hiring an outside consultant to work with you as you meet with top management and write the communication plan. Even if your experience qualifies you to do all the work yourself, having an outside "expert" will often lend credence to your recommendations. Locate a competent consultant with background in the area of your interest. You'll probably find that his or her specialization and objectivity will make significant, innovative contributions to your program or project.

Writing Message Statements

In addition to establishing objectives for what you want to accomplish, it is worthwhile to write a precise statement of what you want to *say*. Ask yourself, "What would I communicate to everyone if I had only one sentence to use for that communication?" The answer to that question can become your basic message statement—a statement that contains the essence of your total communication message. The basic message statement should be used in the annual report, in brochures, as a final paragraph in each news release, and in other communications.

After you have a workable basic message statement, work on "customized" message statements for each audience and for each activity directed to them. If you analyze your employee publications, you should be able to summarize the thrust of your communication efforts in a series of phrases like these:

> "Our organization rewards loyal employees."

> "Our benefits programs are outstanding."

> "This is an interesting and challenging place to work."

> "We encourage employees to continue their education and develop leadership/management potentials."

> "Our management team is composed of personable individuals dedicated to leadership within our industry."

> "Research and development keep us ahead of our competition."

By writing a series of such statements (which *must* be honest), you establish criteria for evaluating ideas for future articles and photographs. If a potential article or photo doesn't help communicate one of the statements, it's probably not worth using. By restricting the number and complexity of the messages you convey, you can assure that the most important messages are effectively communicated.

After you understand your organization's objectives and have established communication objectives, defined audiences and established message statements, you can begin to determine which media will be most effective in reaching each target audience (see chapter 7). Unfortunately, many communicators select media without understanding objectives and audiences. That process is as risky as having a physician prescribe medication without diagnosing the illness. The result will be effective only by chance. Every medium of communication should be analyzed and evaluated in terms of the organization's objectives and the medium's capabilities relative to audiences, message statements and, of course, staff and budget.

Preparing the Communication Plan

The written plan is a "road map" that is essential to measuring progress toward objectives for a specific project or an ongoing program. If the plan is written after consultation with top management, their expectations of communication performance will be more realistic. Having the written plan approved by management allows you to devote staff time and budget to important activities, protecting you from unrealistic requests from division and department heads who often want "extras" from your budget.

Every communication plan is structured differently, reflecting the needs of the organization and its people, but the following topics should be considered for inclusion in the plan:

1. *Background.* This section provides the communicator with an opportunity to "play back" in writing a discussion of his or her understanding of how the organization reached its present situation. Generally it is worthwhile to include a brief description of the organization and its management. By writing such a discussion, the communicator cements his or her own understanding and offers it to the organization for correction or confirmation.

2. *The present situation.* Where is the organization now in terms of its overall situation and its communication program? The first part of this section might discuss what makes the organization unique, its position in its field, in its community, and so on. Include both negative and positive factors, utilizing information from discussions with top management and department heads.

3. *Discussion of the communication process.* This section may be included when the communicator determines that the people within the organization do not have professional communication training and do not understand the communication process and the function of public relations. Discuss the importance of communication and outline the process, perhaps utilizing a "model" of communication.

4. *Why a communication plan?* In some organizations, one or two people are interested in establishing an organized communication function, while others are cool or even hostile to the idea. This section of the plan should explain why there should be an organized communication function and the importance of the communication plan in accomplishing that goal.

5. *Message reinforcement.* This is an optional section for organizations in which the people do not understand the need for consistency in the communication process. It gives you the opportunity to make a pitch for a unified "identity" program within the organization and to emphasize the importance of repeating, with variations, one basic message statement over and over again.

6. *An introduction to the plan.* This section gives the professional communicator the opportunity to discuss the philosophy represented in the plan—reasons for the thinking contained in the plan.

7. *Objectives.* Relate the organizational objectives and discuss how

the communication program will contribute to them. List the main objective of the communication program. List and discuss intermediate goals that will assist in accomplishing the main objective.

8. *Message statement*. Present the one basic message statement to which all the activities in the plan will contribute.

9. *Audiences and messages*. List audiences in order of importance. When possible, use demographic data and other information to discuss each audience's "predisposition," or "the things that turn them on." Write a one- or two-sentence message statement for each audience, a brief summary of exactly what you want to communicate to each audience, in line with your basic message statement.

10. *Strategy*. Discuss the way you recommend the plan be implemented. You may, for example, have a strategy to position your management as experts in specific fields to contribute to the organizational objective of building confidence in your management. This strategy might be executed by involving your top executives in a series of activities (e.g., seminars, speeches), each of which would play a role in accomplishing the objective. You may need more than one statement of strategy to deal with a comprehensive program.

11. *Activities, responsibilities and budget*. List the activities designed to accomplish each objective, the person or persons responsible, the timing (completion date), and the estimated cost of each activity. Sometimes it is not possible to include all this information; include as much as possible.

12. *Research and follow-up*. Describe fact finding and formal research that will be conducted and how it will be used. If you do not plan to conduct formal research, change the heading to "Measuring Effectiveness" and include information on the techniques you will use to determine how well you accomplish your objectives.

The Communication Plan as a Communication Tool

In preparing a communication plan, remember that the executives to whom you present the plan for approval are your audience. Look closely at their backgrounds and interests before you complete the plan. A large percentage of management executives—especially in business—come from the ranks of engineering, law and business administration and probably have never examined how the process of communication works.

As you prepare your plan, be sure to comment on your efforts to obtain management input and how the plan supports management's objectives for the organization. Be sure the plan looks like the reports and documents that executives are accustomed to seeing. Engineers, for example, have unique formats for project scheduling. If your company president is an engineer, he will relate well to your schedules if they are in this familiar format. Go to an engineer to find out what is most appropriate.

If you are presenting a budget, be sure your format follows the standard budget style used by vice presidents and division heads. Ask your accounting department about the format of typical departmental or divisional budgets, and follow it.

Presenting the Communication Plan

Once your communication plan is complete, you'll need to present it for approval to your organization's chief executive officer, the management committee, the board of directors or some other appropriate group. Have copies for each person at the meeting, but avoid handing out any copies until your presentation and request for approval are completed, or you risk losing control of the conference as people leaf through the printed plan, lose interest in what you are saying, and ask questions on topics you intended to cover in a sequence. Keep the copies in a folder until you are ready to distribute them.

If you need illustrations, use flip-charts or photostatic enlargements of typed information for small groups; for ten or more participants, overhead transparencies or slides should be used.

Communication Budgeting by Objective

The simple secret to success in originating and managing a communication budget (and any other budget, for that matter) is to decide what's worth doing and what's *not* worth doing. Once you have decided what's worth doing, list these activities in order of importance (with the most important listed first). After obtaining cost estimates for each, you have a budget for one project.

What about a budget for your communication department? Let's take a look at how to go about it, using a "zero base" technique that will

FIGURE 5.1 Communication by Objective

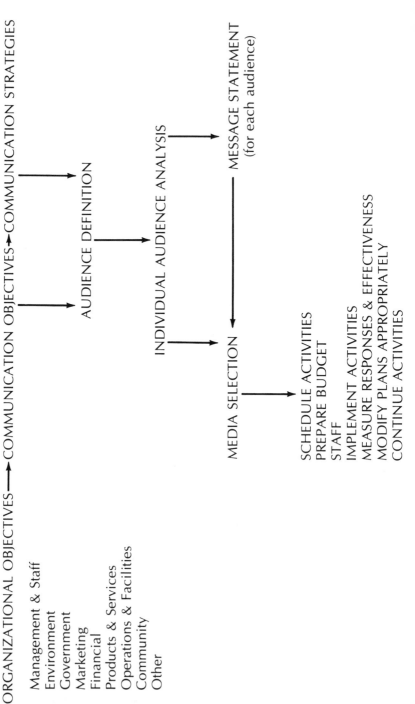

ORGANIZATIONAL OBJECTIVES ⟶ COMMUNICATION OBJECTIVES ⟶ COMMUNICATION STRATEGIES

Management & Staff
Environment
Government
Marketing
Financial
Products & Services
Operations & Facilities
Community
Other

AUDIENCE DEFINITION

INDIVIDUAL AUDIENCE ANALYSIS

MESSAGE STATEMENT
(for each audience)

MEDIA SELECTION

SCHEDULE ACTIVITIES
PREPARE BUDGET
STAFF
IMPLEMENT ACTIVITIES
MEASURE RESPONSES & EFFECTIVENESS
MODIFY PLANS APPROPRIATELY
CONTINUE ACTIVITIES

allow you to budget according to the relative importance of your communication objectives. Your communication objectives were designed to support organizational objectives, so this technique will assist you in securing management approval for communication activities.

After you have studied your organization's objectives and determined how communication can assist in their accomplishment, do the following:

- List all your audiences in order or importance, with the most important at the top of the list.
- For *each* audience, list the communication media and activities you plan to use during the next twelve months to reach that audience. Put in order of relative importance—the most important first.
- Indicate what it costs to use each medium one time.
- List the number of times during the next twelve months you plan to use the medium (e.g., how many newsletter issues will you print?).
- Multiply the number of times by the unit cost, to reach a total cost for the year for each medium.
- Do the same thing for each communication medium, audience by audience.
- Add up the total cost for the year for *each* audience, dropping out the costs for media that repeat from one audience to the next. (A newsletter might be distributed to several different audiences; include its basic cost only once, the first time it appears. Add additional printing and postage costs for each additional audience for which it is used.)
- Add *all* the totals for all the audiences. Add to your total the cost of overhead expenses that cannot logically be appropriated to the cost of communicating with individual audiences. Overhead items will vary from organization to organization but will include such expenses as salaries, staff benefits, rent, utilities, equipment and supplies. The total is your *desired* communication budget for the year.

If the total is too big, you have two choices: eliminate audiences, starting at the bottom of the list with the least important audience; or eliminate media, starting at the bottom of the list for each audience. Be sure to make a comparison with present expenditures. Organizations that never prepared an overall communication budget are often surprised to learn how much money they have been spending on ineffective materials and activities!

Once you have determined how your budget will be allocated, on

FIGURE 5.2 Budgeting—"Stack of Money Concept"

Audience: I. _____

A. Media:	B. Unit cost:	C. Times per year:	D. Cost:
1. _____	1. _____	1. _____	1. $ _____
2. _____	2. _____	2. _____	2. $ _____
3. _____	3. _____	3. _____	3. $ _____
4. _____	4. _____	4. _____	4. $ _____
5. _____	5. _____	5. _____	5. $ _____
6. _____	6. _____	6. _____	6. $ _____

Audience I Total Cost...........$ _____

Audience: II. _____

A. Media:	B. Unit cost:	C. Times per year:	D. Cost:
1. _____	1. _____	1. _____	1. $ _____
2. _____	2. _____	2. _____	2. $ _____
3. _____	3. _____	3. _____	3. $ _____
4. _____	4. _____	4. _____	4. $ _____
5. _____	5. _____	5. _____	5. $ _____
6. _____	6. _____	6. _____	6. $ _____

Audience II Total Cost...........$ _____

(Continue with Audience III, etc.)
All overhead expenses after combining totals for all audiences.

the basis of audience and media priorities, reassemble it for accounting purposes. Most organizations have standard budget classifications that must be used for budgets of all departments so that accounting can be computerized. If such is the case in your organization, you will be provided a list of such categories and will have to live with them as best you can.

Project Budgeting

To produce reliable budgets for major projects, break the project into categories and establish separate cost estimates for each category. For a printed piece like an annual report or an employee publication, the categories might be

Concept development and design
Layout (thumbnail sketches, rough comp or tight comp)
Writing and editing, including travel, research and interviews
Typesetting and photostats
Photography and illustrations, including travel, models, prints, retouching, etc.
Mechanical art
Printing (including color separations, negatives, proofs)
Distribution

Refuse to "guess" at estimates in advance of agreement on design. When someone asks how much a brochure will cost before it is designed, respond that an accurate figure can be determined only by submitting the completed design to typesetters, photographers and printers for written estimates. If *they* want to "guesstimate," let them, but avoid the temptation to do so yourself; it can do nothing but produce misunderstandings.

Try to complete the design a week or more ahead of the presentation for management approval. Submit the design sketches or comp to qualified printers, photographers and typesetters and obtain written estimates. If you're using in-house services, obtain written estimates of the number of hours and related interdepartmental charges you can expect. If you're using outside people for design, mechanical art and photography, get written estimates for each. Add to the totals an amount for supplies, travel and retouching. Then add a 10 to 15 percent contingency for expenses you cannot anticipate—additional photography, overtime

FIGURE 5.3 Typical Budget

Expenditures:	Jan	Feb	Mar	Apr	May	Jun	6 Mo. Totals	Jul	Aug	Sep	Oct	Nov	Dec	12 Mo. Totals
Staff:														
Salaries														
Benefits														
Expenses														
Part-time help														
Office:														
Rent or space allocation														
Utilities														
Equipment:														
Maintenance & Repair														
Purchases														
Rental														
Communications:														
Telephone														
Telegraph, TWX, Telecopier, Etc.														
Messenger service														
Postage														
Production:														
Design services														
Typesetting														
Photography														
Printing														
Media space														
(Other)														
TOTALS														

typesetting, and the like. Prepare a written cost estimate (a better title than "budget" since "cost estimate" sounds more subject to refinement) for each category.

If any decisions are made in the presentation conference (or at a later date) that affect total costs, indicate that the changes will cost additional money. Document decisions made in the meeting with a memo, sending copies to those present and others involved, and request revised cost estimates once the changes have been incorporated into the design. Design changes (e.g., addition of photos, changes in paper quality) and increases in quantities are the principal reasons for projects exceeding cost estimates. Eager-to-please communicators too often simply say changes can be accommodated, failing to note that any change will affect total costs and time of delivery.

Even without computer support, project costs can be monitored easily. If you establish functional categories for your project budget (design, writing and editing, etc.), you can use these categories to monitor and report the project's budget status. To do this, use a four-column accounting ledger and list functional categories as captions, leaving several inches of space between the captions. Beside each, post in the first column the functional cost estimate. At the end of each month, post total costs for each function in the second column and keep a "cost to date" total in the third column. In the fourth column, post a current budget balance. With this system, you will be able to prepare reports to management at the beginning of each month. It increases confidence levels and prevents end-of-project "surprises."

Of course, any time a change is made, you will need to document in writing what was changed, who made the decision, and what effect the change has on cost estimates and on the project schedule. If the change is minor, you can post the costs related to the change to the category established for "contingencies." If it is a major change, you may need to revise your total budget.

Monitoring Budgets

Monitoring budgets, especially in a large organization, can be more difficult and time-consuming than preparing the original budget. Usually, the organization's accounting department will provide a computer printout showing actual expenditures compared to budgeted amounts in each category, by account codes, for the previous month and for year to date.

Some will also indicate the amount and percent under or over the budget for each category. Unfortunately, such reports are of little help to the communication manager attempting to keep costs for each project in line with budgets.

To better organize the communication function to monitor budgets, try the following:

- Establish your own departmental code of accounts, related to projects rather than functions. Use a numeric code containing a two-digit year indication followed by a three-or four-digit project code. Set up a code-control log and designate sequential code numbers for projects as they are begun: the first project in 1981 would be assigned code 81-0001, the second would be assigned code 81-0002, and so on.
- Write the project code number on each invoice for each project.
- Check with your accounting department and see if their monthly reporting format has unused columns. If so, ask them to add your departmental code to the computer postings for your invoices as they are made. If they can do so, they will be able to print out a report for each of your departmental codes each month, and you automatically will have information on project budget status.
- If your organization's accounting department cannot or will not cooperate, you are on your own. Set up a folder for each major project (e.g., monthly employee publication, annual report, audiovisual presentation) and "category" folders for other projects (e.g., news releases). Then, as invoices arrive, post your departmental code on them and file a copy of the invoice in the appropriate folder. Run monthly totals to make sure project budgets are kept in line.
- In large organizations with in-house service functions such as graphic design, typesetting, photography and printing, inter-departmental charges can make your budget difficult to monitor. However, the departmental codes described above can be used to keep charges in line with budgets and to prevent unauthorized charges. Implementing the plan will require the cooperation of the accounting department.

Be sure to reach agreement with the accounting department staff that no interdepartmental charges will be made to your budget units unless the department charging your budget uses one of your project-control codes. Then, as you assign work to the service organizations, agree in advance on the total amount of time and materials to be involved and give them a project code number to use. Their charges can then be included in the monthly reports from the accounting department, or you can request from each of the service departments a report on what charges they are making to each of your project code numbers.

Communication Department Staffing

An appropriate organization and level of staffing for communication should be an expected outgrowth of the development of the communication plan. The plan focuses in on the organization's needs and gives specific direction to communication activities designed to contribute to those needs.

While the plan is being developed, it is logical to group similar functions and estimate the number of person-hours per week needed to perform each function. Obviously, if the requirements estimated for any one function exceed forty hours a week, more than one staff position may be necessary. Perhaps a staff "section" of several people may be appropriate.

Once requirements are defined, write job descriptions for each of the positions needed. List qualifications for the position and determine a salary level in keeping with the skills required and local market conditions.

Finally, prepare a communication department organization chart, showing reporting levels, staff functions with titles, and summaries of responsibilities for each function. (More detailed information on staffing is presented in chapter 6.)

Building Management Confidence

Top management controls the destiny of communicators. Our positions within the organization, salaries, professional development expenses and operating budgets must all be approved by them. It is obviously in your best interest to attempt to understand management's needs and how communication can assist in accomplishing their goals. Communicators should treat management as their most important audience. To do so, study the demographics backgrounds and predispositions of the people at the top and prepare a communication approach most acceptable to them.

Management often is confused about what to expect from communicators, who must gain management's respect by consistently *acting like managers,* demonstrating that they can plan and budget and control and report with the same precision and professionalism that management expects from every other department within the organization. The alternative is limping along, day after day, decade after decade, complaining about how hard we work and how little respect and reward we receive for our efforts.

The reality of your situation may be that by understanding your organization, knowing your management as people, and involving them in the communication process which you manage, you can work more effectively and play a more important role in your organization. But you cannot do so haphazardly; you must get organized—*today.*

Jim Haynes, APR, is a communications consultant for Hay Communications, a division of Hay Associates, in Dallas, Texas. He is accredited by the Public Relations Society of America.

CHAPTER 6

Staffing the Communication Department

LINDA PETERSON and JAMES R. DODGE

Historically, people who performed communication functions for organizations were a cadre of Flying Dutchmen. In whose country should they reside? Traditional ties with personnel and employee relations landed them in personnel, industrial relations and any number of related departments. Anyone who could write or shoot pictures or fish the organization out of a mess after the mess was made was likely to be found in the public relations department, often solely a publicity department. The recognition that communication has an important part to play in policy making, as well as in managing publicity and crises already at hand, led to a parallel discovery that communication has many vital audiences and services.

Responding to those changes, more and more organizations are both segmenting and centralizing their communication efforts. The new look is a corporate communication department, headed by a senior or executive vice president. Within that department, organizations are likely to be divided into functional areas that meet different audience needs. Public affairs, for example, might include lobbyists and legislative analysts, consumer and/or customer relations for organizations which deal directly with the public, and regulatory relations for organizations subject to government regulation. Press relations typically is staffed by people able to meet media demands and, in large organizations, maintain constant contact with the media. The staff might be subdivided into print and electronic specialties. Organizational communication, recognizing employees as an important constituency, includes both all-employee and targeted groups such as union-represented, management and retirees. Financial relations targets communication for both shareholders and members of the financial community such as analysts and investment bankers. Advertising might fit into communication or marketing departments.

Organizations with very special communication needs are breaking with traditional lines to meet those needs. Pacific Telephone, for example, uses an "account executive" concept. Communicators with reporting relationships in the public relations department are assigned as "special counsel" to the three major operating divisions of the company. The marketing department has an in-house communication expert, someone equipped with communication skills who is especially attuned to the needs and problems of the marketing organization, to provide communication tools to help solve operating problems there.

Obviously, these organizational descriptions fit best with medium-to-large corporations. Smaller companies, nonprofit agencies, governmental bodies, privately held corporations with few employees and little or no general public contact or exposure have somewhat different needs. They tend to be staffed with generalists who can perform a variety of communication functions.

The department's organization and the way it fits into the overall plan of the institution are as individual as fingerprints. Organization charts, with all the intricacies of dotted and straight lines indicating who reports to whom, are necessary, to be sure. The structure and the staffing that supports it should all be aimed at getting and keeping access to top-management decision making. The communication staff should be organized to provide solutions to operating problems, rather than simply perpetuate communication vehicles.

This means, for example, that the senior member of the department should be part of the officer policy-making body, whether it is an advisory group, a formal policy review committee, or simply an informal network. The organization he or she heads needs to be structured to provide good, current information on the state of the environments, both internal and external.

Giving communication people the opportunity to break role, to join an inter- or intradepartmental problem-solving team, forces them to think outside the mold. If it's interdepartmental, it has the advantage of exposing the communication pro to line organizations (and vice versa), enabling that person to see, firsthand, mainstream problems of the business. If it's a multidiscipline intradepartmental team, for example, it can expose a print person to other media or a "management communicator" to the problems and techniques of communicating with blue-collar workers. All these opportunities protect senior members of the communication department from isolation and from a sense of being outside the main concerns of the business. It provides them with good, current information and a staff comfortable in any organizational environment.

Organizations are organizations, and even creative people fit into categories. When it comes time to match people to jobs, it's useful to keep each job and the abilities it requires in mind. We will look later at interviewing and hiring people for positions in each category. First, let's examine the kinds of persons in the various levels of the communication department.

Donald F. McLaughlin, director of media relations at AT&T, identifies three layers in a typical communication organization. First, there are the craftspersons or practitioners. Most professional communicators start here, either directly from school or from an allied field—newspapers, television and radio, advertising, marketing or teaching. Craftspeople, McLaughlin says, are those who "do" for a living. They are primarily writers, photographers, designers, illustrators, assistant editors. They may have some administrative duties, but essentially they are producers.

The next level or layer includes creative/administrative people. They are likely to have the title of editor or manager and are likely to be both doers and supervisors. They are still involved in the craft—supervising a publications staff, editing a magazine and managing its staff, running an audiovisual shop—but they are also charged with supervising people, programs, or both.

Next, there's the creative/administrative/executive layer. This is usually occupied by persons who have a strong craft background, have supervised both creative and administrative types, and have made the move to management. Don McLaughlin says that the men and women at this level can do more than turn out good copy and nifty layouts and effectively supervise an amalgam of others doing the same. They also have sufficient interpersonal communication skills, deductive reasoning ability, knowledge and savvy to convince others in the organization—horizontally and vertically—that what they're doing is making or saving money for the organization. Their titles range from director to department head to vice president. In large organizations, the layers may have many people in these levels. There may be writers and senior writers in level 1; supervisors, administrators, managers and editors in level 2; and directors, assistant vice presidents, vice presidents and executive vice presidents in level 3. In small ones, one or two persons may handle all the tasks.

Why do these layers matter? Concern with them doesn't mean an obsession with pigeonholing people and their capabilities. Rather, knowing what kinds of skills—professional, technical, administrative, managerial—a job requires makes filling it with the right people less risky. If you're after a practitioner, for example, you are probably concerned primarily with professional credentials. Can he or she write, interview, edit, design, shoot pictures? If you're after an administrator, can he or she motivate, manage, guide; relate to superiors and subordinates? If you're after a director, can he or she translate top-management concerns into communication solutions? Does she or he see communication programs as management tools, deploy resources—time, money, people—to get the best return on investment? Can he or she lead an organization?

There's a myth that implies supervising creative people is somehow so different that none of the rules that apply to supervising "regular people" fit. Nonsense. There are some tricks for establishing and maintaining an environment in which creative people can flourish, but before they get pulled out of the hat, the tried-and-true rules about managing people need to be functioning. These are

> *Define responsibilities.* Not knowing what you're supposed to do, when you're supposed to do it, and who you're supposed to do it for are leading causes of anxiety and dissatisfaction attacks. Job descriptions do not have to be couched in stultifying institutional language. They should describe the job and the expectations that go with it.

> *Establish methods to measure.* People like to be paid for what they do, not for how they smile at the boss. Creative jobs are not unmeasurable, especially if they are based on a well-developed set of departmental and corporate objectives and are well-defined. Dale McConkey's *MBO for Staff Managers* is a good introduction to organizing nonline management jobs.

> *Don't make unnecessary rules.* Aside from providing the basics— decent salaries and work areas and the opportunity to grow—the secret to managing creative people probably lies in the maxim of the Bauhaus designers: less is more. Flextime, relaxed dress codes when there's no public contact, think time—all of these recognize the non-assembly-line aspects of the creative process. Of course, that doesn't mean releasing "blocked" writers to Big Sur, the Poconos or the Laurentians for unlimited periods of time.

> *Create an open, nonthreatening atmosphere.* With highly motivated, independent subordinates, the one who bosses best probably bosses least. The manager should function as a facilitator,

providing access to information and resources up and down the organization, setting a climate as free of secrets, threats and reprisals as possible. While these are good rules to follow for running almost any organization of independent people, they are especially critical rules for supervising creative people. Nothing maims or mutilates the creative process as badly as the conviction that the products always have to "play" to a certain audience. Managers need to play politics, of course, but political considerations shouldn't color the beginning, middle and end of every creative process.

Encourage intelligent risk-taking. Caution breeds expectability and its first cousin, boredom. No two communication problems are alike, and if a communication staff is going to come up with innovative solutions tailored to specific problems, they shouldn't be hamstrung by convention and tradition. If they are, a computer can probably be programmed to generate the solutions. That doesn't mean the manager should suspend critical judgment—garbage in, garbage out, to borrow from the computer people—but at the brainstorming, problem-solving stages, nonevaluative acceptance keeps the juices flowing. The time for "reality testing," criticism, and fine-tuning comes when the field has been narrowed. Subordinates should feel comfortable raising any idea—no matter how crazy. Ideally, their first thoughts should be, "I wonder if . . ." not, "Oh, no, the boss will never go for that."

The manager, in other words, is there to make problem solving easier, to encourage a certain amount of risk-taking, and to act as facilitator.

Now that the atmosphere's in place, the next step is finding the right people and putting them in the right places.

Interviewing and Hiring

To find, interview and hire the best people, begin with job specifications. These are more than job descriptions. They detail exactly what the group needs to accomplish and what kind of person it will probably take to accomplish the results.

There are two kinds of job specs—the make-or-break and the nice-to-have. If the job opening is for a writer, make-or-break is a proven ability to write. Nice-to-have might be a degree in economics or journalism or animal husbandry or chemistry—whatever seems appropriate for the organization. It is important to distinguish between the two categories of specs. To determine what they should be, look at the organization's objectives, review job responsibilities, consider past and current job holders, think about possible changes. Ask the boss, ask peers, think about what product or program the candidate may need to turn out a month after he or she is hired. Then prepare the specifications.

Once the job specs are defined, develop questions designed to elicit the information needed to make a decision. For example, if speech making will be a part of the job, the manager should ask: "Have you given speeches before? What kinds of groups? How do you get ready for one? May I see a copy (or better yet, a videotape)?" Later on, the hiring manager might want to arrange for final candidates to give mini presentations.

Of course, the questions need to relate directly to the level of the job. In other words, if the opening is for a craft professional, writing samples, recommendations, reputation, and so on will probably suffice. If the job is for an administrative/craft person, the extra credentials and experience for managing need to be explored. For the third level, the director or senior manager, all the above plus the services of an executive search firm might be called into action.

Entire books have been written on the fine art of interviewing. In all, these key points emerge:

- *Have an agenda.* Know what information you need and ask questions to get it.
- *Ask open, probing questions.* Who, what, why, how? Can you give me an example? How would you do that differently now?
- *Give the candidate time to talk.* Don't cut off responses.
- *Keep control.* The interview should be a two-way process, but the manager needs to control the flow.
- *Remember the law.* Questions must be directly related to job performance.

After each interview, summarize key points. Make lists of items that need further exploration, people to talk with, work samples to review, and so forth.

Role plays, case studies and writing tests can be useful. If, for instance, the candidate would serve as company spokesperson, the interviewer might ask, "Suppose the EPA announces that one of our local mills is under investigation. I'm going to play the role of newspaper reporter and ask you to answer some questions." Or, the interviewer

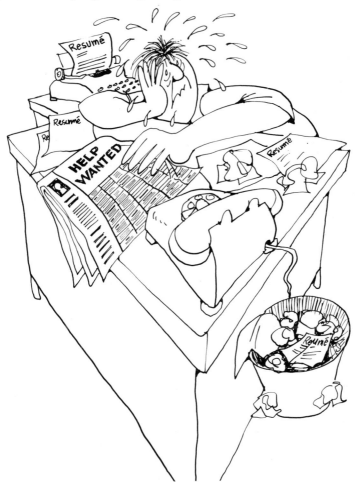

Matching the right communicator with the right job avoids both personal and managerial headaches.

might pose an ongoing problem—inadequate horizontal communication at middle management—and ask for the candidate's thoughts on the subject. Finally, the interviewer might leave the candidate with data and typewriter and ask him or her to come up with a feature article or news story, or both, on a designated topic. All these techniques are legitimate if they relate to the job opening. They are useful if the interviewer has the expertise to evaluate them.

Once a decision to hire has been made, it is important to present the job offer in as much detail as possible. The job, its responsibilities, salary, benefits, and opportunities for growth need to be explained fully. The job candidate should be encouraged to discuss them.

Promoting

Given the right people in the right places in the right environment, how do you recognize who should move up and when? Identifying potential and developing it merits more space than this chapter can devote to it. Still, since it is so critical a part of a manager's job, it is worth identifying a few signposts that point to potential.

"The complete subordinate's" work arrives on the boss's desk without loose ends. Research is thorough: it is well developed and accurate. Obstacles are anticipated and follow-up and contingency plans are built in.

"The catalyst" can bring a group together and can persuade others to do things without arousing hostility or resentment. He or she can resolve conflicts and is a credit-giver rather than a glory-grabber.

"The decision maker" is willing to make decisions and accept their consequences. He or she doesn't shoot from the hip, but gathers information and makes a good, defensible decision without running to the boss for guidance at every step.

Once potential is identified, it's the joint responsibility of boss and subordinate to develop it further. Task force assignments, "opportunity" assignments that stretch talents and abilities that need further growth, and evening classes are possibilities they should discuss. Together they should decide what is appropriate to pursue.

If the subordinate is a craftsperson, interested in making the transition from doer to manager, supervisory and managerial skills can be developed with "acting" assignments—filling in for the boss. If the subordinate wants to climb the next rung in the specialist ladder or develop another craft specialty, classes, self-development programs or "apprenticeship" arrangements might work out best. Whatever the goal, the development process has to be a joint effort, with the boss providing resources and opportunities and feedback and the subordinate doing the rest.

Firing

This being not the best of all possible worlds, from time to time the right person might not end up in the right place. Then what? If the manager has done a good and conscientious job of establishing expectations and performance standards and then measured by those standards, the most painful variety of separation—the surprise—should never take place.

Exit interviews should never include a scenario of departing subordinate protesting, "But I thought I was doing so well."

Performance appraisals or reviews, held at least quarterly, are more than an ounce of prevention. They let people know exactly where they stand, where problems exist (if they do), and what the boss is prepared to do to help the subordinate measure up.

While the content of boss/subordinate conversations surely does not need to be formalized, the structure or system for dealing with performance problems probably should be. Borrowing a leaf from union-management relations, here are four steps to follow:

1. *Counsel.* This is the first "we've got a problem" conversation. After the informal chats fail, it's probably a good idea to begin by describing the problem and asking the subordinate for ideas on how to solve it. Does he or she know how the job should be done? Maybe the problem is training. Is it a lack of interest? If the work is dull, maybe the boss can do something. If not, it might be an early warning signal that a job search could be coming. Is it an interpersonal problem? Perhaps some friendly advice from the boss or someone else will help. The key is getting the subordinate's ideas and commitment for solving the problem.

2. *Warn.* If step 1 doesn't produce improvement, the problem needs to be reexamined. The boss needs to restate expectations and the subordinate needs to know what the consequences will be if improvement doesn't result.

3. *Job on the line.* When 1 and 2 fail, the subordinate needs to know it's "shape up or ship out" time. Obviously, the boss needs to keep documentation on this conversation and should have supporting material (e.g., assignments, performance appraisals).

4. *Dismissal.* Sometimes it happens, though probably not often enough. If there's a poor match between job and employee, in the long run there will be less trauma and ego damage if job and incumbent come to a parting of the ways. If the steps described above are followed, the separation can take place with minimal damage to the individual and the organization. Don't belabor the parting. Get it over with.

Career Pathing

Having the right people in the right place at the right time doesn't mean maintaining the status quo. People change, jobs change, organizations change. For some reasons, in organizational communication, this is a tough concept to swallow. So, traditionally this has been a business of job hopping. Professionals move from job to job, from organization to organization, because they don't see a career path where they are.

That path doesn't have to be up, but it does have to lead somewhere. Even in a three-person department there should be opportunities for growth within the job, within the group. Developing a game of "musical jobs" just to keep people fresh probably isn't terribly effective, but a certain amount of cross-training, joint problem solving and sharing administrative tasks develops people and keeps the wolf of boredom away from the door. Discuss these possibilities and the way they fit the particular talents and energies and ambitions of subordinates. Career pathing, like development, needs to be a joint responsibility of boss and subordinate.

One critical shortcoming of the business right now is the inadequate system of rewards for specialists/professionals. Many communicators haven't the slightest interest in moving up, either in management within their own specialty or "breaking out" into other management positions in the organization. Does that mean doing the same job with the same level of responsibility for the same salary forever? It shouldn't. That kind of prospect drives good people to job hopping because the possibilities in their own organization look bleak or dull or both. "Senior" titles, rotating assignments in other disciplines and educational sabbaticals all are possibilities that wise communication managers should explore.

Using Outside Suppliers

The masthead of a West Coast company magazine recently carried its staff of four full-time regulars and then a list crediting the creative contributions of twenty-two writers, illustrators and photographers from the "outside." Behind the scenes of entire communication departments, a small, relatively unsung, but assignment-hungry corps of designers, illustrators, writers and photographers comes forth as needed to become the "unseen" members of the staff. Communicators today regularly call on their reserves to augment the in-house regulars to accomplish what cannot be done inside, and to rechannel disrupted work flows and soothe ruffled budgets.

It follows, of course, that outside help cannot be deployed indiscriminately. Experienced communication managers hang on to projects that are best handled in-house and farm out projects outsiders can accomplish just as easily. They bring in outside support when an extraspecial touch is required that can't be found on staff; and when it seems smarter, from a budget or deadline standpoint, to call on a specialist whose expertise will get a project off the ground faster and cheaper.

Getting the most out of outside creative service is an art; the following dialog is not: Word Smith, a communicator, is giving Lynn Smith, a photographer, the business. What is *said* is in quotes. What is *meant* is in parentheses.

"Ah, Lynn, you're just the person I wanted to see." (Actually, I called three photographers and you were the first to get back to me.)

"Really." (If he's got another of those company picnic gigs, I'll slit my throat.)

"Saturday is our annual Hayloft Jamboree and Greased Pig chase, and—" (If she cuts it with this, she gets the rafting-the-Colorado piece.)

"How do you want to handle it?" (So, I won't slit my throat, but please, some ideas.)

"Give it a photojournalistic approach. You know, shoot it as it happens and give me a good selection of prints for the *Bulletin*." (I'll leave it up to her and hope it comes out OK.)

"Check." (Hey, I've got carte blanche. This guy's all right.)

"And, now . . . ahem, hum, er . . ." (What's your day rate?)

Six weeks later, Lynn delivered the assignment—a thigh-thwacking, embarrassing selection of prints showing the company's principal officers in the mud in what appear to be blearly-eyed, compromising embraces with slickered-up pigs—great for the *National Enquirer*, but not for the company *Bulletin*. Moreover, Lynn, whose specialty is sports news, used a motor-driven shutter and, as was her style, shot up 20 roles of film from which she made 75 prints for a total of $295, which, to Word's surprise, was tacked to the normal day-rate charges.

Later, over lunch with his colleagues, Word defended the tardiness of the latest issue of the *Bulletin* by placing the blame squarely on Lynn; her failure to meet the deadline (it was left purely to chance), her sense of news (conditioned, no doubt, by her sports news background), and her ability to exploit the dollar (the business arrangements were self-consciously kicked aside).

The real problem was that Word Smith didn't know what he was buying and didn't know how to manage the project. Word's success could have been guaranteed if he had known more about outside services and how to deal with them.

To Market, to Market . . .

It's wise to plan ahead for those occasions when outside creative talent is needed. Develop lists of photographers, writers, designers and illustrators and assess their special strengths well before the time you need them.

Portfolio showings are the primary means of getting the seller together with the buyer. In metropolitan areas with large communities of creative people, communicators often have set times of the week or month for portfolio sessions. Ganging them, so to speak, avoids scattered interruptions and establishes a framework for comparing style and approach among the portfolios.

Assessment of style is the most important factor. Sports photography is hardly appropriate for covering a facilities dedication, nor is landscape or travel experience necessarily going to pull off a tough candidates' night assignment. The same goes for writing, design and illustration. Some creative suppliers are flexible, however. A certain illustrator, for example, might make the transition from hard edge to watercolor wash with ease. The portfolio will show the degree of the artist's flexibility.

As the interview session (usually about 30 minutes) comes to an end, important questions should be addressed—fees, rights to the creative product, contracts, and purchase orders, for instance. Don't leave anything to chance. Hammering out details of an assignment begins with a thorough understanding of the objective of the assignment and a healthy appreciation of the style and operating philosophy of the sponsoring organization. The process ends with a detailed schedule of deadlines and fees. If clearances and releases are to be handled by the supplier, it should be with the understanding that the ultimate responsibility for them still resides in-house.

Outside creative suppliers have well-developed conditions on which they base their fees. Writers, traditionally paid by the word, are shifting to day rates. Photographers charge by the hour, day and even half-day. Illustrators charge according to the complexity of the product and its end use. Designers' fees are based on size and complexity of the project; production people, on the basis of time and material. But virtually all will work against a bid if asked. Many will negotiate charges if a project interests them enough and the deadline is not tomorrow. Often a fee will hinge on how and where the work will be used. Advertising art, for instance, usually commands more than editorial art.

Even after a fee schedule is negotiated, communicators are often buffeted by the unexpected. Fees might not include per diem and travel expenses, film and processing, stats, and special-order typography and authors' changes. Growing numbers of photographers and artists will accept a commission only on the basis of one-time use.

Having completed the business arrangements, the creative supplier begins the assignment. The communicator and the supplier should maintain continuing contact throughout. The writer completes the research, submits an outline, and, perhaps, a sample of how the section or piece should be styled. The illustrator submits tissues showing concept and technique. The designer comes to an understanding of the objective and works with the communicator to select and organize materials for emphasis and editorial thrust. If there's time, the photographer might submit a selection of Polaroids.

As the project moves along, the communicator exercises judgment and discretion and indulges hunches. A gnawing doubt is never ignored. Flexibility to turn a project to accommodate serendipity is allowed. Creative forces are unleashed, but under the control and guidance of the individual in charge.

Of all the contributions to the communications project, writing seems the most flexible and easy to change. A word or a letter can be moved, replaced or blotted out much more easily than a photo image or a line of type. Editors and communicators, recognizing that excess editing often weakens the final product, sometimes use writers only at certain stages of the process. One who is strong at research, for instance, might be commissioned to do the legwork. A good organizer might take a cut at the first draft; a graceful writer, style a manuscript.

The emerging breed of organizational communicators is relatively unfamiliar to illustrators, especially those who move primarily in advertising circles and are used to heavy art direction. Communicators, after their first exposure to the community of illustrators, are quickly developing the savvy needed to get results.

Matters of determining format and blending with other elements require involvement of designers, for one thing. Will it be flatwork? (The separation cost is then borne by the printer.) Or will it be done on color overlays? (Then the artist should be paid extra.) These are questions that should also involve the printer. It is unlikely the concept will come from the illustrator. Thus, communicator and designer should work together to direct the project.

Working with photographers is especially risky when dealing with the unknown over long distances. Remote assignments call for both rigid art direction, to assure that minimal standards are met, and enough flexibility to take advantage of the delightfully unexpected or the photographer's own special skills and insights and that might bring a marginal assignment to life. Photographers like to be worked hard when sent out on location; and they usually don't object, when asked, to shoot for the files during waiting time or during the hours between the completion of the assignment and dusk.

Ideally, an editorial designer not only reads but also has a sense of what the piece is all about. Good editorial designers are fairly new to the scene. They understand the essence of the content and play to it. They should get involved early and stay on the project until the final press check. Editors with design sense are also growing in numbers. They understand the power of visual images and the economies of playing to them.

The community of "outside" suppliers has become more than just a luxury affordable only by the big and the well-budgeted. The flexibility, the extra measure, the economies and efficiencies the small creative entrepreneur brings to the communication environment have earned him a permanent and much regarded position on the "unseen" staff.

Linda Peterson and *James R. Dodge* are principals of Peterson & Dodge, a San Francisco communication consulting firm.

PART **III**

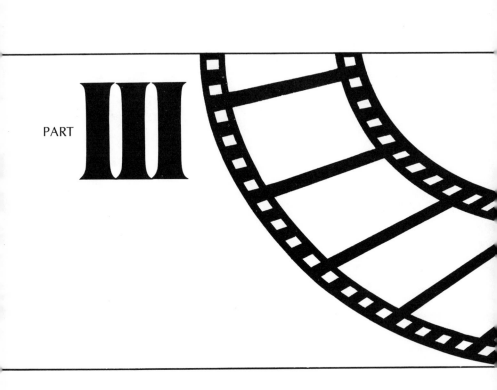

SELECTING AND USING VARIOUS MEDIA AND METHODS

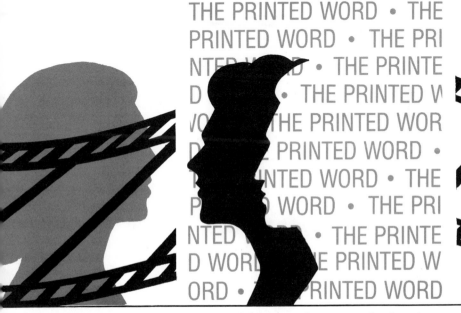

THE PRINTED WORD • THE PRINTED WORD • THE PRI NTED WORD • THE PRINTE D • THE PRINTED W VO THE PRINTED WOR D PRINTED WORD • NTED WORD • THE P WORD • THE PRI NTED • THE PRINTE D WORD E PRINTED W ORD RINTED WORD

The bewildering array of media available to today's organizational communicator is limited only by his or her needs and creativity—printed media, electronic media, face-to-face communication opportunities. The chapters in this section look first at the question of which medium or media for which audience and then, how to put the communication "package" together.

CHAPTER 7

Matching Media with Audience and Message

CAMILLE EMIG

Years ago, if an organization even thought about internal communication, it probably resulted in a directive to start a "house organ." An editor was recruited, maybe from personnel or secretarial ranks, and he or she then started looking for a printer and for people who could provide information on babies, bowling scores and retirements. Although somewhat exaggerated, unfortunately in many cases this scenario was not far from the truth.

Part of the reason for the changing role of the business communicator—from "house organ editor" to communication specialist in areas from writing to videotape production—has been the expansion and sophistication of the media the professional uses. Years ago, there was good reason to call the person "house organ editor." In most cases that's exactly what he or she was. Today, the communicator has a realm of media tools with which to work—everything from magazines and employee annual reports to closed-circuit television and telephone information systems.

Print—An Overview

Although there has been a dramatic expansion of media in recent years, print is still the most widely used. But it too has undergone many changes in content and format. No longer are there only company magazines or newspapers. Paycheck stuffers, magapapers, employee annual reports and posters are all being used effectively to communicate with specific audiences. The descendants of the "house organ" rival daily newspapers and general-interest magazines in professional expertise and interest.

The tradition of the "company publication" has deep historical roots, with evidence of forerunners of today's publications dating back to eleventh-century Chinese feudal lords. Today there are thousands of business and organizational publications of various sizes and formats.

Magazines remain the most popular print medium, but from organization to organization the size, number of pages, use of color and illustrations, frequency, audiences and purposes differ greatly. Internal magazines usually are aimed at an organization's employees or members and contain a variety of articles, from those on company programs and policies to others on the hobbies or life styles of employees. They usually seek to inform, recognize employee or member contributions to the organization, and motivate and show employees that their organization is a good one to be associated with. Some internal publications are also distributed to selected external audiences.

The Ralston Purina Magazine, for example, is a two-color bimonthly magazine for about 23,000 employees and friends of Ralston Purina Company. It contains company and people-related articles and uses photos liberally. Its editor is convinced that this format best reaches its diverse audience because a magazine can be viewed at leisure and shared with family members.

Another two-color bimonthly magazine, *Postal Life,* is sent to the homes of about 670,000 postal employees throughout the United States. Its editors estimate its readership at about 2 million since it's also read by family and friends. *Postal Life* contains articles dealing with post office policy and with people on and off the job.

At New Jersey Bell, a quarterly corporate magazine reaches 40,000 active and retired employees and selected outside audiences. *New Jersey Bell Magazine* is four-color and contains company news and articles on topics that are issues within or outside the company that affect employees in some way. New Jersey Bell uses a number of media to communicate to its employees, but the magazine provides the vehicle for more in-depth, philosophical discussions of items that may be announced as news in their closed-circuit television program or elsewhere.

External magazines are directed to "outside" audiences such as shareholders, sponsors, distributors, customers or other nonemployee, nonmember audiences. *The Review,* published in English and French by Imperial Oil Limited, Toronto, goes to about 150,000 "thought leaders" in Canada. The four-color bimonthly publication is an opinion

Part of the communication process is suiting the medium to the message. Magazines, comic strips and audiovisuals each can be matched to an audience.

forum that contains articles relating to social and cultural topics as well as current issues such as energy.

An external magazine with far different objectives is *Team Talk*, published by Anheuser-Busch for its beer wholesalers. The four-color bimonthly shares marketing ideas among the brewery's 900-plus independent distributors. Its articles deal with brewery programs and wholesaler accomplishments, all aimed at providing information that can be used to make wholesalers' businesses more successful and, bottom line, to sell more product.

The second most popular print media used by the business communicator are the newspaper and magapaper. Most organizational newspapers are tabloid size (11 × 15½ inches) and feature short articles in a format similar to a daily newspaper. The magapaper is a combination newspaper and magazine that contains a mix of news articles and longer features and uses photos liberally. The design is more in the magazine style. Sometimes there is a fine line between the newspaper and magapaper.

A good corporate newspaper is the *ArcoSpark*, published weekly for Atlantic Richfield Company employees and retirees. The publication contains company and industry-related news and articles about employees and their jobs. The editor chose the newspaper format because he wanted a timely, topical publication that could compete well with other publications employees read.

Most magapapers are published less frequently than newspapers. *Today*, distributed to employees, staff and volunteers of Methodist Hospital in Brooklyn, is bimonthly. It contains a mixture of human-interest articles and news affecting the hospital, such as hospital cost information. The editor chose this medium because of its visual effectiveness and attraction.

The fastest-growing print medium in business and organizational communication is the newsletter. Usually smaller than the newspaper, less formal and quickly produced, part of the newsletter's popularity can be attributed to the need to reach audiences already bombarded with information with easily readable messages. Newsletters usually contain short, newsy items and are designed so that readers can quickly go from cover to cover, which is usually only four or eight pages.

The Port of San Diego produces a monthly two-color newsletter, *Port Talk*, for about 2,500 people who are interested in what's happening in the port area. The editor uses the newsletter format for a number of reasons, including budget. The liberal use of photos and feature articles has increased the acceptance of *Port Talk*, says the editor.

A variety of other printed materials—for paycheck stuffers, special informational brochures and employee handbooks and annual reports to posters, mobiles and T-shirts—are described in chapters that follow.

Publications Are Not Alone

In most organizations, publications are not used alone to communicate ideas and information. They are used in conjunction with other publications or within the entire multimedia communication program. For example, *New Jersey Bell Magazine* is part of that company's overall multimedia program, which includes daily and weekly news programs on closed-circuit television, a weekly employee newspaper, and a twice monthly management newsletter. Also news bulletins, closed-circuit TV programs, face-to-face discussions and seminars are all used on an "as-needed" basis.

At St. Francis General Hospital in Pittsburgh, two publications, a newsheet called *Bulletin* and a magapaper called *Probe,* work together to communicate with employees biweekly and bimonthly respectively. *Bulletin* contains short news items that are of interest to employees; many of the items come from employees. *Probe* mixes news and people-oriented features that explain more fully what is happening at the hospital. *Probe* also goes to friends of the hospital.

Paycheck stuffers are a sure way to get a piece of printed material into the employees' hands. They usually fit inside a paycheck envelope and can contain information on a variety of subjects from benefits to current issues. Bill stuffers share information with customers. Posters on topics from safety to those promoting a specific campaign or other subjects are produced for bulletin boards and other stragegic locations in the organization.

Audiovisuals

During the past few years the trend has been toward expanded media use. It's not surprising to find that in a world dominated by visual communication, audiovisuals are growing in importance. In most cases, the audiovisual programs do not replace print.

Slide/tape programs are currently used by business and organizational communicators in a number of areas: orientation, training, fund appeals and various meetings. The slide and/or tape presentation can be as simple as a one-screen, one-projector setup with audiotape to a five-screen, thirty-projector show with synchronized audio. Amazing results can be produced with slide/tape programs; movement can be created on the screens that can make audiences think they are viewing a film instead of a "still" slide show.

Many organizations are reaching their audiences through video presentations, which are highly credible, have immediate impact and communicate a sense of being "newsy." SmithKline in Philadelphia has one of the oldest corporate news programs in the United States. The

The same medium can be used for different audiences.

weekly 5- to 7-minute employee news programs, started in 1971, are produced on tape in-house. They are aired for employees in lobbies and lounges.

Alberta Telephone Company uses video programs for training purposes, maintaining that the medium reduces training time 30 to 50 percent and increases retention of information because it is presented visually as well as verbally. The Hartford Insurance Group uses video programs to reach employees in fifty-three offices scattered throughout the United States and Canada. Video playback equipment has been installed in each regional office so that field employees can view programs produced at headquarters.

At Exxon's New York headquarters, employees can view a twice-monthly in-depth interview and feature program called "Exxon Conversations." Programs have looked at profits, the corporation's search for oil in the Atlantic, and regulations. At Exxon USA in Houston, "This Week at Exxon" follows a standard TV news format and uses approximately sixty employee volunteers as reporters.

Others use video to flash timely messages to employees. Four television monitors in employee cafeterias and lobbies at the St. Regis plant in Jacksonville, Florida, operate 24 hours a day, 7 days a week. They include safety updates, production figures, and dates and schedules of employee meetings.

Sound film is used by organizations for everything from employee orientation to public goodwill. Filmstrips with sound are another segment of this medium.

Some communicators combine the categories of the audiovisuals to create multiimage presentations. For example, these can include the use of slide/tape and film in one program. These are also sometimes referred to as "multimedia," although that terminology could also include print. Chapter 12 describes audiovisuals more completely.

Face-to-Face Communication/Feedback

Face-to-face communication and feedback programs can take on a variety of forms from encounters between two employees or members to organized systems that allow employees to ask company-related questions and receive confidential answers. They are all founded on the premise that you cannot have communication if only one party is doing the communicating.

Obviously, there is a need for the downward flow of information that is generally provided through the various print and audiovisual programs. But people are demanding more, so many organizations are using feedback programs (described in chapter 17). Most organizations recognize that feedback programs are not a solution to overall poor internal communication, but they can contribute to a healthy communication environment.

At Indiana Bell, group "rap" sessions are held as a means of opening up two-way communications. The purpose of the sessions is to pass on information about a work group's operation—what is being done by the group that is worth sharing with others in the company, what problems the work group is having in doing its job, and how operations might be improved.

Avon Products uses communication clinics to obtain face-to-face feedback in its communication programs. Small groups of employees discuss what they like and dislike about current programs.

At New Orleans Public Service, employee briefing sessions provide input for feedback programs and update the 2,800 employees on topics of current interest. Leaders, trained in communication skills and briefed on meeting topics, introduce discussion and answer questions from employees in two-hour sessions. Questions that cannot be answered on the spot are forwarded to the program director for response by other appropriate persons. Questions and answers appear in the employee tabloid and on flyers distributed to staff and posted on bulletin boards three times a month.

A number of other organizations are sponsoring programs that psychologists label "sensing sessions." These are management/employee meetings that involve voicing opinions, asking questions and simply complaining. Programs vary from company to company, but their major purpose is to provide both management and employees with information. For example, at General Electric, employees are randomly chosen for the sessions. The names of participants are published beforehand in the employee newsletter, and those not attending are encouraged to submit questions to those who are. Selected questions and answers from each session are printed in the weekly newsletter.

Other Media

In addition to print, audiovisuals and various forms of face-to-face programs, there are a variety of other media available to the business communicator. The bulletin board is one obvious communication vehicle because most organizations have bulletin boards. But the key to using them effectively is having a program that puts the communicator in control of the boards, as explained in chapter 11. A communication vehicle we all use frequently is also finding a niche in the internal communication area. Many companies are using the telephone to communicate with their audiences on everything from medical benefits to strike information. An instant communication device, the telephone can give fast access to company news; help quell rumors; answer questions; and zero in on needs, ideas and gripes, as described in chapter 11. Ohio Bell's "Newsline" updated information no less than 27 times during an unauthorized employee walkout and handled 2,200 calls daily. Typically, the utility's hotline—a 24-hour statewide, toll-free number—gets several hundred calls daily. The minute taped message, airing the latest Ohio Bell and Bell System news, changes twice a day.

Another way to communicate information to large groups of people is through informational meetings. These differ from the meetings discussed in the section on feedback in that their purpose is to communicate information and not to receive feedback, although through questions and answers, some feedback does result. These meetings usually are attended by large groups of people, and usually feature a presentation (slide or film).

Most of the media discussed and the examples given were, in a sense, taken out of context because in most cases, none of the media is used alone. Most communicators have found that no one program—whether it be a newsletter or a video news program—can, alone, do the entire communication job. However, a thorough knowledge of the available media is the first step toward meeting communication objectives and solving communication problems.

Tailoring the Message

After reviewing the media available to the business communicator, it is easy to see that the job has become complex. Not only are there more media available to get the job done, but the nature of the job itself is more complicated. The "house organ editor" has become the communication professional charged with meeting needs or solving problems within organizations. No longer can he or she use the old "let's run an article in the company magazine" formula to solve the many communication problems facing organizations today.

In deciding which media to use, internal communicators must know what they want to communicate, why they're communicating, whom they're communicating with, and what results they hope to get from the effort. It means having goals and objectives and the plans to achieve them. The importance of having written communication objectives for any program or project was emphasized in previous chapters. Communication objectives must be meshed with management objectives, and they must have management's stamp of approval.

Once objectives are established and approved, the communicator can tackle the problem of what to communicate to achieve the objectives. Because communication is a two-way street—in other words, there is no communication if the message is not received—an in-depth knowledge of who you're communicating with is a key factor in deciding what to communicate. As discussed in chapter 3, knowing your audience—their needs, values, interests—is an essential step in tailoring your message.

There are a number of ways to get to know your audience. Every organization has records that can provide demographic information (e.g.,

age, sex, years of service). Surveys on atttitudes, readership of publications and use of other media can be conducted.

A survey of your audience is not going to give pat answers on the
kinds of information to communicate. But knowing your audience's perceived needs will help in making the decision on the message content
and how to deliver it. Obviously, you won't always be able to communicate exactly what the audience asks for. For example, in a multilocation
situation that must be reached by one "umbrella" publication, you cannot run an article on "Joe Blow's best bowling series." It may interest
Joe and his friends, but bore the remainder of the readers. In a publication like this, the information that is of most interest to the most readers
must be communicated. Possibly another medium can be used to communicate local happenings to Joe and friends.

You can take a marketing strategy in communication and segment
your audience. For example, there may be a need for special communication to management-level employees. There are some things that are
of interest to all employees; others may interest the supervisor but not
the man or woman on the production line. Segmentation can also be
done by division or geographic location, in addition to job responsibility.

Once you've done your research and analysis of the audience and
its needs and meshed the information with the organization's communication objectives, you've finally come to the point where you can begin
making your decision on the media you will use.

Choosing the Media

The choice of which media to use is not a game of eeny-meeny-miney-
moe. Using print because "that's the way it's always been done," or
video because "its's the thing to do" are not valid reasons for choosing
either.

There is no magic formula. It takes an analysis of the advantages
and disadvantages of each medium, meshed with the decisions you've
already made about what to communicate and to whom. Look at the
strengths and weaknesses of each medium in three key areas: effectiveness in communicating your message, distribution problems, and budget
considerations. Print media are "lasting"—written messages can be retained, filed, passed on, and referred to later. Print media are
"traditional"—people are accustomed to reading magazines, newspaper
and books. Reading often helps in the retention of certain kinds of in

formation. Photos are also usually a part of the print medium and can work with the printed word to communicate effectively.

On the other hand, a printed piece can take a long time in production, limiting its ability to communicate real "news." The fact that it is printed, and therefore rather permanent, makes management hesitant to put certain information "in concrete." This can make it difficult to obtain facts and get approvals.

Among the print media, each publication also has its own attributes. Magazines can provide for longer, in-depth information. They also have that "keep me" characteristic, and people have the tendency to keep them and share them with others. Newspapers and newsletters provide information for the "skimmer." They allow readers to be selective in their reading choices because they offer a wide variety of shorter items from which to choose. One reason for the growth of the newsletter has been attributed to the squeeze on readers' time. Very often, newsletters will be read while magazines and even newspapers wait for time that never comes. The audiovisual media's biggest attribute is its ability to make an impact on audiences and provide immediate impressions. These media can involve the use of two senses—sight and hearing, instead of sight only, and can also reach the emotions more than print.

It makes sense to consider the audiovisual media, for people that organizations communicate with are becoming more and more visually oriented. Audiovideo, for example, is a highly credible medium because it "shows" something beyond the printed word. But audiovisual programs cannot be carried home and saved; they require special equipment.

Face-to-face communications are recognized as the most effective form of communication. They practically assure receipt of the message and usually result in immediate feedback. They also require more time and effort to implement, reach smaller audiences, and may require a lot of time to solve logistical problems.

Bulletin boards offer a means to get information out quickly (a news item can be typed, copied and mailed in hours) to a variety of locations. If properly placed and attractively done, bulletin boards can corral a lot of "readers." Bulletin boards cannot assure that the message will be received by all the audience because they rely on people making an effort to get to the boards, then stopping and reading what is on them. Telephone information systems also provide a quick way to get news out. Again they require the employee or member to take action (use the phone) to get the message.

Generally, most communicators use print as the basis of their communication programs and use video, film, telephone or face-to-face programs to complement the basic work. Some experts think this situation will reverse in the future, but most agree that neither medium will ever replace the other. For example, a magazine communicates in-depth information about an organization, explains programs, and features employees on and off the job; a video program brings weekly news; a telephone system has daily information; and a face-to-face program provides the important two-way vehicle that nurtures a healthy communication environment.

What Will It Cost?

Let's say you've done your homework. You have your objectives, you feel that you have a thorough knowledge of your audience or audiences and know what you want to communicate. You've analyzed the advantages and disadvantages of the various media. You've chosen those you want to use. You're almost to the home stretch—except for one very important consideration. Budget.

All the research, analysis and planning in the world is useless if the communication program or project cannot get an approved budget. The lucky communicator can sell a program to management on its merit and be able to work with the budget needed to get the job done. Others will have a certain amount allotted to do the job. Whichever situation the communicator is in, the important thing is getting the message across in a cost-effective manner.

What does it cost to produce a bimonthly four-color magazine, compared with the cost of a black-and-white newsletter or a weekly video program? Unfortunately, that's a question that cannot be answered without more specific information. A number of factors influence the cost of a publication: circulation, size, paper, design, use of color, use of art, frequency, and so on. Manner of distribution is also a consideration. Mailing is expensive, yet has advantages over delivering in bulk to various locations and relying on some method of distribution there.

One method of comparing costs of publications is to take the total costs for producing the publication (usually excluding staff salaries and travel) and divide it by the number of copies printed. A recent study done by the University of Georgia's Grady School of Journalism and Mass Communication, using a cost-per-copy formula based on printing costs and number of copies printed, produced the following information: the average cost of the magazines studied was 56 cents per copy; costs ranged from 6.5 cents to $1.40 per copy. Cost of magapapers ranged from 9 cents to 60 cents per copy; cost of newspapers, from 2.7 cents to $1.27; newsletters, from 6.7 cents to 50 cents. Obviously, production costs vary significantly from area to area and the above statistics must be understood in that context.

Generally, magazines are the most expensive print medium, followed by magapapers, newspapers and then newsletters. But remember, a newspaper or magapaper can cost more than a magazine, depending on the sophistication of the publication, the press run and the location.

The same variables that make comparison of publication costs difficult apply to the audiovisual media. If you take the same subject matter, however, the cost of communicating it would be progressively higher as you go from slide/tape to video and to 16-mm film, the most expensive. In addition to production costs, there are other variables to consider in the audiovisual field. One big cost factor in this area is the hardware: cameras, playback equipment, and the like. For example, if you need to communicate company-wide and have one hundred locations, the cost of buying the hardware may be prohibitive. Over a number of years, however, the investment may be worth it if your goal is instant communication and you replace another medium not meeting this objective.

The annual budget for the SmithKline black-and-white weekly video news program discussed earlier is $55,000 per year. Alberta Telephone Company found that using video reduced training time. Because time is money, the use of video saved that organization money in the long run.

Comparing costs of the various media is usually like comparing apples with oranges. Dollars spent is not necessarily the yardstick by which to measure effective communication—cost effectiveness is the key.

Conclusion

A knowledge of the media available; what each medium can do; which media can get your message to the audience when, where and how you want it communicated and in the most cost-effective manner; these are all prerequisites for the communicator who must match the media with the audience and the message. It's not an easy assignment, but it is necessary to ensure the most effective communication program or project possible. Yes, the business communicator has a much tougher and more challenging job than the "house organ editor" he or she succeeded. But few business communicators would trade places.

Camille Emig is manager of internal communication for Anheuser-Busch Companies, St. Louis. She has served on the executive board of the International Association of Business Communicators.

EXAMPLE: *ATLANTIC RICHFIELD*

Atlantic Richfield Company's employee communciations staff faced a new challenge when it reported for work January 2, 1979. The centralized Atlantic Richfield organization that had existed only a few days before was gone. In its place—with less than a month's notice—was a new organization, consisting of eight separate companies under the ARCO corporate umbrella.

The staff was aware that each of the eight companies would want to establish its own identity; that each of the eight individuals now heading up these companies would have ideas about communication. It was one thing, after all, to be the vice president of the North American Producing Division; the staff would now be dealing with the president of ARCO Oil and Gas Company. The same individual, but perhaps a whole new outlook toward communication for *his* or *her* company.

The months that followed brought no drastic changes in employee communications' media efforts. *ArcoSpark,* distributed weekly to all employees and retirees around the world (more than 70,000), would continue. Other established publications would continue. Field offices, staffed by employee communications personnel in Dallas, Denver, and Philadelphia, would continue to report directly to corporate headquarters in Los Angeles for the time being, at least.

. . .

Atlantic Richfield's overall communication objective did not change. Put simply, the company believes that informed employees who take pride in their company, their jobs, their fellow employees and themselves are better workers.

Ongoing efforts to meet this objective have included reshaping a multifaceted communication program to respond to the specific needs of a changing organization.

The department uses the *ArcoSpark*—through such subtle methods as boldfacing individual company names in the "Around the Company" news summary, and through consciously balancing coverage according to a pro rata share of total employee population—to emphasize new company identities. Readers of *min*—the management information newsletter—were surveyed and their comments and suggestions helped make it an improved publication. Articles in *mgr,* a management journal, examined individual company units for the benefit of all the corporation's managers and supervisors.

Telephone information programs at numerous locations provide employees with an outlet for their opinions to be heard—and their questions answered. Bulletin boards continue to be effective means of communication, and lunchtime forums and panel discussions—laced with occasional film and video highlights—promote personal, face-to-face communication.

. . .

Atlantic Richfield's individual companies had some of their own communication needs too: Anaconda Industries—which came from the consolidation of several smaller units—needed a booklet to tell its employees what their new company was all about. Several of the companies joined together to produce a booklet for MBA recruitment—with employee communications coordinating the project. Others were having difficulty in relocating employees to Los Angeles so a booklet, *Look at L.A.!,* was prepared.

The response continues. ARCO Coal Company now has a new employee information booklet; a benefits summary for all Anaconda companies is off the press. Anaconda Copper company's executives will be introduced to employees through a videotape: and ARCO Chemical Company has a quarterly publication to keep employees informed about activities that are not appropriate for *ArcoSpark.*

—by Dave Orman
Manager, Employee Communication
Atlantic Richfield Company

CHAPTER 8

Publications: What's in the Package

JOAN KAMPE and LYN CHRISTENSON

Even amid cries of "We've entered the electronic age" and "People don't read anymore," organizational communicators continue to produce a variety of publications to inform and persuade diverse audiences. In the company with a significant array of communication tools, printed materials enjoy a special reputation in terms of long-lasting influence.

Publications issued on regular schedules offer a broad format for comprehensive explanation and analysis. They also offer permanence and efficacy in delivering precise messages to large and often geographically dispersed audiences.

Trends in Publications

During the past decade there was an obvious shift in organizational publications, away from the purely entertaining articles and toward those with more meaning and substance. Specifically, editors concerned with producing meaningful publications began to take a sharp look at content. The world has been beset with problems of economic uncertainty, significant social change and personal self-examination in times of changing major values. Editors who clung to the "safe" topics of the 1960s and earlier and who failed to accommodate to the tremendous changes going on around them found themselves decidedly out of step with reader interests and needs. In short, editors who failed to recognize the very real human issues that concern their audiences—where is my organization going; what's my role and what does it all mean in the larger context of my life?—found themselves out of touch with the real needs of their readers.

Enlightened editors, on the other hand, looked at the changes affecting organizations and saw them as opportunities to revamp their publications, making them more timely, honest and relevant and at the same time meeting the interests and preferences of their audiences. That is, in an effort to provide greater meaning to the events affecting the organization, it is essential to avoid the trap of becoming "too corporate" and insensitive to the human side of the organization.

Principal Kinds of Organizational Publications

Organizations use four main kinds of publications: newspapers, newsletters, magazines and magapapers. These vary in appearance, cost and complexity—and also objectives.

> *Newsletter.* Simplest, fastest and least complicated of all periodical forms, newsletters are produced by rank amateurs and seasoned professionals. Smaller and with fewer pages than a newspaper, the format of a newsletter is generally more flexible and the writing brief but not rigid. They are particularly appropriate for meeting information needs of smaller or specialized organizations and audiences.
>
> *Newspaper.* Somewhat more complex than newsletters, newspapers often look much like a city newspaper, carry hard (often late-breaking) news and features and use illustrations sparsely. Quick to produce and economical, newspapers are often used for timely news to supplement less frequently issued magazines.
>
> *Magazine.* These generally contain carefully selected material targeted to a specific audience. Using a feature treatment, interpretive writing, liberal use of photos and art, they generally are produced less frequently—monthly, bimonthly or quarterly, as a rule—than other publications.
>
> *Magapaper.* A hybrid of newspapers and magazines (also called *newsines*), magapapers combine the feature approach of a magazine with newspaper design. They are, in many ways, newspapers straddling the fence between news and information and feature and in-depth treatment.

According to a recent survey conducted by IABC, 35.1 percent of organizational publications were magazines, 18.5 percent were newspapers, 17.7 percent were magapapers and 26 percent were newsletters.

Audience needs can dictate both the frequency and format of a publication. Ingalls Memorial Hospital favors a quarterly magazine and Atlantic Richfield's *ArcoSpark* is a weekly tabloid.

Because they are fastest to produce, newspapers and newsletters are used to bring current news to the organizational audiences. Because they are often the least expensive of the common kinds of publications, they can be used by virtually every organization—from the small company that relies on the newsletter as its sole publication to the large corporation that publishes newsletters and newspapers as local or regional supplements to widely distributed company publications. Magapapers frequently look much like newspapers but combine news coverage with magazine-style features. Thus, an editor who does not want to produce a magazine can still provide expanded coverage of important issues. Magazines vary from black and white to full color and from coverage of a small college to a corporation with operations around the world.

Whatever the format, organizational publications share a common goal: to focus on key issues of the organization, interpreting and humanizing significant policies and activities and putting them into perspective for employees, members and others. Often, too, individuals are singled out for helping the organization achieve its objectives.

Determining the Publication's Contents: The Editor's Role

Once the purpose for the publication has been established, the next step in organizing the publication is to review the areas of emphasis. This could be the organization's business results, employee relations, cost control or the importance of individual initiative. Then determine what standing columns or sections will be required. For example, if one of the publication's objectives is to provide recognition for employees with long service, or members with consistent affiliation, it would be appropriate to include a section called "Anniversaries." Or, if another of the publication's objectives is to provide recognition for individual achievements, a section for milestones within the organization, such as promotions, community achievement awards, speeches presented or patents earned, may be included.

If another of the publication's objectives is to explain business results, it may be appropriate to include a message from the chief executive officer. To produce such a column, the editor can interview the executive or the executive may write the copy. To make such a column credible in any organizational publication, the contents must reflect the genuine commitment and reactions of the executive. The column loses a tremendous amount of value if it is passed down the line to a junior staff person to prepare. After all, ostensibly the purpose of such a column is to open up communication with the leader of the organization. If the leader fails to participate, the column is relatively meaningless.

Similar columns—medical advice, for example—in organizational publications elicit the greatest interest when they discuss topics of interest to readers, not simply the initiator of the column. The editor must consider every aspect of the editorial contents in terms of "what interest is this to my readers?" Of course, organizational politics often dictate that certain topics be covered in a publication. In these cases it is probably preferable to meet with those in management who want a particular topic covered, then identify what it is they want to accomplish by examining the topic in the organization's publication. From there, look at other publications and seek creative ways to present material.

Localize the News

Inserts tailored to a region or local area are frequently useful in publications of large organizations. They can range in subject matter and appearance from a few paragraphs summarizing local news events to several pages cataloging annual benefit program changes. Inserts allow publications covering a large geographical area to be personalized for each region within that area. They may also be an economy measure, since the insert that combines photos and several kinds of news may make separate publications at each company location unnecessary.

A multidivision company, for example, may produce a tabloid newspaper for employees at several locations. The outer pages may contain information of interest company-wide, such as corporate news, benefits changes and employment opportunities available on a corporate-wide basis. Perhaps several different divisions want to communicate with their employees about how an issue affects their segment of the business, or about news of interest to only a segment of the corporate-wide audience. In that case, a separate insert fills the bill. Special inserts can also treat benefits, business results and other topics requiring in-depth explanation.

Gathering the News

Once the issues affecting the organization have been clearly spelled out and objectives for the publication have been formalized, the next step is to create a system for gathering information. Say, for example, the following issues have been clearly identified as "most important" to a company: (1) business results, (2) employee relations, (3) social responsibility, (4) employee safety and health, (5) affirmative action, (6) energy conservation, (7) cost control and (8) individual initiative. Who are the newsmakers within the organization who can serve as your news sources?

Begin to keep abreast of business results by cultivating relationships with the senior decision makers. Meet with them on a regular basis to review their problems, priorities, concerns and exposures. Read the financial reports and planning documents compiled for senior management. Certainly, the more information you have access to, and the greater trust and rapport you are able to establish with your organization's decision makers, the greater the likelihood your publication will accurately reflect the business climate.

In simplest terms, this means establish "a beat." Who are the people in your organization who are the best sources of information? In a corporation, look to the executives who oversee the daily operations of each business unit. In organizations where getting an appointment with such a person is about as difficult as buying a ticket to a sold-out athletic event, consider second-string news sources. Contact "the rising stars" who report to the busy executive. Consider similar opportunities in non-profit organizations.

For information about employee relations, include people in the organization who are responsible for managing the area. For example, look to the personnel staff for assistance in reporting and interpreting issues related to labor relations, safety, affirmative action, employee benefits, and wage and salaries. Certainly such contacts are a two-way street: you keep abreast of what's happening in your organization, and the people responsible for implementing programs stand a substantially better chance of telling their story accurately in the organization's publications.

As your organization develops greater and greater awareness of social responsibility, look to the people charged with administering programs in community relations. Similarly, look for those who are conducting programs for cost reduction, energy conservation and other issues affecting your organization. Be as creative as possible as you draw up your lists of news sources.

Creating a Correspondent's Network

That's only half the story. Once you've identified your "beats" and those people who can keep you abreast of the major issues affecting your organization, how can you develop material that is warm, lively, human and responsive? For example, if you're interested in communicating about safety in your organization, how can you approach the topic in a manner that is meaningful and interesting to your readers? Many organizations have found the solution in developing a network of correspondents. Such a string of reporters allows the editor to emphasize the people in the organization and to focus on company issues in human terms. To pretend that the creation of a reporter network will solve the problems of "What's going on in our Memphis office?" or "Are there any employees with newsworthy interests in the Supply Department?" would be an exaggeration. But it is one more technique in the editorial bag of tricks to stimulate interest and involve readers in your publication. Clearly, it is a two-way street. Readers in far-flung locations receive recognition and the editor gets good story leads.

The mechanics of establishing a correspondents' network are simple and straightforward. At Foremost-McKesson, a San Francisco-based corporation with operations in two hundred locations in the United States and overseas, the editorial staff of *Direction* magazine sought the assistance of the manager at each facility in selecting a correspondent. Using a form letter with a tear-off portion on which the manager was to indicate the name and work number of the selected correspondent, the editorial staff outlined the desirable qualifications: Someone with "a nose for news" and a sensitivity toward the interests of all employees, not just an immediate circle of friends. The letter served as a means of involving the manager and eliciting support for the correspondents' activities.

For editors whose publications are circulated at a single location, the selection process is somewhat simpler. Sometimes correspondents can be chosen by the editor, though it still makes good sense to involve a correspondent's supervisor in the selection process in order to keep him or her "in the loop."

A good cross-section of correspondents clearly increases the odds of producing a diversified list of story possibilities for a publication. For that reason, correspondents should be selected from among secretaries, plant workers, cafeteria workers, truck drivers, forklift operators and marketing managers, or their counterparts in other types of organizations. Take care not to thrust the responsibility on someone who is already overburdened and who really lacks enthusiasm and interest for the assignment.

Once the correspondents have been selected, compile a set of clear instructions for them. One of the best ways to familiarize them with their role is to produce a brochure or handbook outlining their responsibilities. For *Direction* correspondents, for example, the editorial staff distributes a brochure that is divided into sections: *Let's take it from the top* (a description of the magazine that emphasizes the role of the correspondents), *Newsworthy Events to Watch for and Report, the Human Interest Angle of Feature Articles, What to Do with Your News or Feature Idea Once You've Found It, Why Accuracy in Reporting Counts, A Word About Round-up Stories, What* Direction *Can't Use, Photographs*

Wrap-Up is a magapaper distributed to the international division of Diamond Shamrock Corporation. Public statement of the publication's goals and objectives by the division vice-president establishes *Wrap-Up* as an official source of information.

that Enhance Your Story Idea, Where to Dig for News, A Word About Deadlines, What If Your Story Doesn't Run? and *Now That You've Got It All Together.* Such a brochure should do two things: provide a summary of what you're trying to accomplish with the publication, and describe specific topics that are inappropriate. If correspondents are to write the articles, explain how it can be done. If they are to supply information, explain how an editor will use the data.

The *Direction Correspondents Notebook* includes a comment about the importance of timeliness in reporting events. "Story ideas with a time limit, unless they're received well in advance of the season, are not appropriate. For example, Christmas stories, no matter how heart-warming, would lose their appeal in the Spring issue. But if your group has a holiday tradition, such as organizing a Christmas food drive for the elderly, alert us at least two months in advance." Such a brochure can add prestige and professionalism to the role of the correspondent. In effect, you're saying to these people that you take their role seriously enough to prepare a special brochure.

To complement a *Direction Correspondents Notebook*, the editorial staff also created a *Direction Correspondents Newsletter* to solicit leads for specific upcoming feature stories in the magazine and single out individual correspondents for recognition. For example, through the newsletter, correspondents have been asked to find co-workers who use the corporation's tuition assistance program, people involved in their local communities and others who participate in regular fitness projects.

It is critical to be specific. To ask correspondents, "Any news this month?" is fruitless. They require specific instructions because they're generally not communication professionals and are performing other functions in the organization. "Keep it simple" are probably the strongest bywords. Requests for suggestions about people to include in stories may occasionally result in very little response from correspondents. For example, instead of preparing a feature article on the health hazards associated with smoking, the editor of one publication asked correspondents whether there had been a Stamp Out Smoking campaign at their work facilities. Only one correspondent responded, but from that lead a story on the decision to prohibit smoking at a company warehouse was developed.

Editors who have difficulty eliciting meaningful story leads from correspondents should consider adding additional correspondents if it is a case of too many people being covered by too few reporters. At the same time, review the guidance, direction and feedback you're providing your network of correspondents. Recognize your correspondents by listing them on the masthead of the publication and consider other forms of recognition. Company product samples, Christmas gifts and wall plaques that designate someone as a correspondent are appropriate thank-yous. Use as much flourish as you can afford.

If you receive inappropriate material, acknowledge it by explaining to the correspondent why the material won't see print. Perhaps the item is of interest to a small, local audience. Return it with a suggestion to post it in an area bulletin board. If it is something of interest to one segment of your readership that is perhaps served by another publication—such as a local unit's newsletter—route the material to the alternate publication. But be sure to acknowledge the effort; unpaid, unrewarded volunteer correspondents won't persist without recognition.

By taking the initiative to seek out story leads from people in the organization and from a network of correspondents, the editor maintains sharper control of the contents of a publication. Instead of reacting to requests for "a story on energy conservation," for example, you can produce a warmer, livelier story about employees who are clever energy conservers. It's one way to avoid stories that are dull, boring and not read.

How Some Organizations Get the Word Out

The purpose of *JD Journal*, the worldwide employee magazine of John Deere & Co., is "to inform employees of the company's goals, policies, accomplishments, needs and concerns in an honest, readable manner. In so doing, employees and their families will gain a sense of belonging to the same corporate family, that their good work does make a difference, and that they work for a good, responsible, successful employer that cares about their interest and is worthy of their efforts." Other goals of the *JD Journal* are "to create goodwill for the company among outside readers by conveying to them the kind of company John Deere is and how it's meeting its business, social and human responsibilities," and to "stimulate thought and dialog among employees and outside readers, broaden their interest and keep them abreast of current issues that affect them and John Deere."

How can publications professionals carry out their goals, and demonstrate to senior management that they can help solve the major problems of the organization? At Methodist Hospital in Brooklyn, the Public Affairs staff offers these steps for focusing management's attention on the role publications can play:

1. *Investigate.* Determine what problems management sees as crucial and judge where communications skills can best be applied to do something about them. Trust and respect are gained by taking on the difficult challenges.

2. *Know the character of management.* Know its prejudices, its objectives, its interests.

3. *Identify the organization's opinion leaders.* Who can help? Who can hurt your efforts? Cultivate those who can help. Work to make believers out of those who would prefer that you be an employee of some other organization, or not working at all.

Employee communication needs in hospitals and other medical institutions parallel those in other organizations. At Methodist Hospital, Public Affairs Director Bob Chandler uses *Today* as the principal communication vehicle for reaching 20,000 persons, including employees, the medical staff and various community opinion leaders. Chandler selected the magapaper format for bimonthly *Today* because it emphasizes visual attractiveness and can include believable photos that motivate people to pick it up and read it. "A hospital is not like any other business," Chandler says. "The words and illustrations carried in hospital publications should believably portray the special relationships between people. The focus should not be on doctors, patients, CAT scanners, beds, policies or new programs. Publications that communicate should focus on what a nurse did for a patient, what the association administrator thinks the new Blue Cross reimbursement rate will do to operating costs. Publications should present reality. And editors should let them."

Reality, human relationships and the hospital's role in the community were all graphically portrayed by a front-page *Today* feature on a new expectant parents' handbook titled "Life Begins at the Methodist Hospital." Opened by the touching photo of a mother holding her brand-new daughter (actually the cover of the new brochure), the article described Methodist Hospital's obstetrical services. Other *Today* articles have spotlighted free medical care offered to people on limited incomes; staff members' impression of work with geriatric patients; and the care and planning which go into an important, but frequently criticized, part of hospital stays—the meals.

Chandler says it is important to keep in mind that employee publications often do double duty with other audiences. "The employee publications may be more folksy than other publications, but should not be so folksy as to be wholly irrelevant to other publics." Many other persons see employee publications, he points out, and "by generalizing publications a bit, making certain sections relevant for more than one audience, the hospital can increase contact or exposure to its various publics."

At Exxon U.S.A., the public affairs staff meets with management to identify the major issues affecting the organization. They set communication goals that are tied to the issues and then plan story possibilities to meet these goals. The editors of *Profile*, the magazine for Exxon employees and retirees, prepare editorial contents to reflect those issues and concerns.

Although publications share a common purpose, the best means for achieving an organization's goals can differ from one another. In selecting the best publication format, Anheuser-Busch in St. Louis elected to change *Focus on St. Louis* from a monthly two-color, twelve-page magazine to a biweekly newsletter. Editor Irene Hannon says one of her most important tasks is to provide St. Louis plant employees with timely information on company events. "A magazine just did not seem the right way to accomplish these goals," she recalls. "The magazine format lends itself more toward features, and we wanted to stress news—timely information."

The new *Focus*, an eight-page two-color newsletter, has a shorter production schedule and a format that allows for last-minute changes. Hannon's objectives encompass the principal areas of importance in structuring an organizational publications program:

1. Keep St. Louis employees informed about Company news, activities and policies as they relate to the St. Louis plant.
2. Build a sense of teamwork by creating an awareness on the part of employees that whether they are hourly or salaried, men or women, they share common interests and problems.
3. Provide information on departments and specific jobs to promote an understanding of every individual's importance as part of the team.
4. Humanize the organization by featuring "people" stories, stressing the individuals within the various groups that comprise the company.
5. Recognize employees for outstanding achievements on and off the job.
6. Build employee pride in the company and increase enthusiasm by always stressing quality and by making each employee feel that he or she is an important part of the company.

Articles in *Focus* address these objectives. In a feature on the Anheuser-Busch St. Louis Chip Cellars, where beer is aged and carbonated, *Focus* stressed the importance of teamwork. The process involves 250 people at seven different areas at the same complex, who are responsible for aging beer to consistent quality standards. A closing quote by the general foreman sums up the theme: "Without the contributions of all the employees, we couldn't get the job done. It is a team effort all the way."

A story about Anheuser-Busch merchandising personnel described the long development cycle for the point-of-sale (POS) promotional signs and print pieces most employees take for granted as part of grocery store and restaurant decor. Reading about the tremendous complexity in developing POS material that conform to frequently conflicting state laws, for example, informs St. Louis employees about their company. It can also help make them proud to be associated with other people who successfully perform complex tasks for the company.

ArcoSpark is a major part of Atlantic Richfield's program to bring company news to 76,000 employees and retirees throughout the world. The weekly paper replaced a quarterly magazine and various divisional publications in 1973, according to Editor Ken Estes, because "we are in an age of quick communication. We have an obligation to communicate with our people in a timely, topical and credible manner." Because issues affecting companies in energy-related fields receive frequent coverage in the mass print and broadcast media, Atlantic Richfield stresses the importance of informing employees about the company's stand on key topics. This intention, along with other generally recognized communication objectives, is cited in the company's statement of purpose for its internal print communications program: "It continues to be Atlantic Richfield's belief that informed employees are better workers, more loyal spokesmen for their employer in their communities, happier human beings, and better able to contribute to the profitability of the corporation." This statement is supplemented by specific program objectives which include the importance of recognizing employees' informational needs and their contributions and the need to present company communications creatively and attractively.

ArcoSpark articles cover news and issues in the straightforward, matter-of-fact style that epitomizes the maturation of the company publication from its origin as a "house organ" emphasizing chit-chat. An Arco employee was murdered and thousands of dollars were stolen in a California service station holdup. *ArcoSpark* published an article about the incident to show the need for the company's national crime deterrent program, initiated in 1978. The consolidation of several company operations in a new city and the attendant relocation problems are often facts of corporate life. This does not make them any easier for the employees involved, however, and a company can do a great deal to ease the transition. A company division's research and development operations consolidation was the subject of an *ArcoSpark* feature that emphasized company assistance offered to make the relocation less painful. Group presentations, individual counseling and a weekend visiting the new research center site helped some who were in a quandary about accepting a transfer decide to make the move.

Articles such as these are included in the *ArcoSpark* to show that the company recognizes the importance of meeting people's needs. Employees today are demanding this sort of recognition from their employers, and programs such as Arco's relocation programs show that organizations can make the changes demanded by business conditions in ways that minimize the disruptions to employees and their families.

Stanford University's Alumni Association makes excellent use of the magazine format. Magazines produced by organizations vary greatly in size and cost, but the format is one of the most universally used, either as the single organizational publication or as part of a larger publications program. Della van Heyst, editor of *The Stanford Magazine*, says that it is not intended to be timely (a Stanford newspaper has that objective) but strives to capture the intellectual excitement of an educational institution, portray student life and focus on the visual appeal of the campus. The semiannual magazine combines full-color and black-and-white spreads and averages eighty pages an issue. It is printed on heavy stock that offers good photo reproduction and is durable. "Our surveys show 35 percent of our readers have saved all the issues since 1973," van Heyst says. "The money and effort that go into the magazine's design, photography, writing and production are all dictated by our principal goal—to project a quality image and capture the essence of our institution: excellence."

The Stanford Magazine's introductory issue in 1973 featured an interview with Ralph Heintz, inventor of the nonpolluting Heintz Straticharge engine and holder of more than two hundred patents. Heintz, a 1920 Stanford graduate, has given the engine's patents to the university, which may bring Stanford several million dollars. In a recent issue, a Stanford art historian related the fascinating story of the planning and construction of the original university buildings in the late nineteenth century by Governor and Mrs. Leland Stanford, who founded the school as a memorial to their son.

The editor of any publication sets the pace on contents and on writing and editing skills. The newcomer in the editorial office has the same responsibilities in this regard as the veteran. He or she must develop copy that is appropriate to the organization, the audience or audiences and the publication, and also must have the skill to combine words and illustrations meaningfully. Some persons learn and polish these skills in schools, others hone their abilities on the job. In either case, genuine interest in good writing and editing is vital and never-ending. Study good publications and compare your work with them. Keep aware of the trends in writing and editing.

Joan Kampe is manager of internal communication at Foremost-McKesson, a multi-division corporation based in San Francisco.

Lyn Christenson is manager of communication programs for Syntex Corporation in Palo Alto, California.

A survey among European house journal editors revealed that those who publish controversial articles and "bad news" range from only 18 percent in France to 86 percent in Sweden. An inescapable conclusion is that far too many—between a quarter and a half—of the 6,000 journals in the ten countries surveyed manage to exist without reporting events that inevitably can go wrong in companies and industries.*

It sounds incredible because is there any factory, works, building site or office where everything always goes right? What do readers think of the paper that reports only "good" or "neutral" news? How can it be credible? The house journal must be a mirror of the company, the industry at work, reflecting the real things that happen on the job and outside it.

Coal News is a tabloid family newspaper sold for 5 pence every month to 250,000 mine workers and other employees in Britain's coal industry. There is a three-way split of the sales money among the publishers, the salesman at each workplace and a local good cause chosen by the miners. By changing 6 of the 16 pages in each of the 12 monthly editions the paper tells readers what is happening down their own colliery and in their own community.

Coal News is published by the boss—the National Coal Board—but it is not a boss's paper. Of course it reports what the NCB is saying and doing; it also presents the views of miners and their families and reactions of the trade unions.

The industry at work fills half the paper's editorial content. Human-interest topics fill the other half—sport, letters, cartoons (drawn by mining artists), and a monthly competition page; the Coal Queen of Britain contest, which the newspaper promotes; miners who work for charity, become mayors, weigh 17 stone and win £300,000 on the football pools. . . . A quarter of the space is taken by advertisements, which help communication and offset running costs. There has always been a page-one leader comment (editorial) speaking up for the coal industry and mining people.

One of the real tests of credible communication in any organization comes when the editor contacts the industrial relations manager at a crunch point in the yearly wage negotiations and says, "We're going to press tomorrow—let's report the latest negotiations." Does the chief negotiator cry out: "Get lost!" Or does he say, "Our employees need to know what is going on, so let's tell them." Certainly union leaders aren't reluctant to give their views.

* Compiled for the Federation of European Industrial Editors' Associations by the Danish Association.

Coal News fully reports industrial relations topics and our readers expect it. An example is the 1979-80 miners' wage negotiations. Coalfield editions started reporting early in the year what local miners' leaders were expecting to get. The July issue covered the National Union of Mineworkers conference debate under the headline: Call for £140 on Face, £80 on Surface. The October front page gave details of the union's five-point claim, with the NCB's reply presented the following month.

When the union decided to hold a coalfield ballot on the negotiated settlement, the Coal News team worked around the clock to bring out an immediate four-page special issue, which was given away to everyone in the industry. It included a detailed table of pay raises for all grades so that everyone knew what he would get. The Coal Board chairman and the miners' president were, of course, quoted. In December the ballot result was reported on the front page—a majority vote for the offer and against industrial action. Next month, the payout arrangements were explained.

Safety in the mines is another priority topic and Coal News reported the industry's special year-long campaign called Think Safety. The four major accident causes—haulage and transport, surface locations, machinery and rock falls underground—were examined in detail. Miners and managers were interviewed so that action could be taken to prevent "carbon copies" of accidents recurring.

Many other events were being reported: an agreement with the power station board to use two-thirds of total coal output; action to find new markets for coking coal lost by the steel industry slump; opening new mines, closing exhausted ones; a production drive called Target '79 to get the most from sophisticated coalface machines; a family Mining Festival at Blackpool resort for 25,000 people (another Coal News promotion); the courageous story of little Fiona Bell, once handicapped but determined to skip and dance her way back to a normal life. . . .

Let's not dodge the $64,000 question—how to assess the results of another year of communicating. There is no simple answer. The paper is bought by two out of every three miners—just about saturation point in this family industry where father and son often work at the same mine. They wouldn't buy the paper if they didn't like it. Selling the paper helps keep the editorial team on its toes and ensures that it remains a lively tabloid. Readers write letters, which are printed, and talk to our writers, who report their views. There is no other effective way of keeping in regular contact with employers throughout the country on such a wide range of issues.

—by Norman Woodhouse
Managing Editor, Coal News
National Coal Board

CHAPTER 9

Publications: Putting the Package Together

WILLIAM E. KORBUS

Organizational communication usually deals with one or more of four basic publication forms: newsletter, newspaper, magapaper, magazine. Your organization's particular needs may dictate which form to use. If, for example, you have many short articles, the newsletter form is probably most appropriate. If you have both short and feature-length articles, which can be supplemented with visual material, you may find the newspaper or magapaper more useful. Magazines offer the most flexibility because they provide an opportunity to use a number of short pieces, with or without images, or long feature-length material.

This discussion is primarily from the viewpoint of magazine design because magazine design can be adapted to other media. In other words, if you can design a magazine, you can design the others by making some modifications. All the principles that follow apply to all forms of design—posters, direct mail pieces, newsletters, tabloids, books, and so forth. The same holds true for the layout principles. The example may be magazine, but it could easily be newsletter or tabloid.

Format

One of the first decisions to make in the design of a publication is what format to use. This includes number of columns per page, horizontal and vertical grid patterns, type style for body copy, and headlines and column form (justified or ragged).

The number of columns per page has a great deal to do with how the publication is perceived. A two-column format has a symmetrical, formal look (fig. 9.1) that is well suited to an institution concerned about a stable image, such as a hospital, a church, or an educational, insurance or financial institution. A three-column format allows for a more asymmetrical or informal treatment (fig. 9.2). This does not preclude the possibility of a bank using a three-column format and still giving a stable, secure look. A three-column format can be balanced symmetrically.

A three- or four-column format allows greater design flexibility than a two-column. Multicolumn formats allow a choice between symmetrical and asymmetrical and also go together more quickly and easily than a two-column because the choices are greater. Images can be cropped to one column and have a vertical appearance; they can be cropped to three columns and have a horizontal feeling; a square configuration can be achieved that appears neutral on the page. In other words, when creating a modular system—the modules being words, images, headlines, negative space—there are many choices, which allow for a varied layout.

The communicator will also have to choose an appropriate column

FIGURE 9.1 The illustration extends from left to right margin jumping the gutter, while the headline and body copy create a base for the layout. *Design by William Korbus.*

FIGURE 9.2   Balancing the body on a solid base of photographs, but leaving the left-hand column virtually blank creates a dynamism in this layout. *Design by Judith Martens.*

structure. Will the columns be justified (even), projecting a sense of order and formality? Or will they be flush left/ragged right, projecting an informal quality, eliminating word breaks and allowing additional white space to make its way into the layout?

The variables just examined are not all the possibilities needing attention. You may want to use rules between columns, box entire pages containing feature material or use "mood" headlines.

The next decision to be made is whether or not to use a grid pattern to maintain a standardized design. Somewhat of a grid is established by the column structure. For example, the page will have a two-, three-, or four-column structure that divides the area into vertical modules. If those vertical modules are then divided top to bottom at regular intervals, a complete grid is formed. All images can begin one inch from the top of the page, headlines can appear two inches from the top, and no body copy will be any higher than three inches from the top. These one-inch intervals can extend to the bottom of the column and be used for cropping photos, subheads, and the like. Alan Hurlburt's *The Grid* offers an extensive examination of this particular design technique. I've been content with using only the column structure, and in some cases a specified "sink" at the top of the page, but not extending the restraints further into a vertical as well as horizontal grid pattern.

While you may be thinking that this kind of rigid structure would cause pages to be monotonous and uninteresting, you actually will have created a sound skeleton on which to arrange the design elements of type and/or images. Instead of monotony, there is a great deal of order and an opportunity to carry the reader systematically through the material.

Just as a column structure projects a sense of dignity or informality, a similar image comes about through the type chosen for body copy. A sans-serif typeface projects an image of contemporary, no-nonsense efficiency. A serif typeface gives the impression of a traditional, conservative and formal organization. Square-serif typefaces, depending on their weight, can have the attributes of either sans-serif or serif typefaces; they tend more toward sans serif, however.

The typeface you use for the text (or "body") should be easy to read. Don't use a script or italic as the dominant style for body copy because the legibility is low compared to the traditional Roman posture. Italics are better used for captions or cutlines, in a slightly smaller size than the body copy. Italics are preferable to boldface because italics call less attention to themselves and detract less from the important elements on the page. Reverse type, which prints white letters on black or a color, is difficult to read and should be used sparingly.

Similar consideration should be given to the typeface you use for headlines. Don't be afraid to mix a sans-serif head with a serif body, or vice versa. The style of your publication can contain all serif heads and sans-serif body copy and cause no style or legibility problems.

Design Principles

The basic design principles are balance, contrast, harmony, proportion, theme and movement. "Movement" can be further divided into rhythmic or direct movement.

Balance is either symmetrical (formal) or asymmetrical (informal). People's faces, for example, are symmetrically balanced on an axis passing vertically from the chin through the center of the nose to the top of the head. On a layout, the left and right sides of a page can be balanced in much the same way, by placing elements of equal size, weight, tone or texture equidistant from the center of the design (fig. 9.3). The design

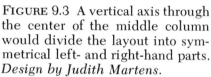

FIGURE 9.3 A vertical axis through the center of the middle column would divide the layout into symmetrical left- and right-hand parts. *Design by Judith Martens.*

FIGURE 9.4 The large heavy image in the lower left corner is balanced by the headline extending across the layout and the unequal columns of body copy. *Design by William Korbus.*

also can be balanced top to bottom along a horizontal axis through the center of the layout and thus be symmetrical both horizontally and vertically.

An asymmetrical layout is also balanced, but in an uneven way (fig. 9.4). Almost everyone has played on a teeter-totter at one time or another and realized that if one person weighs less than the person on the other end, the heavier person will have to sit closer to the center to be balanced on the teeter-totter. The same is true in doing an asymmetrical layout; that is, elements of a "heavier" nature (larger, colored, irregularly shaped) should be placed closer to the balance point than elements that are "lighter" (smaller, monochromatic, regularly shaped).

Contrast may be achieved with one colored element versus a series of monochromatic elements (fig. 9.5). Contrast also may be a layout involving large shapes versus a single smaller shape. Or contrast may be a textured element played against a series of smooth elements. Whatever the case, contrast is the spice that adds interest to a layout.

While contrast promotes sparkle on the page, harmony gives the

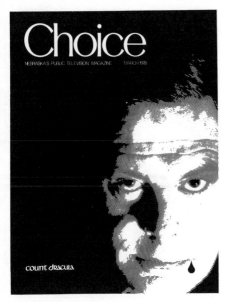

FIGURE 9.5 The cover is black and white except for the single drop of red blood in the lower right corner. *Design by William Korbus.*

FIGURE 9.6 Harmony exists between the illustration and the headline type because both have the same stippled style and are shadowed on the left. *Design by William Korbus.*

layout a feeling of unity. Contrast may be evidenced by variations in type sizes; keeping all sizes in the same type family produces harmony. This harmony gives a cohesive quality to the layout (fig. 9.6).

Proportion exists in design as an external dimension (the vertical proportion of a single page or the horizontal proportion of a two-page spread), as well as between elements in the layout such as body copy to image area, headline to body copy (fig. 9.7). For example, an 8 x 10 page has a proportion of 4 : 5 in external dimension. On that page, a photograph covering half the area with body copy covering the remainder would be a 1 : 1 proportion. Proportions that are easily identified, such as 1 : 1, square, or other equally balanced relationships, are not very interesting. Proportions such as 1 : 3, 2 : 3, or 3 : 5 increase the interest level because these are relationships that are not easily identified by the eye. By using proportions that are a bit unusual, the communicator can add attractiveness to the material.

Theme is still another design element (fig. 9.8). For an article on

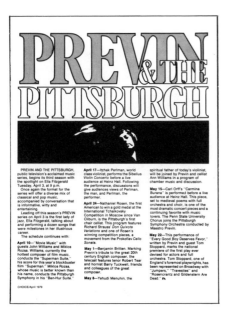

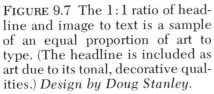

FIGURE 9.7 The 1:1 ratio of head-line and image to text is a sample of an equal proportion of art to type. (The headline is included as art due to its tonal, decorative qualities.) *Design by Doug Stanley.*

FIGURE 9.8 Since the article is about dance, it is appropriate to use a "romantic" type style and treatment along with an illustration-like photo conversion to capture this theme. *Design by Martin Almanza.*

dance, the photographs might be of the stage, of dancers, of dance prepara-tion. In the same way, the headline type style should attempt to ex-press the fluid, graceful quality of the dance. A script or novelty face would be a good choice. In the layout, the images and type should reflect the "dance" theme, drawing the entire design into a cohesive whole.

Movement exists in one of two ways. Movement may be rhythmic, developed through a series of similar units moving, evolving and grow-ing in a particular direction: a line of type, a series of photos or another repetitive element carrying the eye in a prescribed direction (fig. 9.9). Or movement may take on a more direct quality—an arrow pointing or a photo in which movement points in a direction to carry the viewer (fig. 9.10). All these design elements are variables used to carry the reader through the layout, through the story and through the publication in a manner that has been carefully determined.

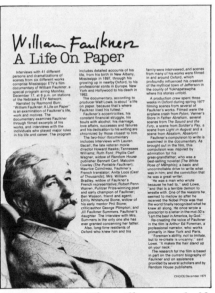

FIGURE 9.9 The animated, staccato of the photos in column three demonstrates rhythmic movement. *Design by William Korbus.*

FIGURE 9.10 The silhouette halftone of Faulkner facing and looking right from the first column "directs" the reader into the article. *Design by Martin Almanza.*

Layout

The basic layout principles are grouping, gridding and alignment. Grouping is the technique of keeping all elements closely associated in the layout. The designer does not allow one element to become fragmented and float off irrationally in the design. If you use good grouping techniques, you will have the sense that the layout is growing from the center, much as a Fourth of July skyrocket explodes in the sky or a flower unfolds—opening from the center outward.

When using the gridding principle, think of the page as being divided into squares or rectangles of a specific length and width, like building blocks. These blocks or modules are then filled by various elements (e.g., photographs, illustrations, headlines and body type). The columns of type, for instance, might be one module wide and a number of modules deep; a photograph might extend across two or three columns or modules and be any number of modules deep.

The alignment principle stresses the need to have one design

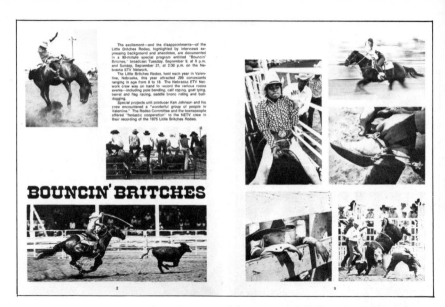

FIGURE 9.11 Horizontal and vertical lines can be drawn along the elements' perimeters throughout this layout, which will then connect photos to photos, photos to type, and type to type. This is alignment. *Design by William Korbus.*

FIGURE 9.12 The zero in 20's acts as a frame for part of the headline. *Design by Mike Buettner.*

FIGURE 9.13 The alphabetical motif stretches across the entire page with the main headline centered to provide an axis between the two columns. *Design by Judith Martens.*

FIGURE 9.14 This flush-left headline aligns with the flush-left introduction and text. *Design by Martin Almanza.*

module align with another so that the entire layout will relate through a series of imaginary vertical and horizontal axes. The headline may be aligned with the top of the body copy, body copy with a photograph, and so on, weaving the entire layout into a single unit (fig. 9.11).

"White space," or negative space, is the noninformation area of a layout. It contains no information elements such as type, photography, illustration or copy. For the new designer, this area should be confined to the margin or along the outer edge where it will not become "trapped white space." White space trapped within the layout calls attention to itself, distracts the reader, and detracts from the message elements being presented to the audience.

Typography

Typography is one of the elements communicators may manipulate according to the design and layout principles. Headline typography in

particular allows you to explore a number of design and layout possibilities. You can use headline type as art, such as in "Upstairs
Downstairs Moves to the Roaring 20's" and "Stories Without Words"
(fig. 9.12), or you can use headline type in a more formal arrangement:
centered, from left to right, and creating a central vertical axis that focuses the reader on that particular layout (fig. 9.13). You might arrange
the headline flush left or flush right in order to get a better grouping
arrangement in the layout (fig. 9.14), or choose a more random headline
style that gives an asymmetrical or informal feeling to the page (fig. 9.15).

A headline should conform to the same restraints used for any other
design element. The headline should stay within a particular margin and
should be aligned and grouped so that it adds a cohesive quality to the
layout. In figure 9.15, the second line is aligned, set flush left, with the
left side of the first line. The third, fourth and fifth lines are set flush
right to the photographs and aligned with the top of the photo. The
headline alone would have a random, unorganized quality. Combined
with the photo, subhead and caption, it is an integral part of an interrelated group of design elements. All the individual units form a cohesive
whole because of grouping and alignment principles.

Another decision relating to headline styles is whether to use the
same type family, size and weight throughout the magazine, creating a
more conservative, harmonious style. An alternative is to attempt a
"mood" headline system for each article, lending a more dramatic quality to the publication. If the first article in a banking publication features
car financing, the designer might choose a sans-serif italic typeface that
projects a feeling of movement, combining it with a car image that is
moving off the page. On the other hand, for an article on stock and bond
investment, the designer may feel more comfortable using a typeface
that promotes a sense of tradition, formality and sturdiness. Either approach is acceptable, but decide on a single approach for that entire
issue. Don't vacillate between mood and constant styles within the same
publication.

Equally important is the type family selected. Roman type styles,
whether old-style, transitional or modern, have dignified, traditional,
conservative qualities. A sans-serif, square-serif Egyptian or modified
serif such as Optima or Serif Gothic would be more appropriate in an
informal contemporary publication. The size of the type used and the
amount of "leading" (space) between lines is also a consideration. In
general, use one or two points of leading when using 9-, 10-, 11-, 12-point
type.

FIGURE 9.15 Notice how the top line of the headline defines the margins. The second line is flush left to the first, with the remaining lines flush right to the photo. The headline has a "random" appearance that is derived of a carefully thought through structure. *Design by Martin Almanza.*

FIGURE 9.16 The silhouette halftone provides vitality to a page that would be less dynamic had a square-cut halftone been used. *Design by Tim Timken.*

Before deciding on body copy, take the time to discuss with your typographer or printer the type styles available. Have several samples set in different faces and line widths, using varying amounts of leading, to see how comfortable the type is for the reader, how well it fits the mood and projected image of the publication, and the texture it creates on the page.

Visuals

Many communicators, whose primary function is writing, do not realize the amount of communication that can take place through the use of good photos and illustrations. Just as words are symbols conveying ideas, visual images also communicate. In some situations these images communicate more effectively than words.

Images can be used to carry information to either support or supplement an article. Either use is appropriate, and the designer should recognize how the image is being used when making the choice for the layout. A photo or illustration also may be used purely for its attention-getting value, or to elicit a predetermined response.

When choosing photographs for a layout, look for photojournalistic qualities—strong photos that contribute to the article yet could stand by themselves. Captions can and should be brief. Do not use bad photographs just because they are available, do not use beautiful photographs if they are inappropriate to what is being communicated. Be discriminating in choosing photographs for a layout so that the photos can do the job they are intended to do: carry supporting information or supplementary material, or attract attention.

When using photographs, be aware that there are two kinds of scale or proportion: internal and external. The external size of a series of photographs may be identical, while the internal scale may vary greatly from close-ups to medium shots to panoramas. The traditional manner of dealing with photographs is through an external scale hierarchy using the most important photo as the largest with secondary photos slightly smaller and tertiary photos smaller still. A hierarchy also can be created by varying the internal scale even though the external scale of the photos is similar.

The use of color in a photo is another consideration. Full-color, duotone, and tint block are three of the alternatives available. Full-color photos printed as process-color are as close to representing reality in print as we can approximate. A duotone results from adding a second color to a black-and-white photo. Printing a duotone of black and brown gives a sepia tone, which can lend a historic feel to the image. A tint block is often used as an accent in a black-and-white photo. It may color the sky, or the primary element, or act as a background to the primary element, thus focusing the reader's attention on the important aspects of the photo.

Photographs can be edited in a number of ways. The most common method is through cropping and sizing to fit a particular layout—eliminating extraneous material by designating only a portion of the photo to be reproduced. Editing also can be done through the caption, using words to focus on the important element in the picture. Various photomechanical means might also be used to direct attention to the important items in a photograph, such as converting the original photograph into a silhouette halftone (fig. 9.16) or vignetting the important

  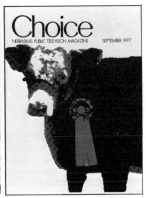

FIGURE 9.17 This mezzotint simplifies the images and allows us to drop out the background to provide an area for dramatic presentation of our body copy. *Design by Martin Almanza.*

FIGURE 9.18 High contrast line conversions present a recognizable abstraction of reality. *Design by Laura Hart.*

FIGURE 9.19 Posterizations are a relatively simple, inexpensive means of presenting continuous tone material with greater impact. *Design by Judith Martens.*

content. Photographs may be altered before halftones are made by retouching and airbrushing them. These techniques require skilled professionals; if retouching or airbrushing is necessary, go to a specialist.

Particularly useful reproduction methods are the use of photoconversion screens when making film negatives or the use of positive photostats for print (fig. 9.17). Photographs used in these ways are viable alternatives to illustrations. Most editors reply on photo halftones and often overlook the dramatic possibilities of silhouette halftones or partial silhouettes to focus on the important aspect of the photo. Using a photo conversion in the form of a line shot (fig. 9.18), straight-line, wavy-line, or "bullseye" screen to attract the reader is still another method. Vignettes, mortices and geometric shapes are other visual alternatives when using photos. Posterized photographs (fig. 9.19) are achieved by varying the exposure and screens when making a photo negative. These options are all frequently bypassed, so communicators lose the advantage of exciting visual possibilities in their designs.

Type can be either printed over (surprinted, fig. 9.20), or reversed out of a photo (fig. 9.21). This combining of elements—type with photograph—can simplify a layout and make it more attractive. Use these techniques in dealing with the image portion of the publication to create

FIGURE 9.20 Surprinting type on a photo allows for combining elements and thus simplifying our layouts. *Design by Mike Buettner.*

FIGURE 9.21 A reverse head integrates type and image for quick identification. *Design by Mike Buettner.*

an exciting contrast of visual elements that readers will find attractive (fig. 9.22).

Photos also can be used as a basis for illustration (fig. 9.23). A photo can be placed on a light table and a piece of layout paper, tracing paper, or paper towel laid over it. By using the photo as the primary image source and tracing the image, an illustration can be created.

Illustration is an area often neglected by the organizational communicator because an illustrator is not on the staff or otherwise readily available. This is unfortunate since a great many sources of illustration are available. Sometimes hiring a nationally recognized professional is the best choice for dealing with a difficult illustration problem. A professional illustrator can be located through an agent or representative in any of the major markets in the country. Call an agent in New York, Los Angeles or any large city and ask for a portfolio of samples of different illustrators' works. After you have chosen the illustrator whose style seems most appropriate for your publication, establish criteria for the specific kind of work needed. Research material may be sent to the illustrator to help complete the assignment. The cost will depend on the complexity of the illustration and the time involved to produce it.

Perhaps the work of a local illustrator has attracted your attention in a local publication or advertisement. Contact the person directly and find out about availability, cost and time requirements for particular illustration needs. A great deal of talent exists in the educational institutions in our cities. It's not difficult to contact the art department of an institution and ask to see the work of a promising student or instructor. It's an opportunity for you to obtain good illustrations and give little-known illustrators the chance to be published and earn a few dollars.

Be wary of the person within the office who has "always wanted to draw." Allowing this person an opportunity to submit material for publication may prove fruitful. If the material is of poor quality, however, it can be an unpleasant experience for both the would-be illustrator and you. This situation is a problem more often than not.

Clip-art is another source of illustration material. Many printers subscribe to clip-art services so they can offer these illustration options to their clients. Most clip-art is not useful for organizational publications, but a bit of it may be appropriate. A good-quality illustration from a clip-art service can be obtained for very few dollars.

FIGURE 9.22 By combining the textures of silhouette halftones, copyright-free illustration, square-cut halftones and line conversions, an interesting and energetic layout is achieved. *Design by Martin Almanza.*

FIGURE 9.23 This wax pencil illustration was done by using tracing paper over a photograph on a lightboard. *Design by William Korbus.*

Most communicators do not realize that copyright-free illustrations are available (fig. 9.24). A number of books have been published containing illustrations that are available for public use without any fee. Dover publications has *1800 Woodcuts by Thomas Bewick and His School, Graphic Trade Symbols by German Designers,* and *Art Deco Designs and Motifs.* Morgan and Morgan has other copyright-free publications: *James Connor's Sons and Electrotype Specimens, 1888.* Hart publishes *The Great Giant Swipe File!, American Designs, The Animal Kingdom, Attention Getters, Compendium, Holidays* and *Trades and Professions.* The copyright-free images can be used individually or combined in montages to create interesting results.

Paper and Ink

Papers most likely to be of interest to business and organizational communicators are bond, book and cover, which all come in a number of sizes, weights and costs. In addition to quality, paper is priced by the pound, so the weight of the paper selected is very important in budgeting a project.

Find a reputable paper company, make an appointment with one of the sales representatives, and discuss any problems or questions you have. Paper salespeople know the current costs and availability, the companies that have the kind of stock you need, and the alternative stocks that may be better to use. A good salesperson can become a valuable asset to you by anticipating the kinds of paper that might be interesting for future use. Printers can also be helpful when you are selecting paper.

Many people, when choosing a paper stock, think of using color; and color stock can be useful and attractive if used properly. Look at the publications of competitors and think about the possibility of choosing a color stock that will make your publication stand out from the rest. This is the real reason for choosing color—to attract your audience. Also keep in mind that color stock used in conjunction with colored ink still must be effective, attractive and have contrast so that the message will be well displayed. If the stock color is close to the ink color, the effect will be very subtle. If delicacy is not what you want, colors too closely matched may make the material appear drab, unappealing and weak.

The communicator should be aware of the special ink choices that are available. The Pantone Matching System (PMS), a must in specifying

FIGURE 9.24 Copyright-free illustration was used for the figures on this award-winning cover. The inset photo of the house was an etch tone conversion to match the style of the rest of the design. *Design by Martin Almanza.*

ink colors, is available through all printers. A good investment for the organizational communicator is to have a PMS ink-sample chart, with inks printed on both dull and glossy-finish stocks.

Two inks with special characteristics are metallic inks and opaque inks. When used properly, metallic inks are attractive and rich and add a great deal of "flash" to printed materials. Opaque inks are very effective on dark stock, or overprinted with halftones to give unusual effects. Consider using metallic and/or opaque inks for their eye-catching qualities.

Resources: Magazines and Annuals

A number of design periodicals can help the communicator stay abreast of current design trends and established and promising designers. Their use also can strengthen your ability to recognize good design, illustration and photography.

> *American Photographer* deals with photography and photographers. It does not focus on the latest in equipment, darkroom techniques or trick photography, as do many other photo magazines. It publishes sound, straightforward reporting of the photography field.

> *Art Direction* magazine has a very strong New York influence and regularly contains columns dealing with ethical questions regarding designer/client relationships; news regarding designer moves and promotions; and articles on trends in art direction, design and illustration.

> *Communication Arts* (CA) monitors trends in publication design, packaging, layout, illustration, photography—almost any facet of visual communication done in the world today—with an emphasis on American design. CA contains a great deal of color material, does profiles on influential designers, covers design trends both past and present, and once a year publishes the *Art Annual* of photography and illustration. At the end of each year a communication annual is compiled, examining television, radio, books, magazines, letterheads, posters and advertisements.

> *Folio,* "the magazine for magazine management," is useful in dealing with areas such as budgeting, circulation, sales and production features. *Folio* also includes design articles and sponsors workshops dealing with all facets of magazine production.

> *Print* magazine does not contain as much color reproduction as

Communication Arts, but does a great deal in examining additional areas of design, such as graphic shows, visual symbol systems and annual reports.

U & lc (upper and lower case), a tabloid published by International Typeface Corporation, is designed by Herb Lubalin, a top-flight American art director and designer. *U & lc* is extremely attractive and wins national and international awards every year for its excellent design.

In addition to the periodicals, several design annuals are particularly useful. *The Annual of Advertising, Editorial and Television Art and Design*, published by the Art Directors Club of New York, contains material from all over the world. *Creativity Annual*, published by the editors and publishers of *Art Direction* magazine, also contains international material. Both publications are fine references for monitoring contemporary design trends, examining particular design styles, and perhaps even finding someone to solve a specific one-time design, illustration or photography problem.

Step by Step

Now that the basic steps and techniques in producing a publication have been introduced, let's follow the process from inception to distribution.

1. The idea takes two forms: verbal and visual.
2. The copy is written and photos or illustrations are generated.
3. Paper of proper texture and tone is chosen and ink color selected.
4. The copy is edited and spec'd for typesetting.
5. Photos are chosen from the contact sheet, enlarged and cropped. Illustrations are completed by the illustrator, chosen from a clip-art service, or selected from a copyright-free source.
6. Black-and-white line art is reproduced as veloxes or photostats.
7. Copy and veloxes are pasted up in camera-ready form and sent to the printer.
8. Continuous-tone photos are prepared as halftone negatives and stripped into the layout as specified.
9. Proofs are produced for and reviewed by the designer/editor.
10. Printing plates are made.
11. Paper is fed to the press and printed.
12. The printed job is folded, collated, bound and trimmed.

13. The finished job is delivered to communicator for proper distribution to the audience.

The printing methods you are likely to encounter are basically three—letterpress, offset and gravure. The largest proportion of work will be run offset. Letterpress printing is declining, and gravure printing requires long runs to make the job economical. The best suggestion I can make is to talk to your printer, clearly outlining the parameters of your problem. Your printer will be able to assess the needs in relation to the presses, paper and personnel available, thus producing the highest quality, most economical product.

William E. Korbus is a nationally recognized designer who teaches visual design in the College of Communication at the University of Texas at Austin.

CHAPTER 10

"Targeted" Media

WILLIAM P. DUNK and PHILIP F. BAMFORTH

In many organizations, communication is a Muzak of words and pictures—low-impact background noise. After a while, people are no longer aware of its presence or may even get bored and tune it out. When this happens, a communication communicates nothing.

The strategy of communication should be to get through, to get noticed, to get above the noise level of the thousands of communications that are bombarding people from all sides, to get out of the mainstream. The strategy should be to get noticed by employees, by investors, by college students, by government representatives, by customers, by consumer advocates, by environmentalists, by town leaders, by teachers, by. . . . In organizational communication, communication strategy means having a continuing plan to affect key audiences in such a way that they will support the organization or at least be neutral toward the long-term objectives of the organization as set out in its operating plan. Messages should not be fired hit or miss—sprayed across the audience landscape with the hope that some of them will hit home.

Finding the Right Position

Any company that is not the largest in its industry faces a special problem in getting noticed. It is fairly easy for people to remember the biggest, but not so easy for them to remember the number-two company, or numbers three or four or eleven. When Avis said it was number two and won a clear position as the company that tries harder, it became the leader in the minds of many people.

To get noticed, an organization should adopt a position. It should have a positioning statement in writing, which then gets imprinted on the minds of key members. From it flows the organization's basic message—altered to suit the interests of each audience.

Chesebrough-Ponds, for example, has for years positioned itself not as a manufacturer of cosmetics but as a company that turns out vital products for the American family. All its communications, whether for investors, employees or customers, flow from that position.

Once an organization has adopted a position, it must communicate it endlessly. To state the position once or twice or five times in the annual report and the employee publication and a booklet and film is not enough. Intrinsic in the information presented must be the perpetual statement of the organization's position in one way or another. In strategic, or "target," communication, you do not simply provide data; you focus target audiences on the company's position. Every document, every speech, and every movie must reinforce the company's communication position.

The Objective Before the Vehicle

The dozens of special communications described in this chapter require intense planning. Too often, communicators start at the wrong end. They should start with the objective: to communicate an attitude, to supply information, to move to action, to move emotionally. Then comes the message; then the vehicle; then the channel and the work to get the message or messages through the channel and to the audience.

Instead of saying, "Let's get out a booklet," the communicator should start by saying, "Let's make the new dental plan understandable to all employees." Then say, "What vehicle will do the job?" And, importantly, "Will the result buttress the company's desired communication objective?"

Making Points

Communication messages and media must make points to be successful. One point or three or six, they should be clearly and obviously spelled out and emphasized. All else is supplemental. Too often, main points and supporting points in a publication are buried in the text, camouflaged in solid body type, overpowered by illustration and color. The main point or points must come through loud and clear, or the message will not communicate.

Once the points are decided, then comes the decision as to how. The vehicle may be a book or a poster or a limerick, a telegram, painting or lapel pin. It may be delivered by mail or by hand or on a TV show, over AP or in an ad. The successful communicator keeps an eye on the communication. He or she should not become obsessed with technique.

In Terms of Audience Interests—Target

Each target medium should be for a distinct audience, and there should be targeted media and communication tactics for at least the top five audiences that the organization has decided it has. Each audience should be analyzed to make sure that it is appropriate and approachable.

Audience analyses can be formal or informal. A telephone survey, for instance, can ask, What, specifically, do you want to know about the organization? What, besides information, do you expect from the organization? What are the strengths and weaknesses of the organization? What are your thoughts about the prospects for the industry? From whom do you normally find out about the organization? What three or four adjectives would you use to describe the organization? Where do you think the organization is headed? What are your feelings about the organization's communication and communicators?

Budgets for special-purpose media should be limited. They call for imagination and ingenuity in planning and execution. At the same time, they offer opportunities to try ambitious new concepts and for reaching out geographically to use low-cost suppliers in remote areas of the country.

Schedules become important, because there is usually no event or limiting date that moves them inexorably forward. Thus, without the exercise of self-discipline, these projects can become strung out in time until they die before they are born.

Some Specific Media

Targeted booklets, targeted letters, targeted ads, targeted media other than publications. Media that drop messages where the ground is fertile, to grow into vital impacts on the specific audiences they are intended to reach. Here are some specifics:

Letters to employees from the plant or office manager can be particularly effective communication if they are not overworked. To most employees, the local manager is the most authoritative, most "real" person in the whole organization. Messages from him or her can have a personal touch that other media do not have and can reach members of the employee's family, who can have an important impact on the views of the employee.

Billboards along highways or in airport terminals that say *Welcome to Middletown, Home of Ace Plastic Corporation* or some similar message about what a company does can communicate the corporate identity effectively. They make a point for the organization or they supply welcome information to the traveler.

Corporate art exhibits in plants or public places can communicate important messages to skeptical publics. They can convey the idea that corporations are not entirely profit-minded and that they can take the lead in advancing an appreciation of the arts. Some are collections of regional art or art in a specialized area. Chesebrough-Ponds communicates an understanding of contemporary fashion and trends vital to a consumer company in its headquarters arts collection. It also supports children's art programs.

Benefit books should furnish their employees with an explanation of those plans in words that can be understood by the average employee. Many companies go too far, pour in all the details, and as a result retard rather than facilitate communication. A benefit handbook should ideally be fifty pages or less for a major corporation to tell the story of its benefits to employees. More than that is too much because employees seldom wade through more.

Benefits films and slide presentations should augment booklets on benefits. Benefits are complex, and audiovisual presentations are excellent instruction tools—if they are kept brief.

Personalized benefit computer printouts can further supplement the message on benefits. They have the special advantage of telling the employee about his or her own personal list of benefits in dollars and cents. Some organizations print a weekly message on paystubs, sometimes announcing benefit charges.

Recruiting booklets. Many companies don't think about their audience when they prepare materials to attract college graduates and others to join their companies. They think in terms of the interests of the corporation; they tell how big the organization is and all the products they make; they talk about "careers" with the organization. Applicants want to know what the organization can do for them. They want to know what

The strategy behind good communication is to get noticed. Whether an audience is made up of employees, management trainees or service station owners, communicators must compete with many other media for attention.

it is like to work for the company, what jobs are available, the pay, the opportunities for advancement and greater responsibility, the opportunities for further study. They want to know what their specific career paths will be in the organization.

Orientation media. For new employees, information about the company and the job can be carried in print and audiovisuals. The first few days and weeks employees are on the job are the most impressionable time of their stay with the organization. They are alert at this stage to sponge up information about the company, its management, its products, its policies and its objectives (see chapter 14). One caution: be alert to the information capacity of the employees and don't overload.

Postcards to employees. One service company in Great Britain effectively uses a series of postcards to employees in place of an employee newspaper or magazine. Once a month a card is sent to employees, giving them a new tip on how they can help render better service to customers.

Pay-envelope stuffers. Many companies deliver paychecks to salaried employees in envelopes and to wage employees "bareback"— without an envelope. The procedure itself communicates the message that the company puts wage employees in a different class from salaried employees. When a paycheck is conveyed in an envelope, a short message, particularly one that relates to pay or benefits, can be enclosed. It should be positive. A simple message can be placed on the envelope as well.

Paycheck stub messages. At the bottom of the paycheck stub there is usually room for a very brief message. It can explain a change in deduction or it can be a wish for a happy vacation or birthday or holiday. (Couldn't the computer be programmed to say "Happy 53rd Birthday!" on the paycheck just before each person's birthday?)

Company histories and anniversary books can be effective communication media if they are strategically planned and executed. They should have a progressive approach. Too often, company books are monuments to the past. Good company histories and anniversary books show company progress and propel the reader into prospects for the future. Or, they show how the passage of time has brought maturity and foresight and strength to deal with change and progress, thus keeping the company in tune with the future. They show what the company has learned from the past concepts that it can use profitably for the future.

Literature for students and teachers. There is always a big demand from students and teachers for educational information. An electrical equipment manufacturer, for example, can supply information about electricity. Elementary and high schools in particular seek special information in the form of illustrated books and booklets, motion pictures, videotapes and slide presentations. Students are at a highly impressionable age; for the rest of their lives, they will remember the information about your organization that came into their classrooms. Offer authentic, useful information with a minimum of plugs for your company. If you get into the educational information field, be prepared for an avalanche of requests for information.

Sample kits. Some companies supply kits of material to students and teachers, usually at a cost of 50 cents to $5. For example, one rubber company's kit contains samples of different kinds of rubber and a small booklet that explains how natural and synthetic rubber are produced and how simple experiments can be performed with the samples. Thousands have been sold.

Dividend stuffers. When the company's dividend checks are mailed to shareholders, an enclosed message gets a free ride—and arrives at a pleasant moment for the shareholder who is receiving a check. A brief message about the company can help reassure shareholders that their investment in the company was a wise one. Perhaps the chief executive officer can take this opportunity to discuss legislation affecting the company and the industry and to invite shareholders to make their feelings known to their representatives in Congress or in Parliament. Combustion Engineering has put questionnaires, address update slips and other data in its stuffers.

Continuing education books. Many organizations offer their employees an opportunity to take courses either for advancement in the organization or for enrichment. A booklet about the programs offered by the company and by nearby educational institutions, and the company's policy on tuition refund, can show the organization as generous and progressive and genuinely interested in the advancement of the employees.

Company scholarship books. Near the top of the list of things employees are proud of is the scholastic achievement of their children. Thus they are particularly receptive to an attractive written explanation of any scholarship program supported by the company for employees' children. To save questions, and possibly some bitter disappointments, make the brochure as complete and explicit as possible, particularly with respect to eligibility for the scholarships and how candidates are selected.

Essay, photo and art contests. Contests get people involved, participating, whether they are essays or coloring by children, or essays or photos or paintings or sculpture by adults. Whatever the vehicle, communication about the contest can build prestige for the organization.

Ad reprints. Not all employees, shareholders or other audiences see the company's advertising messages in newspapers and magazines. Reprints of some of the ads, sent to key audiences or posted on bulletin boards, provide an opportunity to tell these audiences the strategy behind the ad program and to explain the behind-the-scenes story of how they were produced.

Calendars provide a service and often are things of beauty that are on view, not just for a day or a week, but all month long, twelve months a year. If they are strategically planned and tastefully done, they can project a potent and lasting message.

Quizzes and puzzles can help build interest in organizational publications. Whether they work a message about the company into a quiz or puzzle is less important than the fact that the quiz or puzzle is there, drawing readers into the publication and providing entertainment.

The company fact book provides security analysts with all the facts they want to know about the company. The most important role of the fact book, however, particularly if you are in a multiindustry company, is to encourage additional security analysts to become interested in and follow the progress of your company. The fact book should disclose the basics of your business so that analysts will become familiar enough with your company to recommend your stock for purchase. It should not be a collecting point for unwanted or marginal information but should contain genuinely useful information not available elsewhere. The fact book does not need to have the splendor of some annual reports, but it should be attractively designed so as to project your company as an up-to-date, progressive organization.

Portfolio managers' booklets. The managers of investment portfolios have become a most important investment audience. They need a different kind of story about the company than the one addressed to the security analyst. It should provide a macroeconomic perspective of the company, showing how it is affected by business trends and new economic developments. These booklets should discuss corporate goals and objectives, position the company against its competition, and provide other responsive information. They should be easy to scan and read. In short, they should win the trust of portfolio managers by being specifically responsive to their information needs.

Rep books are for registered representatives, the account executives of brokerage firms. Often the representatives will send them to potential shareholders so these marketing brochures should sell your corporation to the reps and give them the ammunition to sell your corporation and its securities to their clients. The rep book should highlight the company's competitive strengths and, if appropriate, indicate why now is a good time to buy the company's stock. Most important, it should impart a clear message quickly—one that can be passed on from the rep to a customer in less than two minutes of telephone time.

Corporate ethics books. In recent years the ethics of businesses and business executives have come under close public scrutiny; the whole gamut of corporate relationships with the public and the motivations of the corporation have been questioned. In response to this trend, many corporations issue books stating company positions on such matters. They contain corporate policy statements; public relations policy and employee communication policy; and the company's position on equal opportunity, consumer relations, the environment, energy, and so forth.

Research and development brochures. Many audiences, including investors, employees and customers, believe that a company's research and development effort and accomplishments are a good indicator of the future success of the company. A booklet that tells the R & D story can make good points for any company.

Key-issues white paper. Rather than sit back and take unwarranted public criticism on the chin, or endure unjustified government attacks and regulations, an organization can issue white papers to tell the true story and the background of a key issue. To be believable and effective, the white paper should be candid, presenting the black along with the white.

Contribution booklets. Some corporations are reluctant to talk about their contributions to schools and charitable organizations. They fear that if they call attention to their gifts, very many other organizations will be stimulated to solicit contributions from them, and that in refusing to contribute they will create more ill will than good. Other corporations believe it is important to underline their citizenship role. They publish booklets outlining their policy on giving to promote understanding in the minds of all parties concerned. Most important, these booklets bring credit to the company and help dispel the notion that the corporation is unfeeling and unresponsive to people's needs.

Industry books. If a book plugging your company appears immodest for certain audiences, do one about your industry for educators, the press, authors, students, college recruits, elected officials and others.

Tour booklets. When people tour your facilities, they may be impressed with the story you have presented to them; but after they leave, they may forget much of your message. A book that visitors can take away with them will remind them of what they saw and heard and can include additional information about the organization. Such a book also will probably be seen by friends and relatives, thus multiplying your audience.

And a partial list of others. Lest this list become much too long, work on your own compilation of other possible target media, such as customer-service books, merger-partner books, coloring books, comic books, questionnaires, corporate advocacy brochures and ads, jingles, games, company architecture, pins, banners, pens and pencils, T-shirts.

Some possible target media are so obvious they're often overlooked—the printed items used in corporate life that people don't think of as communication vehicles. Such things as insurance policies communicate. Unfortunately, they often communicate confusion rather than useful information. Rework them as a way to make points about the company.

Job instructions and standard operating procedures communicate. They need to be written carefully if you wish them to be read and respected and followed. Application forms communicate, although sometimes irritatingly. Signs in parking lots and beside timeclocks and in restrooms also communicate—sometimes bluntly.

Just as there is body language, there is organizational "appearance language"—the housekeeping of its plants and offices; how the boss dresses, walks, smiles; his or her tone of voice; the evident attitudes of employees, their enthusiasm or lack of it. Finally, everything an organization does not say is also communication.

William P. Dunk is president of Corpcom Services, Inc., parent company of Corporate Annual Reports, Inc., and associate editor of *Corporate Communications Report*, a newsletter on investor relations and financial communication.

Philip F. Bamforth is president of Corpcom Productions, an affiliate of Corpcom Services.

CHAPTER 11

Bulletin Boards, Exhibits, Hotlines

WALTER G. ANDERSON, ABC

While bulletin boards have been a traditional means of communication within organizations for years, the use of exhibits and displays is more recent, and telephone hotlines are a development of only the past few years. All three can be popular, but they must be organized and supervised.

Bulletin Boards

Bulletin boards are among the most traditional forms of internal communication. They have the advantage of being relatively inexpensive and easy to maintain and have an immediacy that attracts attention. They do not have the problems of credibility often associated with other methods of controlled communication; employees and others tend to regard them as straightforward public notices of vital events.

Perhaps the most important aspects of bulletin boards are their high visibility and easy accessibility. Bulletin boards should be set up in high-traffic areas to attract maximum attention, and the material should be kept current and interesting. No other medium permits an organization to announce news in printed form so quickly. A flash bulletin can be prepared and posted within minutes, even in a system of multiple boards.

News is generally posted on a regular basis, daily or weekly, but many organizations post news several times a day, depending on the need. Furthermore, boards can be organized so that news can be directed to specific audiences. General company news is posted on all

157

Viewers can readily find the desired material when the bulletin board is organized with specific categories and labeled areas.

bulletin boards, while local news appears only at the location of the activity.

Another important advantage of bulletin boards is their economy. After the initial investment, regular maintenance is generally modest. The only expense is the cost of producing and posting the news and feature material, plus a modest amount for housekeeping to keep the boards clean and in good physical condition.

Physical Appearance of Boards

Bulletin boards vary as widely as the organizations that use them. Indeed, they are often designed to reflect the personality of the sponsoring organization. They can be traditional cork boards or sleek, modern displays of metal, glass, plastic or wood. Some organizations use a variety of boards; the major bulletin boards are more elaborate than those in local areas.

There is a trend to refer to major bulletin boards as information centers. They are often divided into sections for permanent notices (legally required notices about wages and salaries, working conditions, safety, equal employment opportunity), and sections for news or feature material. The most popular format seems to be a horizontal shape, roughly 9 feet by 3 feet, positioned at eye level for people of average height. Information centers may be open or glass-encased to prevent random placement or removal of material. Boards should be well-lighted areas or directly under a standard ceiling light for maximum visibility. Some are back-lighted so that color transparencies may be viewed.

The Herman Miller Company created free-standing kiosks to serve as public notice centers. The four-sided kiosks, made in-house with Herman Miller products, provide 16 square feet of surface. Each kiosk has shelves for literature and a drop box for depositing requests for literature. The information centers have places where employees can get all kinds of information.

Guidelines should be developed for bulletin boards programs. They should define the character of the service and resolve many day-to-day decisions that may arise, such as the purpose and locations of bulletin boards, the kinds of materials to be posted, and the graphics of posted materials. It is essential to obtain management approval and support and to establish the lines of authority for the operation of bulletin boards.

Contents

The contents of bulletin boards depend on the nature of the sponsoring organization and the guidelines established. It is critical, however, to maintain control of bulletin boards to assure that only authorized material is posted.

The biggest weakness of some bulletin boards is that they are open to everyone and can easily become cluttered. Everyone should be informed about the procedures for posting material, and the person authorized to maintain them should remove unofficial and outdated material regularly. Some bulletin boards are under glass and are inaccessible to all but those who maintain them.

The most efficient way to organize material is to establish specific categories and label areas to indicate where various items are to be placed. This directs viewers to the appropriate place for different kinds of news and helps the manager of the program to arrange material. Here is a list of materials commonly posted on company bulletin boards:

Personnel news: appointments, promotions, transfers, wage and salary changes, vacations, holidays, benefits, government regulations, job openings, working hours, plant or office closings, meetings, safety programs, training programs

Company news: new facilities, construction progress, new products, reorganizations, historical events, production achievements, labor relations, research developments, management messages, crises (strikes, floods, snowstorms, fires), company honors and awards, critical problems (inflation, energy, safety), advertising, marketing, sales promotion programs, or financial news (profits, sales, stock prices)

Employee relations: awards to employees for service, safety, news, suggestions, community service

Social and community activities: club meetings, picnics, art and craft shows, campaigns to raise funds

Employee services: classified ads, community services, care agencies available to employees (day-care centers, baby sitters, Alcoholics Anonymous)

Format of Materials

Some organizations standardize the format of all material to appear on information centers and bulletin boards to simplify the preparation of the material and create a better overall appearance. IBM Tucson posts information on preprinted sheets labeled by general news categories. Each sheet may contain only one news item or several, readily identified by category. Herman Miller preprints 4½ x 11 brightly colored cards with such headings as Corporate News, People, Jobs. J. C. Penney labels news by categories and often provides an extra supply of the notices near bulletin boards for employees who want copies.

Feature photographs or other graphic material add another dimension to the boards and enhance visual appeal. Architects' renderings of new or proposed facilities, photos of employees recognized for long service or outstanding accomplishments, and posters promoting a United Way campaign, blood drive or other company-wide program are a few examples. J. I. Case posts a "Photo of the Week," usually taken by a staff photographer and dealing with some aspect of the company. Eastman Kodak and Sperry Corporation post color transparencies on back-lighted boards with supporting copy explaining subjects of long-standing interest, such as company products or benefits.

Many organizations post news releases so that employees can learn news about the company before local media cover it. Alexander and Alexander affixes a special "Newsflash" label to news releases to draw attention to important news. It also affixes the "Newsflash" label to re-

Brightly colored cards with standard headings can simplify preparation and distribution of bulletin board material.

leases sent to the mailroom to attract its attention to important announcements that must be posted quickly.

Other organizations post press clippings about the company that have appeared in newspapers or other publications. Clippings show how the outside media view organizations and have the added value of coming from outside sources. J. I. Case posts articles about the company and also about its competition to remind employees they are competing in the business world.

Maintenance

It is essential for one department or individual to be assigned to maintain bulletin boards. Overall control is usually assigned to the communication department, although physical maintenance may be handled by others, particularly in large, dispersed organizations.

J. C. Penney enlists the aid of porters, who are provided with diagrams of the placement of material so they can place or remove material according to an overall pattern. The Social Security Administration assigns messengers to do the job; receptionists, members of the mailroom staff or security guards are assigned to handle bulletin boards in other organizations.

To be effective news sources, bulletin boards should be changed regularly—daily or weekly—because viewers quickly tire of the old material. The key is to keep them a lively news source. Most organizations have a series of central, or "flagship," bulletin boards and supplement them with local or satellite bulletin boards elsewhere. The flagship boards become recognized as the central sources of information. The satellite boards contain the same basic information and also information of more local interest. J. C. Penney's employees are scattered over more than 50 floors in several New York office buildings and at many local stores or other facilities, so they have thousands of bulletin boards (150 in New York alone), which are changed daily. Memorial Sloan-Kettering Cancer Center in New York has about 5,000 employees scattered over half a dozen facilities; it maintains nearly a dozen information centers to keep everyone informed.

Costs

It is difficult to estimate the cost of bulletin boards because prices vary by region and by the size and format of the boards. J. C. Penney purchased fifty stainless-steel bulletin boards in 1973 at a cost of about $200 each, but estimated that with inflation they probably would cost twice as much today. Penney communicators say that for a communication tool that is so highly regarded by employees, both the total cost and the unit cost per employee is "peanuts" when compared to the cost and effectiveness of other types of media.

Measuring Effectiveness

As with any communication tool, it is wise to measure the effectiveness of information centers and bulletin boards. J. C. Penney includes its bulletin board program in its periodical communication audits. Other communicators simply observe the traffic around bulletin boards as a measure of their popularity, or post an offer of a giveaway or premium (sample company products or tickets to local entertainment) that viewers can request. Communicators who have initiated information centers and bulletin board programs agree that they are among the most popular, effective and economical forms of internal communication.

Exhibits and dislays take the bulletin board concept a step further and can reach both internal and external audiences.

Exhibits and Displays

Another form of internal communication in many organizations today is the exhibit or display, which frequently accompanies an information center. Such exhibits permit an organization to communicate more extensively on a particular subject. They can draw attention to a major subject or event, such as the introduction of a new product, the dedication of a new facility, or the commemoration of an event such as an anniversary.

Exhibits and displays depend heavily on graphic elements such as photographs, transparencies, posters, products or historical memorabilia. "They take the traditional bulletin board concept a step further to meet the more demanding, contemporary communication objectives," says an Eastman Kodak communicator. Kodak has been producing a series of dramatic displays, changed monthly, to broaden employees' knowledge of company operations.

The Kodak project was developed for its Colorado division because employees there are isolated from the mainstream of company operations and the diversity of company operations. The project uses a series of photo displays on a wide variety of company-related activities—including work done in Colorado on six permanent, 5-foot by 8-foot panels installed in various buildings at the Colorado facility. Each year, corporate communications at Rochester sends 9 photo displays, each consisting of 12 to 15 photo enlargements and captions and a descriptive copy block of about 100 words. The print sizes vary and most are in color. All display material is mounted on 1/4-inch stock with Velcro backing that holds firmly to the fabric-covered display panels.

Each new display is posted on the first of the six panels and previous displays are moved to the right so that each display has a life of six months, although the overall display constantly has a new element. Removed displays are returned to company headquarters for secondary uses. Topics featured in the displays have included quality assurance, new products, distribution, papermaking, film manufacture, energy conservation, Kodak and the printing industry, and Kodak regional operations.

The Coca-Cola Company designed exhibit cases that can be used to display notices or other objects. When news is light and there are few employee notices, the information services department prepares significant features such as a collage of advertising campaigns the company has used around the world. Reliance Insurance Company maintains four "bay window" display cases for rotating exhibits that feature company activities and special events. In recent years displays have included educational exhibits on the art of puppetry, deep-sea diving, unusual employee collections, art work on loan from local art schools, and wildfowl decoys. The "bay window" cases, which extend about six inches from the wall, allow for more elaborate displays than are possible on traditional bulletin boards. Displays may also be placed in other high-traffic areas, such as reception rooms, hospital waiting rooms and corridors.

Barnes Hospital has a "History Hall" display of photos, copy, portraits and other memorabilia tracing the history of the hospital. The Ball Corporation display in its entrance hall includes some of the early Ball glass jars used in food preservation and contemporary products. The Amax Corporation has arranged a group of products, ranging from a section of a metal pipeline to a car, in which various Amax products are used. The display is in a room used for receptions and meetings so visitors can become familiar with the company's products and history while participating in social or business functions.

Many organizations that produce elaborate exhibits and displays for trade shows, conventions or meetings get extra mileage by setting them up in-house. Hospitals can put displays in waiting rooms to help educate the public about specific hospital activities or problems.

Organizations that sponsor art and craft shows or photo contests may display entries during or after the event, singling out those that are up for special awards. Or, when an organization has had a special event such as a company anniversary, picnic or service award dinner, photographs taken at the meeting may be displayed in the company lobby or cafeteria.

Exhibits and displays add an extra dimension to more standard channels of communication. They also reach audiences outside the regular staff, thus serving as effective public relations tools.

Telephone Information Programs (Hotlines)

Fast–moving events in large organizations often demand a system for rapid internal communication such as a telephone information program—a "hotline." The essence of hotlines is speed, simplicity and honest reporting with a minimum of interpretation or editorializing. Without moving more than a few steps, an employee can often obtain information immediately about the company's position in a current labor situation, the price of the company's stock, or a variety of current facts about the organization.

Hotlines have the additional advantage of providing live information, that is, information delivered verbally by a human being rather than in print through an impersonal publication or other medium. Even in programs where the caller's voice is tape recorded for reply at a later date or where the hotline provides a taped message, there is a personal touch that makes communication more human.

There are several basic kinds of hotlines. The most popular seems to be the straight news format in which a caller may dial a number and hear a reporter announce the latest news, usually at a specific time. The news may be reported by a "live" announcer or it may be recorded and updated periodically so that the caller always gets the latest news. This is especially useful during crises, such as a strike, plant breakdown, storm or energy failure. In some organizations, personnel not located at the company facility, such as traveling salespersons, employees at home or on vacation or ill or off for the day, or employees' spouses may keep up with recent events. Many hotlines operate 24 hours a day.

Some organizations conduct one telephone information program at company headquarters and another at division locations, with different news for each. Pennsylvania General operates a program called "Newsline" for its main office and three division locations. General Electric conducts a program that can be dialed from several locations in different states. The programs are usually given identifying titles such as "Newsline," "Hotline," "Call-line," "Actionline," "Dial-a-News" or simply a telephone extension number, "3562."

While the basic content of most news programs consists of significant news about the sponsoring organization, a number include what might be called social news—announcements of social functions, banquets, club meetings, picnics, sporting events and announcements of blood drives and community activities.

A second kind of telephone information service is one permitting the employee to call or write in (on special forms) for an immediate reply to a question. The answer is provided by the person who answers, or the inquiry is recorded and the question answered at a later date. Some companies collect common calls and broadcast answers over a public address system the next day. These question-and-answer programs are known variously as "R.S.V.P.," "Call-line" and "Direct-line."

Questions are usually referred anonymously to a qualified person within the organization for reply. The answers are then forwarded by mail to the caller, whose name is known only to the program moderator. This anonymity encourages greater candor in the questions and assures that employees' comments, criticisms or complaints won't be held against them. Callers may ask silly, lewd or ridiculous questions, but these are usually minimal and disappear once the seriousness of the program is established.

Surveys indicate that employees like hotlines, whether they are of the straight news variety or the question-and-answer type. Communicators report that when question-and-answer hotlines are started, there is a deluge of questions, but after a while, when the novelty dies down and most questions are answered satisfactorily, the number of questions declines. One organization compiled the 100 most often asked questions in a booklet that they distributed to callers who ask the same questions and to all new employees. Employees quickly learn that the company is serious about communicating quickly and honestly, and they come to rely on the newslines as a quick, reliable and serious form of communication. Even supervisors, who sometimes look upon telephone information programs as usurping their responsibilities as communicators (or as threats to their authority), learn to accept and even use the programs as often reliable sources of information. Hotlines can improve other communication methods. For instance, supervisors know that if *they* don't inform employees, hotlines will.

Several organizations conduct specialized hotlines to handle subjects of specific interest to the audience. C and P Telephone Company, which conducts a regular "Newsline" program, also has an Equal Employment Opportunity Hotline to answer employee questions about the EEO and affirmative action programs, and another hotline to help employees resolve customer problems—to better serve customers. Hartford Insurance maintains a hotline to help employees and immediate family members with personal and family problems. A psychiatric social worker attempts to resolve the problem directly or refers the caller to a social agency that specializes in counseling of particular personnel or psychiatric problem. Sun Petroleum encouraged employees to call the company president directly; in one day he received a call every six minutes.

Cost

The cost of telephone information programs depends on the scope of the system. Theoretically, there is no extra cost because the program is usually incorporated into the existing telephone system and requires only a special number and some extensions. If one takes into consideration the time it takes for someone to broadcast news or handle inquiries, however, the cost can be substantial. The investment is worthwhile if it provides employees with quick and accurate information that might not be obtainable from other sources.

Measuring Effectiveness

Telephone answering services can be measured simply by electronically counting the number of calls received. A high volume would indicate that people are using the system and that they feel there is a need. General Electric, Philadelphia, receives over 110,000 a year. B. F. Goodrich averages 350 calls a day but has handled as many as 640 calls in a 24-hour period. National Grape Corporation/Welch Foods considers 30 to 40 calls a year good. A low volume might indicate the service has a limited value, people are being informed adequately by other means, or there is no great need for information at that time. If popularity dies down temporarily, it may be revived by in-house publicity in other media. General Telephone's program is constantly promoted. Wilson Foods Corporation in Oklahoma City periodically publicizes its program in the employee magazine and on in-house posters, and has distributed a wallet card containing the hotline number so that employees will have the number wherever they are.

Communicators who have established telephone information services stress that the success of such programs depends on management endorsement and support. Employees are quick to realize that management is not serious if the program does not meet its objectives or their needs. The communicator must get top management to enlist the support of all persons who will be involved, especially the key people who will provide answers to questions. Replies must be substantial, candid and honest; and callers must be assured that their calls will be kept confidential, except to the moderator.

Walter G. Anderson, ABC, is president of The Anderson Press and publisher of *editor's newsletter,* a monthly report on trends and techniques in organizational communication. He is accredited by the International Association of Business Communicators and in 1979 was named an IABC Fellow.

CHAPTER 12

Audiovisuals

STEWART L. BURGE, ABC

Electronic and computer technology have provided so many devices, processes and capabilities that modern audiovisual production is a gadgeteer's dream come true. Used effectively, audiovisual (A/V) hardware adds an exciting new dimension to organizational communication. Sensory involvement of audiences exposed to top-flight audiovisual productions can reach levels of understanding unheard of in years past. Yet, with all the potential for creativity offered by the buttons, switches and meters, this technology sometimes becomes an obstacle to the communication process. Too often, mastery of the hardware becomes an end in itself. The result can be that, amid the flurry of dissolves, wipes and animation, the basic message is overwhelmed or hopelessly lost.

Somewhere in that gray area between message and medium there is a point at which optimum audience impact is attained, whether the format is video, film, multiimage or slide/sound. To reach that point requires a carefully blended marriage of sound aesthetic judgment and refined technical skills.

There is no doubt that the audiences with which organizations must deal today are more sophisticated, better educated, more selective, and more critical than ever before. They also have grown up with television and are oriented to visually based messages, to simplification, to complete subjects (no matter how complex) being reduced to concise hour or half-hour packages. Some critics insist that this has caused a serious decline in the willingness of people to actively seek out information of interest or benefit. Be that as it may, this simplified packaging of information in a visually based format is highly familiar to audiences and, therefore, almost invariably acceptable to them.

It makes sense for communicators to recognize this characteristic in their audiences and turn the familiarity of the telecommunication approach to advantage. That means that when the lights in the meeting room dim and the first few bars of music fill the silence, the complete attention of every person in the room likely will be riveted to the screen—waiting for your message to unfold.

Preproduction Planning

The communicator's first responsibility is to make sure the message to be conveyed gets matched up with the best medium for the job. If new employees aren't getting accurate and timely information about their benefits, it may be that the benefits handbook needs to be revised or a slide/sound program should be developed. Or it may be that the vice president of employee fringes needs to do a better job of briefing new hires.

Whatever the answer, it's the job of the communicator to find out all there is to know about the situation. This is usually best done during a face-to-face discussion with whoever is initiating the project. If the boss wants a videotape, and you believe a multiimage presentation will be more effective, you owe it to the boss—and yourself—to state your position and support your advice with facts.

What's the Purpose?

In order to select the right medium and then assure that the message accomplishes its mission, it is essential to identify the basic purpose of the communication. The purpose should be stated concisely in terms of the desired result. Do you want to motivate? inform? educate? persuade? solve problems? Exactly how do you want members of the audience to feel or behave after seeing the presentation?

When you arrive at an appropriate statement of purpose, it's a good idea to put it in writing so that you can refer to it periodically during the rest of the production process to make sure the approach and treatment coincide with the basic reasons for producing the program. Plan and execute your presentation so that the purpose is constantly supported. No matter how much you know or how clever you are as an A/V producer, if your audience is confused about what you're driving at, your presentation has failed.

Who Will See It?

Take a close look at the audience you intend to reach. Who are they? How old are they? What's their educational level? What are their backgrounds? How much do they already know about the subject? What's their relationship to you? How are they employed? What are their prejudices? The more you know about the audience or audiences, the better your chances of having the program fulfill its purpose. Even if the subject matter is basically the same, two different audiences may well dictate two different versions of an A/V production.

Who Does What to Whom?

To avoid headaches and possible embarrassment, make sure everyone involved is aware of who is responsible for each aspect of the production. This is a critical consideration if you're working under contract with an independent producer.

Who sets deadlines? Who writes the script? shoots the visuals? edits the tape? selects music? pays the bills? An hour before show time, it does little good to have someone say, "Oh, I assumed *you* were going to handle that." False assumptions can ruin the best intentions.

Selecting the Medium

The three most common audiovisual media are videotape, film and sound/slide. Each can be used independently or in combination with the others. Each has its own strengths, weaknesses and devotees.

In the business setting, most communicators turn to an A/V format in response to a stated problem or set of circumstances. Thus, in approaching an A/V project, a fairly clear-cut set of requirements normally evolves. A useful technique for handling these requirements is to divide them into "musts" and "wants." If the sales manager says she *must* have motion in order to demonstrate the functioning of a product, it is obvious that a single-projector slide show will not suffice. If the CEO insists that his end-of-year message *must* be distributed to all locations in *exactly* the same way and on the same date, a live presenter with a script and slides will not work. A "want," on the other hand, is something that should be included, but is not essential. You may want to have a "lip-sync" narrator for your anniversary film, but you may find that a "voice-over" narration will work almost as well—and within budget.

The process of listing "musts" and "wants" is an excellent way to get agreement on what is most important in the production, and what can most easily be deleted without damaging the production's effectiveness. It has been suggested that when starting an A/V production, the communicator should forget about hardware choices, staffing requirements and budget and instead analyze the communication goals. In most cases, hardware, format and other decisions will evolve from it.

Videotape—In the late 1960s and early '70s many organizations jumped on the video bandwagon. Unfortunately, a significant portion of that equipment is gathering dust in closets because organizations bought hardware without looking at alternative media or paying enough attention to their needs or capabilities. There are notable exceptions, however; organizations that have successfully integrated videotape into their total communication programs have backed their hardware decisions with capable staffing and effective use of the medium.

Good video is not cheap, but many organizations have found that the costs of production and distribution are dollars well spent when measured by an "effectiveness of communication" yardstick. Some are able to justify the relatively high front-end cost of video hardware and production facilities in-house. Others find it wiser to lease or rent equipment and produce their own programming, or to call in independent A/V producers to handle projects as the need arises. There is no clear-cut answer as to which approach is correct. It depends on how video is to be used, how often, and for what purpose.

Videotape production generally can be classified according to desired usage into three broad types: *Professional* productions are those in which the quality of the tapes is comparable to that of motion pictures or commercial television. These are normally high-budget programs used to convey documentary-style information to large audiences. *Semiprofessional* productions aren't necessarily amateurish, but nevertheless are characterized by production quality that is somewhat lower than that of commercial TV offerings. Typically, they are produced to present specific information to a captive audience. Employee orientations, news programs aimed at employees, safety programs and executive messages to employees are among the subject areas normally handled with semiprofessional productions. *Extemporaneous* productions are generally used as training aids and make good use of videotape's most alluring aspect—instant playback and review. Public speaking, sales training and helping executives get ready to "meet the press" are a few of the valuable applications of extemporaneous programming.

When you are approaching the first two classes of video production, it is important to consider what will happen to the program when it is completed. How will it be distributed? Under what conditions will it be

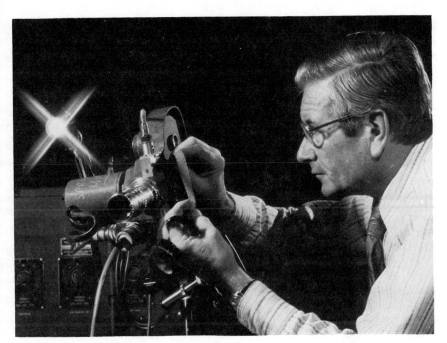

While most 16-mm films are used for "image" communication, videotape can answer multiple needs.

shown? Most video productions will be viewed on normal-size monitors, which means that your audience must be relatively small for each showing or you must arrange for multiple monitors.

Compared with print media and the more common A/V formats (slides and overhead transparencies), the current use of videotape in organizational communication is relatively limited. Future uses promise to be increasingly widespread, imaginative and effective.

Film—Although there are exceptions, 16-mm films tend to be used primarily for "image" communication. Most tend to be more artfully conceived than the other audiovisual formats. This is not to say that aesthetic interpretation is limited to film productions because increasingly video and multiimage productions are using the pleasing, nonliteral, interpretive approaches previously limited to professional film productions. But companies, associations, hospitals and other institutions are, as a rule, more comfortable with precedent than with innovation. The result is that when the need arises for an "image" A/V presentation, people often begin thinking in terms of film.

Few organizations have in-house motion picture capabilities. That

Sound/slide programs enjoy many degrees of sophistication each of which can be extremely effective if properly matched for both message and audience.

means most films are handled by independent producers, which, naturally, must be a consideration when budgeting and planning. Some organizations have turned to Super-8-mm film and equipment as a less expensive way to get into film production. Lessened image quality plus the time and costs involved in duplicating release prints, however, have kept Super-8 from being widely used.

Sound/slide—Sound/slide presentations, although generally simpler and less expensive than either video or film, can be extremely effective. The basic format for a sound/slide presentation consists of a live presenter whose prepared remarks are illustrated by 35-mm (2 x 2-inch) slides. Sometimes the presenter advances the projected slides without help. More frequently, an "assistant" follows a marked script and advances the slides. The next step in convenience and consistency of showing involves the use of a cassette tape recorder that plays a prerecorded sound track while the accompanying slides are advanced manually. This permits the addition of music and sound effects to a standardized narration.

Slide programs used to be limited to these two techniques. Then along came the concept and hardware for automatically synchronizing slide programs and a whole new A/V "family" was born. Developments in slide projectors, synchronizing recorders, programmers and dissolve controls have brought a totally new level of professionalism to slide presentations.

Thousands of organizations today use single-projector programmed slide presentations to good advantage for sales, orientation, training and marketing. These represent the low end of the A/V production budget but, when well conceived and well executed, they can be powerful communication tools. The early 1970s brought a second generation of hardware sophistication, which made possible fast cuts, variable dissolve rates and simpler multi-projector control. In the mid-1970s electronic programming equipment revolutionized the field and ushered in the "multi" phenomenon.

Multiimage usually refers to a programmed presentation that uses 35-mm slides to supply projected visuals on two or more screen surfaces simultaneously. The screen surfaces may be separate parts of the same screen or totally separate screens. A minimum of two projectors may be used, but common projector combinations are four, six, nine and fifteen. Multimedia is used now to describe a programmed show consisting of two or more A/V media such as slides, motion picture film, video, live speakers, actors, with slides normally providing the framework for the presentation.

Electronic programmers are the key to the "multi" area of A/V. They permit producers to manipulate images; to animate; to compress time; to alter space; to provide multiple viewpoints; and to integrate slides, motion pictures, video, light displays and other special effects into automatic, repeatable presentations. Sound/slide programs run the gamut from very simple to monstrously complex; from amazingly inexpensive to extremely costly.

Budgeting

Budgeting for any kind of A/V production can be a slippery proposition. There are so many variables involved that the simple question, How much will an audiovisual program cost? is not unlike asking, How much will a new house cost? The answer can be $20,000, $200,000 or $2,000,000, depending on how luxurious and how big you want it to be. Production costs for an A/V show depend on dozens of interrelated items: what medium you want to use; how long the show will be; how complex it is; the equipment, time and people needed to put it together; the location for showing the production; and how much of the production you can handle yourself.

Arriving at a workable budget requires a combination of two things: production expertise and accurate specifications for the program in question. Production expertise comes with experience. If you've done a dozen videotapes, you should be able to estimate how much the thirteenth will cost. If you are new to the field, you would be wise to call in a "technical adviser" to get you started. Accurate specifications for the program should be readily available if you've completed the "must/want" list described earlier. If the list isn't detailed enough for budgeting, now's the time to fill in the missing information and pin down specific requirements.

Outside Help

No matter how much experience you have as an A/V producer, eventually there will come a time when you don't have the answer to a problem and must call on the service of an outside resource person. Whether you need help from a photographer, film editor, artist, audio engineer, talent agency, or a full-service production house, the question is the same, "Where do I find a *good* one?"

Professional organizations or your telephone directory provide a starting point. Current periodicals often publish lists of "Who's who" in various areas of A/V production. The display and classified ads they carry are additional sources of current information. Perhaps the best method of locating good suppliers, though, is through their reputations and recommendations from other users of A/V services.

Regardless of how you locate your suppliers, ask them for samples and references. If they're truly good at what they do, they will be proud of what they let you see and hear.

What Equipment?

Whether your A/V message is planned for video, motion film, sound/slide or multiimage, it's essential to determine precisely what hardware will be used. It will probably be determined by the equipment you already have on hand or are willing to buy or rent.

A/V hardware is changing fast. For the most current information on hardware, contact local audiovisual suppliers. You can find them through professional contacts or in the telephone directory, and they'll be happy to talk about their wares. Not every dealer handles every brand of A/V hardware, so it's a good idea to talk with several so that you can base your buying decisions on "comparison shopping" facts.

When you talk with a hardware supplier, describe as completely as possible what your requirements are now and what you expect them to be in the foreseeable future. Will the equipment be in constant or occasional use? Do you need a complete system now or will you be adding on next year? Will you be producing programs or simply showing them? Does the equipment have to integrate into an existing A/V set-up? Will it be used in a permanent location or be taken on the road?

Get specific information from the supplier; find out about warranty periods and availability of service and parts, in addition to prices and features of the hardware you need. Once you've narrowed your options, ask the supplier for names of individuals or organizations who are currently using the hardware you're considering. Contact them for evaluations of the equipment *and* the supplier.

The Production Process

The person who develops a trouble free 1-2-3 system for producing audiovisual programs will be rich and famous. The fact is that for even the simplest productions, there are a variety of elements that must be dealt with simultaneously. In the case of sophisticated multiimage or multimedia presentations, the variables multiply in a geometric progression.

The secret to coordinating all the interrelated factors of an A/V program and having them come together in an effective presentation lies largely in thorough planning. And, while there is no single surefire method for planning, there are a number of accepted production practices that should be understood and used.

Outline

Start with an outline that tracks each of the main points of the story line and sketches each important supporting point. There's no need to get specific in the outline. Just note the broad ideas that support your program's basic purpose in the sequence they will be presented. A single typewritten page should be enough for the average outline.

Scriptwriting

This is the point at which many novice A/V producers begin to go astray, because A/V scripting is a special sort of writing requiring a special sort of thinking. Most communicators write in good, effective journalistic style. When they shift to A/V scriptwriting, they tend to turn out programs best described as "talking books." Their newswriting style is polished and their syntax flawless, but they overlook the fact they are writing for listeners and viewers, not readers.

If you write an article, you employ certain specific "signs" to guide the reader. Paragraphs, exclamation points and quotation marks are a few of the signals that let the reader know precisely what you are saying, and how you are saying it. In an A/V script, neither you nor your audience enjoys the luxury of seeing an italicized phrase or the end of a paragraph. Nor can you break into the script for the aural equivalent of a footnote. Finally, your audience has no time to return to a preceding sentence to clarify a point they may have missed. An A/V script is a linear medium—once the information it contains is gone, there's no going back.

The scriptwriter not only bears the burden of writing factually and interestingly, but also must develop a clear, concise and logical flow of both visual and audible information. The entire script must be developed in a smooth, easy-to-follow sequence. Sentences have to be straightforward and easy to understand.

There are a number of simple ways to check scripts for understandability. Read the script aloud; record it on tape, then play it back and listen critically; or read it aloud to someone who will tell you "it stinks" if it really does. Go back and simplify the passages that don't quite live up to your expectations. Recast the ideas in words that are as straightforward as possible.

The Shooting Script—Some experts recommend the development of a storyboard early in the production process, even before drafting a script. Others say that the story line normally is guided by the specific information to be conveyed so visualization must *follow* scripting. There are times when words dictate imagery, and times when visual images prescribe the words to be used. The goal is to weave the separate elements together in such a way that the total effect is greater than the sum of the individual parts.

The shooting script is used to guide production of a program and tie together the audio and visual elements. The most common format for a shooting script consists of blank rectangles (representing the screen format) down the left side of an 8½ x 11 page. Indicate in each rectangle, using words or sketches, each different visual called for. Production notes such as "long shot" or "extreme close-up" should be indicated where necessary. Each shot should be numbered sequentially.

The right side of the page is used for the audio: narration, sound effects, music, and so on. Narrative copy should be typed in upper and lower case and double spaced. Production notes regarding music and sound effect cues should be included at appropriate spots within the narrative.

Revisions—Script revisions are unavoidable, irritating and time-consuming. But they can improve the program's flow and pacing. Don't be insulted or intimidated by script revisions. If you feel strongly about the wisdom of a change, defend your original position and ask the "critic" to prove his or her point.

The Visuals You Need

The sense of sight is powerful. It gives most of us our personal view of reality. It's little wonder, then, that visuals are the "guts" of an A/V presentation. They are what people react to, what they evaluate, and what they remember. Make every effort to ensure that the technical and creative quality of the visuals in a presentation are the best available.

If you will be shooting your own visuals and are not experienced in the field, get some good books on the subject, study them, and gain some experience before jumping into a project with a deadline hanging over your head. If you are using an outside photographer, cinematographer or videographer, make sure that the person is well qualified. Check samples of previous work and references.

Subject matter is limitless. Sorting through the possibilities and selecting the "right" visuals is the challenge. The task of determining *what* visuals to use and *how* to use them should be approached with this simple question in mind: "What do I want my audience to understand or feel?" Aside from obvious technical skills, effective visual interpretation requires sound aesthetic judgment, a thorough understanding of the program and its audience, and experience.

Generally, visuals may be classified according to where they originate and whether they are "live" or illustrated. Visuals obtained on location suggest the photojournalistic style and emphasize the candid, natural presentation of people, things and events. Location shooting conveys a "real life" feeling to the production, even though the sequences are usually well planned and rehearsed. They work best, of course, when they don't appear to have been "staged." Visuals shot in a studio make no attempt to capture the loose, natural feel of location photography. Studio sequences may involve people (a monologue or interview situation) or things (new products, demonstration of how a machine works).

The other broad classification of visuals involves reality versus graphic representation of reality. For example, you may want to show live footage of a heart bypass operation, then switch to an artist's cutaway drawing to show the portions of the heart involved in the procedure. Or you could do an entire production with cartoon figures or summarize sales and earnings data with charts and graphs.

Titles and graphics deserve special mention because they appear in almost every A/V production and are frequently misused. The key to successful titles and graphics is simplicity. Crowding, excessive ornamentation, poor spacing and complex design can kill their effectiveness. Used intelligently, titles and graphics can fortify the message, clarify visual data or simplify complex ideas.

Individual graphics should contain no more information than can be easily absorbed in 5 to 10 seconds. All lines, letters and numbers should contrast well with the background and have distinct separation of the various tones. Colors should be bright and complementary. Letters and symbols should be simple, with a minimum number of small openings and curlicues. Proven typefaces for A/V work include Helvetica, Univers, Optima and other readable sans-serif faces.

Structure and Program Content

In order to take advantage of the powerful communicative potential of visual images, the A/V producer must depend on a strong point of view to provide a backbone for the production. In the selection of visuals, a unified point of view helps clarify, define and delineate the purpose of the program. So, knowing what you are looking for permits you to adapt the subject matter to your needs at the very time of its recording on film or tape, thereby sharpening and controlling both the materials and their treatment.

Dramatization is probably the simplest and most obvious means of approaching A/V material. Close attention must be paid to proportion and balance, however, to avoid having the dramatic impact overpower the content or having it force viewers to draw conclusions different from those intended.

Dramatization can be handled in many different ways. You might, for example, want to base a videotape program on a simple interview that, though unexciting, contains important information. To avoid a monotonous "talking head" presentation, the program might open with the interviewee in a dramatic situation related to the program's theme. Such an opening offers significantly higher audience appeal and helps lay the groundwork for the interview. Once the interview begins, "cutaway" shots can be used to dramatize the points being raised. At the end, the interviewee can again be shown in a dramatic location shot indicating what action should be taken based on the material developed during the interview.

No matter what visual devices are used, they must be used to construct a clear, logical path for the viewer to follow. The structure of this path may center on emotional progression, problem solving, geographical arrangement, progression through space, chronology, physical groupings, or combinations of these.

In addition to structuring the visuals to provide a smooth progression, the A/V producer is faced with building and reaching a thematic climax without resorting to devices that alter the truth or distort facts. As the project moves from shooting script to actual production, specific story units, or sequences, should be created. These are the A/V building blocks with which scenes are built. The scenes, in turn, are the production high points (i.e., its major premises). As such they must be bridged with transitional material to lead the viewer smoothly and easily from beginning to end. Transitions can be highly effective or deadly dull. They should be treated as important parts of a production.

The degree of communication expressed through an A/V program depends heavily on the selection and arrangement of its visual elements. Each shot must be included for its informational and emotional connotations and relationships. By paying careful attention to this rule, remarkable communication results can be achieved.

Do You Hear What I Hear?

Too often, it seems, the audio side of the A/V equation is ignored during planning production. It is tacked on almost as an afterthought. That's a shame, because a good sound track can be a potent force in influencing an audience and driving home your message. Sound—voice, music, sound effects, silence—is an integral part of an audiovisual program. It plays a vital role in providing information about the mood, the characters, the places and the theme of the production.

Voice—Selecting the appropriate voice, then using it to best advantage, is mostly a matter of good judgment on the part of the producer. In choosing an off-camera narrator, it's wise to listen to a variety of "demo" tapes, available from the potential narrators themselves, or from talent agencies or recording studios. Listen for the style, tone and range of the narrator's voice. For on-camera personalities, of course, make sure the person's appearance and presence are appropriate, as well. Suitable voices frequently can be found at local radio stations, commercial recording studios, or at college drama and broadcasting departments.

When the time comes to record the voice portion of the audio track, everyone involved—narrator, producer, audio engineer—should have a full, detailed script from which to work. The studio engineer will assume responsibility for the technical quality of the recording, leaving you free to concentrate on directing the narrator.

During the recording session, listen critically to the delivery, pacing, pauses, conversational tone and other aspects not actually written into the script. Because the issue here is one of subjective interpretation, this is no time to be shy. These are your words and your ideas being recorded. No one knows them better than you. Don't hesitate to offer guidance and constructive criticism.

Music, Sound Effects and Silence—Music and sound effects are to an audio track what lighting and composition are to a photograph. They are important for conveying the desired mood and "tone." Because each A/V production is unique, your use of music and sound effects will vary according to what you intend to convey. For some productions, a simple musical opening and closing will work. For others, musical bridges may be invaluable as transitions between sequences, or a musical "bed" running through the presentation may be advisable.

Music used in an A/V production should not compete with other elements for the audience's attention. It should augment, reinforce and complement. It can help establish, change or intensify the mood of a production. The question of where to obtain music for A/V productions inevitably arises in "how-to" discussions. The answer usually falls into two categories: from original sources or from prerecorded sources.

If your budget allows, an original musical score composed, performed and recorded specifically for your presentation is ideal. It is surprising how many producers never explore this option, thinking that recording original music in a studio is prohibitively expensive. Frequently, one or two instruments played by competent musicians and enhanced by a good audio engineer can result in a sound track ideally suited for an A/V presentation.

By using original music you are assured of a sound track tailored to your needs and free of copyright problems. Some producers continue to skate on thin legal ice by "borrowing" music from commercial records and tapes without permission. The copyright law requires producers to obtain written authorization to use copyrighted materials *prior* to use. The rules apply to in-house, not-for-profit, nontheatrical subjects as well as to "on-air" use for large audiences.

As an alternative to custom-made musical scores, prerecorded library music offers good quality at reasonable prices. Commercial music libraries deal in "generic" music produced, recorded and sold to anyone with cash in hand, so you may hear the music you select for your program used in someone else's program. Still, music libraries offer a huge selection of music and sound effects records. Library music rates vary from about $40 to $100 per needle drop, depending upon how the sound will be used.

Two other facts argue in favor of using prerecorded library music: the music is intended to be used in A/V-type situations and is written and recorded to fill that function; and it is recorded with a suitably reduced dynamic range to accommodate the audio limitations of standard audiovisual playback equipment.

Sound effects can be obtained simply by recording "wild" sound on your shooting locations with a good-quality tape recorder. Except for lip-sync sequences for a motion picture, this procedure normally yields acceptable quality and can add valuable "presence" to your program at practically no cost. An alternative is to use commercially recorded sound effects available from music libraries.

The fourth potential element of A/V sound is actually a lack thereof. Silence in a sound track may be thought of as the equivalent of white space in a publication. While technically it is "nothing," experienced producers often make good use of silence to punctuate, emphasize or define the accompanying "real" elements.

Once it is understood that sound is not a tacked-on "extra," most A/V producers begin using it with great care. Although a good sound track cannot salvage an otherwise second-rate production, it has the potential of making a good A/V program significantly better by reinforcing the mood and adding richness and color to the message.

Putting the Track Together—Once all the necessary elements are selected and recorded, it's time to put them together in a single, cohesive mix. Mixing is usually handled by a trained audio technician in a studio where multitrack recording equipment is available. By using individual recording channels for each audio component, a skilled engineer can weave the elements together into a smooth, balanced sound track. Nonetheless, it is the producer's responsibility to oversee the final mix-down and bring the benefit of his or her knowledge of the production to bear on the finished product.

The Challenge

The challenge to the A/V producer, whether novice or experienced, is to "get inside" the technical and artistic characteristics of all the elements involved in a production, then to select and use those that best carry the message and support the program's basic purpose. Audiovisual communication stands as the new frontier for organizational communication. Whether it serves as a dynamic motivational tool or a stumbling block to the communication process depends on the diligence of the individuals responsible for its use.

Stewart L. Burge, ABC, is Manager–Communication Programs for GTE Automatic Electric Inc., in Northlake, Illinois. He is accredited by the International Association of Business Communicators and has served on IABC's Executive Board.

EXAMPLE: *THE AEROSPACE NETWORK*

Prior to 1971, employee communication at Boeing Aerospace Company in Seattle, WA followed traditional lines—a companywide newspaper, the *Boeing News,* supplemented by specialized publications, surveys, and occasional audiovisual programs. In mid-1971, as a result of economic pressure, Boeing's defense and space arm experimented with an electronic solution—an in-plant public address system news program—to a widespread morale problem. The newscast experiment, nine years and three communication awards later, operates as an integral part of the internal communication effort.

Born of Hard Times

The Aerospace newscast came to life during the "Boeing Bust"—the period in the late 1960s and early '70s marked by massive layoffs at the major Seattle employer triggered by the cancellation of the U.S. supersonic transport program and the winding down of the manned space program. Over a few months, Boeing's work force plummeted from more than 110,000 to about 30,000. Morale was best summed up by the now famous local freeway billboard, "Will the last person in Seattle please turn out the lights?"

After hitting bottom in mid-1971, the remaining employees turned business around by winning small contracts in nontraditional Boeing areas such as hydrofoil boatbuilding, energy and agribusiness. Within months the business base improved. But with a devastated communicators' force and a one-person newspaper staff working on a biweekly schedule, how could the improving news be spread quickly among the work force? Aerospace employee communication manager Jim Douglas proposed an experiment—a two- to three-minute news program, broadcast during business hours, using the plant's paging system.

The Price Was Right

The idea was approved by management. It had considerable appeal, not the least of which was cost. The paging system, already installed for security and safety reasons, reached nearly all of the company's Seattle locations. Because it was not an actual broadcast station, the "studio" required was nothing more than an audiovisual tape recorder connected to a paging outlet by a telephone device that cost 50 cents a month. One staff member could prepare and broadcast the program in less than two hours. It was just the sort of communication boost needed by a technology company down on its luck.

Getting the Word Out

Once the system was established, there was little problem finding news. Information was supplied by company personnel and industrial relations groups. Among the biggest contributors were division managers, who rivaled among themselves for morale-boosting exposure for their organizations. They all wanted the immediate recognition the daily audio newscast could provide.

The Electronic Advantage

In a working environment still smarting from the threats of constant layoff, rumors flourished, resulting in considerable lost time. The company switchboard was often jammed with employees calling outside to find out what was going on. The problem was compounded by a constant communication worry of the defense contractor—releasing news concerning its government customers. Government contractors frequently have no control over the timing of news releases. There were frequent fast news breaks and employees complained they often had to wait for days to find out what happened that day at work. The short response time of the newscast worked to eliminate those complaints. Unlike a telephone dial-in system, the network's "live" nature could carry a message to thousands of employees within minutes, freeing telephones for company business.

New Directions

Since its early days as a two- to three-times-a-week program, the network has grown into a daily channel for a variety of employee-related information, some of it aimed at specific audiences. On occasion, the system is used to relay emergency traffic or weather information to homeward-bound employees and to broadcast short public service announcements about energy conservation. In 1979 the network supported a campaign to eliminate unnecessary company paperwork.

In recent years, a special effort has been made to include more of the employee audience in the communication process. Coverage of employee activity has been increased and telephone recording equipment has been added to allow the use of the actual "voices" of the employee newsmakers whenever possible. Listeners now hear more from people like themselves, not just from the company spokesman or management.

They Do Listen

The Aerospace newscast has shown up in surveys as a major source for employees' company news. On a daily basis, the newscast's impact is measured by response to news items. A historic example was a story concerning the company's efforts on the Trans-Alaskan pipeline. Within hours of a broadcast about a need for 100 engineers with specific skills to move to the Far North, more than 500 qualified applicants responded.

—by John Kvasnosky
Supervisor, Employee Communication
Boeing Aerospace Company

CHAPTER 13
Face-to-Face Communication

JERRY TARVER, Ph.D.

Most of us do so much talking and listening that we tend to take face-to-face communication for granted. We don't get around to studying our speaking behaviors. Let's begin by recognizing that we engage in three primary kinds of face-to-face communication, as illustrated in these three hypothetical situations.

Interpersonal Communication—Monday. Today I want you to join me for lunch simply because I enjoy your company or because for some reason, it is important for us to get along well. The only real objective for lunching together is to maintain, or improve, our relationship.

Our interaction will be pretty much one-on-one. You and I, I and you. We'll sit by ourselves but if others drift to our table we can interact with them without losing our contact with each other. (Look at the big table in the corner. Eleven people, but most of the talk is in groups of two or three).

We may talk business, but we don't have to stay on one subject very long. A lot of sentences don't get finished; a lot of ideas get dropped. We'll probably behave just as we would if we were talking in the hall or having a chat in the office. We may say some things that are quite personal. I may admit a secret worry or brag about something of which I'm proud. You might let out some hostility or confide your feelings about a friend.

If everything goes well, each of us will let the other know (with or without words) that "it was a nice lunch."

Group Communication—Tuesday. Is it OK with you if we schedule that committee meeting during lunch today? We've got six people, and the noon hour seems to be the only time we can get together.

The tone of our talk at the table is a little more formal than it was yesterday. People who seem to be heading our way realize we're having a meeting and they find another place to sit. You and I can still exchange comments, but today we are aware of the impact of what we say on all the others in the group. When we speak now, we are in a "one with a few" situation.

We are more organized today. We have a leader and a recorder has been appointed to take notes. Handouts have been prepared, and an agenda lists the topics we hope to cover. We have lost some of our freedom to make personal comments. Expressions of my private fears or our deepest feelings might attract a stern glance from our leader if they don't bear on the subject at hand.

I understood the committee was appointed to solve a problem our organization is facing, but another person thinks we should simply gather relevant data and report it back to the organization. It's up to our leader to see the group comes to a common understanding of our tasks. Then we will measure our results by the amount and quality of the data we collect or by the viability of our proposed solution. (At lunch yesterday, I don't recall either of us using the terms "viability" or "data collection.") Obviously, we are more purposeful today than we were yesterday.

Public Communication—Wednesday. I am pleased to be in the audience today for the speech you are delivering to the club after lunch. The occasion becomes much more formal than it was on Monday or Tuesday. There is some kidding around but, obviously, the procedures being followed are quite rigid. You rate an introduction to the group, even though many of us already know you. You sit in a designated place before the talk, and you are expected to stand at the microphone when you speak. There is a smattering of conversation in the audience and it quickly dies away. You have the attention of everyone in the room.

I find the ideas in your talk well organized. The points you make emerge more sharply than when you were speaking in the committee yesterday. Then, you were willing to go along with the committee's decisions; today, I see you as an advocate of the point of view expressed in your speech. You seem to want to influence my thinking.

In broad outline, the chart that follows indicates the distinctions among the three kinds of communication examined:

	INTERPERSONAL COMMUNICATION	GROUP COMMUNICATION	PUBLIC COMMUNICATION
INTERACTION	one-to-one	one-to-few	one-to-many
PURPOSE	enhance relationships	learn or solve problems	influence an audience
SETTING	casual	informal	formal

Next we need to discuss how we can best function in each situation.

Public Speaking

You should speak only on subjects you know and care about. If you don't have the interest or the time to prepare, don't agree to speak. If you are writing a talk for someone else, be sure you are allowed enough time to do the job and can write for the other person. Keep the topic simple and limited because most speeches these days do not last more than 15 or 20 minutes.

Preparation of the Speech

Don't prepare speeches merely to take up an audience's time; plan to do something for them. Perhaps you want to *inform;* perhaps, to *stimulate* or stir up feelings. Some occasions call for you to change beliefs—to give a speech to *convince;* others, to cause *action.*

To know what effect you want to have, study your audience with care. Collect facts about age, sex, education, ethnic background. Find out how many people will be in your audience. One writer prepared an address about energy at the height of an energy crisis and was later told that the college audience he was writing for would have in it a large number of students from Iran. Obviously, knowing that fact would have been a great help to him.

Learn about the speaking situation. Consider the time of day, the exact length of the speech, whether to allot time for questions and answers. Ask about other speakers on the program, the physical arrangements for the meeting, the type of microphone. During the Vietnam war I prepared a talk on "Humor in Communication" without finding out I was to follow a speech by the wife of well-known prisoner of war. Don't let that sort of thing happen to you.

A speech should do something for an audience other than just take up their time.

Do the best you can to learn the attitudes of your audience. Will they be friendly, hostile, open-minded, uninterested? If they are negative, avoid the speech to get action and settle for a talk to inform. If the audience is favorably inclined, you may have a good opportunity to call for action.

Knowing about your audience can help you select the right material and language for your talk. Good speeches fit the specific audience and usually cannot be used for another occasion without rewriting. Knowing your audience can also cushion you against surprises and give you a psychological advantage.

Good speech writing should almost always follow a logical pattern. The listener cannot stop and "replay" a speech if an idea fails to stand out clearly, so careful organization, as outlined below, is important.

The *opening* precedes the solid content of the speech and probably should not last for more than a minute or two. If you start with an acknowledgment of the speech of introduction, it should be brief and simple. It can be planned ahead. A plain statement, "Thanks for your words of welcome, Alice," helps the audience begin to tune you in. Next, say something pleasant to gain goodwill. Include material in your opening that will attract and hold attention.

Here are some techniques for openings. They are frequently used, but they won't be trite or boring if the speaker uses a little imagination. Select as many from the list as you think the occasion requires.

Honest compliment. When you can sincerely say something nice about your audience, do it. Comment directly on audience accomplishments or characteristics or choose indirect references to your host city or even something as routine as a local athletic team.

Common ground. Mention an interest you and your audience share. We often begin conversation with strangers by asking, "Do you know so and so?" A mutual bond always helps start the flow of communication.

A story. Telling a story arouses curiosity and gets people involved in your speech. A president of a major corporation once began an important speech by describing a conversation he had at a cocktail party. He got the audience's attention and moved smoothly into his subject.

Humor. Be cautious in opening with humor because it's hard to know what makes people laugh. There is no agony quite like standing alone in the awful silence following a joke that failed. Be especially careful not to offend anyone. Often, the safe approach is to poke fun at yourself or some group to which you obviously belong. Consider using a "one-liner" rather than an elaborate anecdote. Good jokes travel fast, and speakers cannot ask, "Have you heard the one about . . .?" If you use humor, you don't need to have people rolling in the aisles. A few smiles and chuckles should be enough.

References to your subject. Start by mentioning the topic of your talk only if your audience has a strong positive attitude toward your subject. "I'm here tonight to tell you how to save five hundred dollars" is better than "I am sure all of you are interested in knowing why we are adding ten percent to your next bill."

After you have the attention of your audience and your listeners are in a friendly mood, tell them the theme of your speech. Describe very briefly what you intend to cover. Sometimes you might elaborate by adding a concise preview of the major ideas, or "points," in your talk.

The main points should stand out clearly. As a rule, don't develop more than two to five major points. They should be of approximately equal weight and should evolve in a logical sequence.

You can present your points or ideas in chronological order, as we see in this example:

1. Gather your material. (*discuss*)
2. Build the product. (*discuss*)
3. Market your creation. (*discuss*)

You can organize ideas in a spatial relationship:

1. Let's consider the inner city. (*discuss*)
2. Let's examine the suburbs. (*discuss*)

You can divide a topic into its "natural" or "logical" parts, with each part becoming a main point. For a speech on the topic "Who benefits from profit?" you might identify the groups who benefit and make each group the subject of a point:

1. Stockholders. (*discuss*)
2. Customers. (*discuss*)
3. Employees. (*discuss*)

Sometimes you can use a "problem–solution" pattern of organization. For the annual safety talk, begin with a point that emphasizes a problem and follow with a point that offers solutions.

The conclusion to your speech should be short and positive: a restatement of your main idea, a summary of your points, a quotation that captures the theme of your talk, a brief illustration that will leave your audience with a vivid final impression. Avoid ending a speech with "thank you." If you want to express your appreciation to your audience, do so with a sentence or two that has some substance to it.

Delivery of the Speech

Body language is important when you stand before an audience. Consider eye contact, posture, gestures and voice. Look at the people before you as you speak. See their responses. If they appear restless, speak louder and use more action. If they look puzzled, restate your idea or give a few more examples. Look directly at several people in the audience; don't focus all your attention on one or two.

Stand with your weight on both feet. Don't take the one-legged position of a stork, and don't lean on the speaker's stand. Don't twist or sway.

You can solve the problem of what to do with your hands in three ways: let them hang comfortably at your sides, let them rest lightly on the stand, or put them in your pockets if you have pockets of comfortable size and can use them without distorting your posture. Use your hands to gesture when you feel it naturally appropriate to emphasize, to describe, or to hold interest. Don't plan your gestures in advance. Unless you are an actor, "canned" gestures almost always destroy timing and make your gestures appear awkward.

Speak in your natural voice. Don't strain or try to reach a lower key than you normally use. Remember, most people don't like their own voices, but audiences soon grow accustomed to a speaker's particular sound. You will be tempted to talk too fast, so make an effort to slow down to a listenable pace. Don't be afraid to pause occasionally to look at notes or let an idea sink in.

Try to speak from an outline rather than a manuscript. Except for extremely short speeches, never memorize a talk. Your outline should be on note cards. The function of the outline is to remind you of your next idea. Glance at your outline and then express the idea in a conversational style. Key words and incomplete sentences are all you usually need.

The content of a speech should be specific and personal. Find concrete examples, illustrations, statistics, quotations and comparisons to explain the ideas set forth in your main points. Draw the material from your own experience whenever possible. Instead of, "The latest figures show," say, "The figures I read in the last week show. . . ."

A public speech is "an enlarged conversation," so use short words, contractions, colloquialisms. It usually takes more words to express an idea in speech than it does in writing. For example, you might replace "management audits attest to our efficiency" with "I've read a study on the way we run our company that shows we are doing a first-rate job." Note that the second statement would not be suitable for a written report; it is designed for the ear rather than the eye, and it sounds better than it looks.

Writing a Speech for Others

Most of the public speaking skills previously discussed can be applied to writing a speech for someone else. You need to be concerned with delivery only if you are involved as your speaker's coach after the manuscript has been accepted, but the principles of audience analysis, goal setting, content and language are the same no matter who gives the speech.

One of the unique problems speech writers face is the challenge of making the speech fit the speaker. Your starting point should be to make sure you have adequate access to the speaker during the time you are writing and to determine what the speaker wants to accomplish in the speech before you start to write. Beware of the intermediary who will try to speak for the speaker. Direct contact between speaker and writer offers the best means of finding out what the speaker actually wants to say.

Give yourself time to write. We all appreciate the boost we get from an approaching deadline, but remember speech writing involves a lot of research and thinking before you sit down to hammer out the final product. Because of the variables involved, it is hard to say exactly how long it takes "to write a speech." After the research has been done, many writers find an hour of writing time for each minute of the speech is not a bad rule of thumb. You probably have other duties to perform, so don't forget to spread out the writing time. Some writers have agreements that all speech-writing assignments are made six weeks in advance.

Capturing another person's style is often difficult. Read your speaker's earlier speeches. Listen to him or her talk. When it is feasible, have the speaker read an early draft aloud to catch phrases that sound out of character. By all means, try to hear the speaker give each speech you write. The experience may be painful, but you will benefit in the long run.

You might want to use a large typeface for the manuscript your speaker will take to the podium. Leave a wide left-hand margin for the speaker to make notes. Use only the top two-thirds of the page so the audience won't be treated to a view of the top of your speaker's head as his or her eyes travel all the way to the bottom of the page. End each page with a complete sentence so the speaker's thought won't be interrupted as each sheet of paper is turned.

Group Communication

Committees and other groups would waste less time in meetings if they determined the purpose of their meetings and established reasonable procedures to follow. Why do groups meet? Two answers might be to solve a problem and to gather and exchange information. Here is a procedure to follow for problem solving:

> *State the question.* Be sure everyone knows exactly what problem is to be solved. Don't assume that everyone knows the issue confronting the group, and don't assume everyone understands the terms used to state the problem. Get necessary background information before the group. What is the history of the problem? What limitations of budget or time will affect proposed solutions? By what standards will a solution be judged to determine if it is successful?
>
> *List all possible solutions.* The emphasis in this step is on listing, so don't stop to discuss any proposal. Try to get as many ideas before the group as possible, and don't worry about overlapping or con-

tradictory ideas. Have someone serve as recorder to write down each idea.

Discuss the advantages and disadvantages of each proposed solution. Take up each suggestion in order and get from the group all the good and bad points of each idea. Try to avoid argument; the group should be working toward a joint solution, and there should be no "winners" or "losers" when the final decision is reached. During this stage, do what you can to spread the talk around so that no one person does all the talking.

Choose the best solution. A group should aim for consensus rather than compromise in making a final decision. The solution to the group's problem should be agreed upon by all. A number of solutions may be combined in a final answer, but everyone should fully agree. Try not to take votes because once a person is committed to a particular answer by voting for it, he or she may find it hard to see the value of other possibilities.

The above process should be followed as closely as possible, although you will often find that groups have a habit of wandering off the subject and getting ahead of the agenda. Do your part; prod gently to keep participants on the track. You can use this process with a group as small as three or four or as large as six to eight. Larger groups are difficult to work with and should be broken into smaller units.

A manager often finds it better to assign a group to solve a problem than to solve it alone because groups have a stronger commitment to ideas if they are involved in producing them. So, if there is a controversy about next year's vacation schedule, resist the temptation to issue an edict. Ask the concerned parties to sit down with you and solve the problem as a group.

In some situations, a group rather than a single speaker offers the best means for transferring information to an audience. To plan a "panel discussion," take the total time allotted for the presentation and divide it into two parts. During the first part, have the panelists discuss the information. Each person can give a brief formal presentation, or the panelists can engage in a conversation for the audience. During the second time period, allow the audience to ask questions or make comments.

A panel discussion is a dynamic communication activity that allows, even promotes, listener involvement. Make sure the audience is aware of the procedures being used.

Only in most unusual circumstances will a panel solve a problem. The usual aim is to generate information and get people thinking. You might use a panel instead of a speech for the annual safety message or to present a new program or procedure.

Interpersonal Communication

Do you say, "You don't understand what I am saying?" A far better choice in most cases is, "I'm sorry, I didn't make myself clear." An appreciation of how "understanding" comes about should show that the responsibility for getting a message across rests more with the communicator than with the receiver.

Since there is no way to transfer a message directly from the mind of one person to the mind of another, we must rely on "symbols" to carry our meaning, and the person who sends the symbol should know that the receiver may not interpret it in the same way the sender does. Consider the following dialogue:

"Do I turn left here?"

"Right!"

Obviously, "Right" can mean either "Yes, turn left" or "No, don't turn left." The sender knew exactly what was meant, but to the poor receiver "right" is merely a symbol that must be interpreted. All too often the interpretation is followed by a heated argument.

In interpersonal communication, it is especially important to remember the role of symbols in transmitting ideas and feelings. Be careful in your choice of symbols and tolerant if a listener fails to attach your intended meaning to your words. If you choose the wrong words, your intentions won't count for much. To illustrate, look at the problem of sexism in language. A friend told me of a salesperson who invited a husband and wife to ride with him to look at some property. As the three of them got to the car, he said, "And the little lady can sit in the back." The salesperson *intended* to be courteous and friendly. But the words were interpreted as, "I regard you as an inferior person in this important transaction." The salesperson didn't have a chance of making a sale after that.

When someone fails to convey a message, it is easy to become defensive. For instance, a supervisor says, "You didn't get it right," rather than, "I didn't explain it clearly," and the listener's defense mechanism is tripped. To reduce defensiveness, find the symbols that will make sense to the other person.

One important distinction between two classes of word symbols can be useful in interpersonal communication. Some symbols are "descriptive" and others are "evaluative." As a rule, descriptive statements will cause less resentment. For example, "Tom, there are six changes I need in this report," uses descriptive symbols or words. One way to handle the problem of evaluative statements is to cast your opinions in terms of your own perception. Say, "I don't enjoy slide talks," instead of, "Slide talks are terrible."

Of course, people use symbols other than words to send messages. Body movement, tone of voice, and a variety of other nonverbal symbols may often be more important than language in sending messages. Consider the case where you ask a friend, "Will you help me work on this project?" Even if the answer is yes, you may drop the request if you pick up unspoken clues suggesting the *real* answer is, "I don't want to do it." There might be a slight pause before the answer, or perhaps the voice sounds weary, or your friend may avoid eye contact in giving the reply, or facial expression may show distaste for your suggestion. The tongue said yes, but the rest of the body said no.

For good interpersonal relationships, be sensitive to these nonverbal messages: If you say to a friend, "You look upset, what's the matter?" and your friend answers, "Nothing," the reply may satisfy you or may suggest that your friend has a serious problem. The true answer is in the sound of the voice rather than the choice of words. Most persons have little trouble recognizing the importance of vocal tone in instances where the vocal emphasis is strong. We need to be alert to cases where the voice transmits a more subtle message. The first warning of a problem may well be a slight chill in the way someone says "Good morning."

Watch your own use of vocal tone in sending messages. Be alert to detect that hollow sound in your voice that tells you and your listener that you aren't really interested in the conversation. Don't let the annoyance or boredom of the moment slip into your voice when you answer the telephone. The party on the other end may get messages you did not intend to transmit.

You only have to observe people in your next elevator ride to remember that people tend to be cool to the message sent by strangers touching in public. A firm handshake is almost always in order, although some people occasionally pump the other person's hand too forcefully and too long. Backslapping is limited to fairly close friends (or teammates), and the person who pounds away at casual acquaintances is likely to offend. There may be differences between the rules for public touching for women and for men, but the best advice is to try to sense what your particular interpersonal partner finds acceptable.

All of us have rather strong feelings about the proper distance to be maintained when we communicate in various circumstances. If you keep a subordinate too far away from you in an office conference, you may hurt the person's feelings; if you get too close, you may frighten the person. Be aware of the other person's zone of private space and don't invade it, but if someone gets too close to you for comfort, or stands too far away, try not to let the behavior interfere with your reception of messages. As a skilled communicator, you should understand what is happening and be able to handle the situation.

Gesture, posture and eye contact are other important areas of body language. One gesture, "steepling" (the fingertips of one hand are pressed against the fingertips of the other) may signal "I've got you where I want you." It may make the other person uncomfortable or wary.

Posture can often give clues regarding the positive or negative thoughts in a person's mind. An angry, frustrated child may sit slumped back deep on the sofa with stiffly crossed arms. That same child, watching an appealing TV commercial, may sit on the edge of the sofa with hands on the knees as though ready to run out and buy the product. These same gestures are seen in business encounters.

Too little eye contact can suggest a person is untrustworthy; too much may make a person squirm. When talking to only one person, shift your gaze occasionally from the person's eyes to objects in the area of your conversation. Don't avoid eye contact by looking off into the distance, except for purposes of reflection, and avoid the shifty look that results from moving your eyes from side to side.

Hair, clothing and jewelry all send messages. Obviously, the circumstances in which you communicate have a great impact on the way symbols of dress and appearance are interpreted. A college professor used his pipe as a dramatic tool in lecturing. He thought the pipe made him impressive. When students evaluated the class, one of the most forceful suggestions was "Get rid of the pipe." When it comes to the way you look, impressiveness should probably take second place to appropriateness.

In analyzing nonverbal signals, look at the total pattern of behavior rather than just one symbol, and consider the range of meanings a symbol may have. For example, drumming the fingers on a desk might mean impatience, but if the person doing it is smiling and talking with animated expressions, maybe the nervous energy signals excitement over your idea.

Successful communication can occur only when someone assigns the intended meaning to the signals you have sent. It is a complicated process whether it takes place at the interpersonal level, in public communication, or during the deliberations of a committee.

In one sense, radio, TV and press interviews are face-to-face communication. In spite of the presence of a camera, mike or note pad, you are talking to a live human being. In another sense, the reporter is a filter through whom your remarks must pass on their way to the ultimate listener or reader. Try to remember your real audience as you answer questions. Know the message *you* want to get over. Except in live interviews, your best points may be edited out, but you can at least try. Here are four tips to remember in any media interview:

1. The reporter may surprise you with nasty questions. This usually is not personal. If you allow yourself to feel hostile, your nonverbal signals, such as vocal tone and facial expression, will make you look bad. Concentrate on a factual answer and don't resort to emotional replies.
2. On the air, time is money. Long answers will be edited out, so try to be brief. Resist the temptation to forestall difficult questions by answering the easy ones at great length.
3. Don't be tempted to guess at an answer, to state boldly what you think the answer *might* be. Resist. Say, "I don't know."
4. A good interviewer can often put you at such ease that you are caught off-guard and make careless remarks. While you must be candid, you cannot assume that anything you say will be off-the-record.

Techniques for facing hostile questions are best learned by practice. Many firms offer workshops for dealing with the media; you may find such training a good investment.

Face-to-face communication in all its forms continues to be important. When David Rockefeller was asked to speculate on the responsibilities of business leaders in the year 2000, he predicted that direct human contact will always be vital in communication. Business communicators should see the challenge they face in Rockefeller's statement that the business leaders of the next century "will have a personal responsibility for advocacy, activism and outspokenness" and must represent their companies and industries "articulately and coherently."

Jerry Tarver, Ph.D., is professor of speech communication and theatre arts at the University of Richmond in Richmond, Virginia, director of the Effective Speech Writing Institute and editor of *The Effective Speech Writer's Newsletter.*

PART **IV**

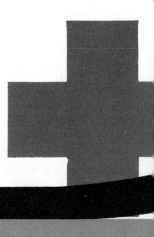

SOME SPECIAL NEEDS AND TECHNIQUES

No matter how well constructed and planned, an organization's communication program will at some time be disrupted by some special needs. Anticipating these needs is the first step toward handling them effectively.

CHAPTER 14

Important Single-Purpose Programs

RAE LEAPER, ABC

Everything a communicator does should have a specific purpose, and the part that purpose plays in the overall plan, and the specific audience addressed should always be clearly in mind. The topics discussed here are specific, and they are also extremely diverse—covering safety campaigns and shareholders' meetings, patient information programs and organizational moves, economic education, and communicating in a crisis. Each one challenges the communicator to be a problem solver. Each one gives the communicator an opportunity to reinforce his or her role as a member of the organization's management team, using communication tools and techniques to solve problems.

This chapter is divided into two sections: (1) special-purpose communication as part of ongoing communication programs; and (2) one-time events, activities or disasters.

Special-Purpose Communication in Ongoing Programs

Employee Orientation

The responsibility for employee orientation generally belongs to the personnel department. However, it is important for the communication department to cooperate in the production of the program, perhaps in a customer-client relationship. Employee orientation is too important to an organization to be done haphazardly. Good employee orientation programs can help reduce turnover, training time and cost, waste, tardiness, absenteeism and even production costs. They also can improve employee loyalty and morale. In addition, well-informed employees are one of the most effective media for telling an organization's story in the community.

The climate of open, two-way communication in an organization should be established early. It gives the communicator a direct and personal interest in the content and presentation of employee orientation.

In the Beginning, There Are Always Goals—An effective orientation program should have a set of goals to direct its development and against which it can be evaluated. One major consulting firm suggests the following as possible goals:

- To provide new employees with a clear picture of what the organization offers them and what it expects from them
- To provide new employees with a basis for sound decisions—on the job, in compensation and benefits, in career planning
- To provide new employees with ongoing access to individuals who have detailed knowledge of various aspects of the organization
- To provide new employees with an introduction to the work and those with the same or similar jobs
- To provide new employees with an awareness of channels available for problem solving

Instead of a program aimed at accomplishing a logical set of goals, too many orientation programs fall into one of the designs identified by Robert W. Hollman of the University of Arizona. The Paperwork Design finds the personnel department saying a brief hello and then devoting its enthusiasm to getting all the necessary forms completed. The Social Darwinism Design throws the new employee almost immediately into the job with the idea that the "most fit" will survive. The Mickey Mouse Design turns the new employee into the department "go-fer" or assigns *all* the organization's policy and procedure manuals. The Overload Design thrusts an elaborate and comprehensive body of information on a new employee in a short time period.

What Goes into an Orientation Program—Employee orientation can be divided into two distinct parts: general orientation to the organi-

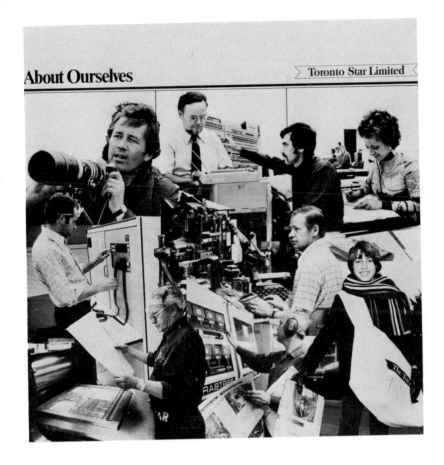

About Ourselves   Toronto Star Limited

Printed materials often are the heart of employee information programs.

zation and specific orientation to the job and department. A general orientation should include an overview of the organization—what it does or makes; its basic organization; its position in the field and history; the organization's policies and procedures on hours, vacations, holidays, training salary and wage information; benefits; and a description of physical facilities. Job and departmental orientation usually includes the department's objectives and activities and how these fit into the overall organization; specific duties, policies and procedures of the department; a tour of the area; and an introduction to others in the department. The first part usually is covered by the organization's formal orientation program; the latter by the new employee's supervisor.

The most common practice is to structure the orientation as a half- or whole-day process during which the person conducting the session uses a variety of printed materials and audiovisual aids. The printed materials are usually the heart of the orientation because employees can use them for later reference when questions arise. When developing printed materials keep in mind the ease with which they can be updated. Two obvious methods are the looseleaf notebooks and packets of individual leaflets or sections. Parts of either of these can be updated without changing the entire contents.

Don't overlook the important role of employee publications in announcing a new or revised orientation program. It's an excellent opportunity to remind all employees of important facts about the organization and to demonstrate that the organization gives attention and consideration to those who work for it.

Many organizations make effective use of films and/or slide presentations. They can be simple—one slide projector and a tape cassette—or complex—a multiprojector slide show, a 16-mm color film, a videotape television program. One advantage of audiovisuals is their impact. They can present what employees need to know in color, pictures, words and sound. They also can bring to the audience people who could not otherwise be there, scenes that employees may never see. And they tell the same story each time—to each group of employees in each location.

How Long and When?—Timing, both in terms of length of the orientation and when it is given, is important, but there is no universal rule. The lengths vary from a couple of hours to several days. Many organizations set an orientation session for the employee's first day on the job. Large corporations have regularly scheduled orientation sessions, and new employees attend the next available one.

It is important to keep in mind that new employees are not able to absorb an infinite amount of information. If it's communication that you're after, orientation should be handled as a long-term process, not a crash program. Orientation should not stop when the film ends, the lights go on, and the handbook is issued. New employees will have questions that occur only as the information sinks in or as they work at their new jobs. Follow-up can take the form of another session or additional printed information. More than likely, it falls to the supervisor to make sure that questions are answered and that important information is restated when it is needed. The communicator can assist by preparing guidelines which help the supervisor to be a better communicator.

Employees who have been on the job for a year or less are good sources of feedback on the effectiveness of an orientation program. Employee turnover statistics, especially if it's a new program or if significant changes have been made, also can provide an excellent means of evaluation.

Safety Campaigns

The role of communication in maintaining safety is clearly recognized. The need for safety must be told and retold; communicators must keep finding effective ways to do it, in cooperation with the department or departments specifically charged with the responsibility for safety.

It's Not Always What You Think—Not all safety campaigns are organization-wide. It's also possible to mount special, short-term efforts to solve particular problems. Be on the lookout for these hot spots and move in with a plan. In fact, the short-term emphasis, even without a trouble spot, is one way to keep the overall program fresh.

There's a tendency to think of safety in terms of heavy equipment, hard hats and safety goggles. Employees who push nothing heavier than a pencil also face hazards, and communicators who work for seemingly "safe" organizations are not exempt from planning and carrying out safety awareness programs. Off-the-job safety campaigns should be developed, as well as plans for such emergencies as fires, earthquakes and tornadoes.

One of the pleasant side effects of a safety campaign is that it can enable the communication department to demonstrate its effectiveness in numbers and dollars. Communicators have put their creativity to good use in devising a seemingly endless list of media to get across the safety message: films, slide/tape presentations, meetings, demonstrations, video programs, booklets, billboards, posters, brochures, contests, drawings, bonuses, awards, decals and stickers, calendars, letters, special days or weeks, bumper stickers, flags and T-shirts.

An organization's publications, of course, play an important role in safety campaigns. They can be used to call attention to the ongoing plan; to announce new plans; to recognize goals, achievements or anniversaries; and to cajole and compliment. Editors are a remarkably resourceful lot, and they have created a wonderful variety of stories and photos to carry the message. And communicators don't have a monopoly on creativity. Involve others and openly recognize their contributions to safety.

Safety programs and achievements are news for the external media as well. But use caution or they may be interpreted as the existence of an unsafe workplace.

Financial Communication

The Annual Report—The flagship of a company's financial communication flotilla is the annual report. On it is lavished the love, money, attention—and perhaps the paranoia—that goes with putting the organization's best foot forward for a very important audience—shareholders and investors.

The pages of the annual report have become a showcase for the printing, paper, photography and design businesses of the world. But, are annual reports read? The beauty of the design and production often seem to be in reverse proportions to the quality of the writing. But that's changing. The annual report is too valuable a communication tool and reaches audiences that are too important to the organization to waste the opportunity to say something significant.

A few organizations have had the courage to speak candidly about a bad year in the pages of their annual reports. A few years ago there would have been a collective corporate coronary if anyone had suggested that the president say, "Last year was not a very good year for XYZ Corp." Now it has been done, and neither the world nor the stockmarket collapsed. In an article in *Coverage*, Washington National Corporation executive Thomas R. Strubbe said, "Our reports today contain enough statistical data to satisfy even the most sophisticated investors, yet much of such information is reserved for a page in the back near the financial statements so that it does not detract from the narrative that is of primary interest to most individual investors."

Corporations are taking advantage of their annual reports to show that they are run by concerned human beings; they are not just successful producers of product and profit, but also participants in their communities.

Quarterly Reports—In the United States, the Securities and Exchange Commission requires many organizations to file quarterly financial data with the SEC. Even though there is no federal requirement to share this information with shareholders, more and more organizations are issuing quarterly reports. Although the primary intent of quarterly reports is to transmit fiscal information about the corporation, most do not neglect appearance.

Some companies also produce quarterly publications for other audiences. Standard Oil of California mails *Chevron World* each quarter to shareholders, employees, the media and others. The four-color magazine includes articles on legislation that affects the industry, the energy shortage and other items of interest to persons within the oil industry.

A number of major organizations send special letters on a variety of topics concerning legislation, regulation, finances, and so on. They keep shareholders informed of major political and legislative developments affecting their company and suggest actions they can take.

Typecast—Until recently, financial communication was almost exclusively the province of the print media. Now communicators are showing that there are other effective and interesting ways to communicate financial news to a corporation's audiences. Closed-circuit television and regional shareholders' meetings are being added to the usual array of print materials.

Ashland Oil in Kentucky provides closed-circuit television coverage of its annual meeting to shareholders and security analysts in New York City. The action was prompted in 1979 by bad weather and a desire to save the security analysts two days of travel to Kentucky. The television coverage has been extended to Columbus, Ohio, where the company has a major facility. Other corporations are putting new life and meaning into the required annual meetings of stockholders by taking them "on the road" to cities where the company has important facilities and substantial concentrations of shareholders.

The Employees' Right to Know—Ironically, only recently have a corporation's employees been considered an important audience for financial information. Today's employees feel they have a right to know about the organization for which they work. They are no longer interested only in chitchat and personals. They want to know how the company's doing and how the competition's doing. They want to know where the company's going and how it plans to get there. They feel they have a right to know about the employment situation and the security of their jobs.

Employees also need to know more about the financial condition of the organization. You can demonstrate this by asking a few people at random to estimate the company's percentage of profit, or what an aver-

Economic education programs should suit the needs and times of each organization's particular audience.

age organization earns. Then ask what profit they think an organization ought to make. If the results you get are anything like the national norm, you'll find that most persons overestimate by a wide margin.

The communicator should recognize this right and need to know and be ready to provide the information through a variety of media. Employee publications and management newsletters are two of the most effective ways of keeping employees up to date on the fiscal health of the organization. Audiovisual presentations, closed-circuit television and meetings are others.

Even if organizations weren't responding to employees' need and right to know, there are now legal requirements for reporting at least some financial information to employees. In the United States, the

Employee Retirement Income Security Act of 1974 (ERISA) requires an annual disclosure of benefit-plan financial information to employees.

The key element in financial communication for employees and all other audiences is credibility. Employees want to know the unfavorable news as well as the favorable. They expect honesty.

Employee Annual Reports—Perhaps nowhere is the recent acknowledgment of the employees' right to know about the organization for which they work more clearly demonstrated than in the increasing popularity of employee annual reports. In most organizations, the employee annual report has developed out of the practice of simply giving employees copies of the annual report for shareholders. Although that is better than no effort at communication, it is an excellent example of mismatching a medium and the intended audience. In a recent study by the Clorox Company of Oakland, California, both the corporate and the employee annual reports were mailed simultaneously to a representative sample of employees. During the following month, an outside consumer research firm conducted 255 telephone interviews. The survey showed that 71 percent preferred the employee report; 81 percent felt that their own report gave them the feeling that Clorox has a positive attitude toward employees.

A review of the field also will quickly show that not all efforts are successful. Many reports are more propaganda than revelation. They tend to be preachy, poorly written, or both; and too often they emphasize how little money the company is making and at the same time heralding the benefits to employees. Such reports may do more harm than good because most of today's employees see right through the veneer of attempted goodwill.

The basis of the employee annual report, like the corporate annual report, is financial. However, there are significant differences in what kind of financial information employees and families are most interested in and how it should be presented. Employees do not want just financial charts and pages of figures. They want an interpretation of the figures in terms of the impact on their jobs.

The following contents of an ideal employee annual report are suggested by one consulting firm:

- A freewheeling discussion by the chief executive of the firm's goals, prospects for reaching them, problems, accomplishments and failures.

- A summation of the year's major events.
- A discussion of employment in the organization, addressing the issue of job security.
- A discussion of trends both in the firm and in the industry.
- A projection of operating results.
- A graphic analysis of expenditures with accompanying narrative explanation. Emphasis should be on expenditures that often confuse employees, such as borrowing money, payments to stockholders and depreciation; the how's and why's of material costs, compensation and benefits, machinery and equipment costs, interest payments, taxes and retained earnings.
- An analysis of income, which is generally easier for most people to understand than a mere statement of income, and an explanation of profits.
- Comments on the contributions various divisions make to the entire organization's financial picture.
- An easy-to-understand explanation of financial jargon.
- If possible, a parallel between "economics" familiar to employees (e.g., budgets, wages) and the "economics" of the firm.
- A tie-in, if possible, to relevant external social, political and general economic issues.

There are many ways to present the information. One way is to build the report around a theme. Another technique is a diary of the year's significant events. To be effective, the events must be truly significant and not trivia selected in order to space comments throughout the year.

Annual reports naturally lend themselves to comparisons—either a long-range (five- or ten-year) historical analysis or a comparison of this year and last. There are many kinds of information that can be compared: employment rates, company growth, diversification, benefits. For years Pitney Bowes has presented charts showing the growth of employees' pay.

One of the most popular approaches to an employee annual report is the photo story. The report is for and about employees, so what better way to illustrate it and tell the year's story than through the photographs of the employees?

No matter what material is included or how it's presented, the element without which all is lost is candor. This means top management must be committed to an honest presentation of the facts. An organization that ignores or skirts sensitive issues is asking for trouble. Employ-

1979 Annual Report
To Employees

Bemis Company, Inc.   BEMIS

Employees want an easy way to understand explanations of corporate finances in their annual report.

ees eventually learn about them, and it's better to have the information come from the organization than through the grapevine or the mass media.

Although print predominates, a few organizations are using other media. Daniel Freeman Memorial Hospital in Inglewood, California, used a slide presentation to supplement its printed report. The 1,500 employees viewed the slide presentation over a three-day period and hospital officials were available at the meetings to answer questions. The slide presentation became a communication technique in itself by bringing employees together for open communication and by giving employees on the night shift a rare opportunity to meet officials and participate in discussions.

Because of all the effort that goes into producing an annual report for employees, it's worth a little more planning and effort to gain added impact at the time of distribution. The regular employee publications, special publications for supervisors and managers and bulletin boards all should be used to stimulate interest in the forthcoming annual report. Employee meetings at the time of distribution also are an excellent way to take maximum advantage of the report.

Economic Education Programs

In spite of the fact that literally decades of economic education programs have failed to shape or change the attitudes of the public, the community, stockholders or employees, there are at least two excellent reasons for initiating economic education programs. Probably the most important reason is the relatively new and almost symbiotic relationship that exists between business and government. Few, if any, major decisions of business today can be made without government approval of some type at the federal, provincial, state or local level. The second reason is the increasing number of sophisticated and probing questions being asked by employees, stockholders and neighbors. And they want clear-cut honest answers.

Both reasons are present in the following statement of the chief executive officer of a large multi-product corporation:

> I go to Washington frequently these days and generally get clobbered whenever I'm there. So, I turn to our employees and shareholders for support. And they're not there. They're sidelining me. . . . As for our employees, they're great on the job, but they seem to change identities as soon as they leave the gate. On the job, they are loyal, devoted and efficient. Off the job, they act as if they don't know their company and stay aloof or even hostile when we lock horns with government.

Few businesses actually have any fairly systematic economic education program. Many are more talk than action and boil down to occasional speeches by executives on the wonders of free enterprise or pamphlets for grade school children. Experts call past attempts at economic education "one of the most spectacular marketing disasters of recent years." The reason for the unenviable track record of most economic education programs is that they have been based on two erroneous assumptions: (1) people, including shareholders and employees, are economically "illiterate"; and (2) people are hostile to business and the free enterprise system.

Although surveys turn up significant gaps in information and knowledge (one of the most significant and consistent is the overestimation of the amount of profits businesses earn), there is no evidence that the public is without interest in, or knowledge of, the economic system. On the contrary, there are many indications that the public today is more knowledgeable about economic trends and developments than ever before; it supports the U.S. economic system and says it is willing to sacrifice in order to preserve it, even though public confidence in American business is low.

Fortunately, a few businesses have programs that seem to be successfully getting their economic messages across. They are designed to restore confidence in business and its leaders, to win "constituency" support for company goals and to answer, in specific ways, the concerns and questions of these constituencies.

Guidelines for Success—In 1977 Towers, Perrin, Forster & Crosby conducted a survey of large corporations for the Financial Executives Research Foundation. Based on an analysis of 130 separate programs reported, Myron Emanuel, Director of Business Communications Programs for TPF&C, offers the following guidelines:

> *There is no universal program.* What works in one place is not always effective in another. Each organization needs to plan its own program to suit the needs of its particular audiences.
>
> *Define the subject.* Economic education does not mean the same thing to everyone, and unless it is clearly defined in management's mind, only confusion can result. For some, economic education means an academic approach that is unbiased and that deals with principles and laws of economics. For others, it means an advocacy approach with political activity the desired result. The better advocacy programs, while not without bias, are even-handed.
>
> *Think small.* The programs that seem to work best aim specific and limited messages at specific audiences; they put general topics into the perspective of "this business."
>
> *Know the audience.* It is important to know which questions people want answered, which existing positive attitudes can be reinforced, which negative attitudes should be addressed, and which gaps in information or knowledge need to be filled. Letters, meetings or surveys can provide answers to these questions and thereby shape the content of the programs being planned and give benchmarks for measuring progress.
>
> *Make it an ongoing program.* One-shot programs are more likely to be seen as self-serving and manipulative.
>
> *Keep it part of the established communication channels.* When an economic education program works well it is usually integrated in an existing communication program. Blaring introductions are usually counterproductive.
>
> *The chief executive must be involved.* Programs that thrive and succeed have the active support of the chief executive officer.
>
> *In employee programs, the first audience should be management at all levels.* It is often overlooked that managers' information needs are just as intense (perhaps more so) as those of rank-and-file employees. Although the differences between the interests and con-

cerns of employees and managers are not great, they are significant.
Don't forget to listen. Employees want to know more about the
business and how it affects them. They want to listen and be lis-
tened to.

Keep it cheap. There is no evidence that expensive programs work
better. Expensive, elaborate productions (films, videotape, four-
color brochures) may provoke hostile questions about costs.

Keep it flexible. Most economic education materials have a "shelf
life" of little more than one year because events move so rapidly
these days. With the exception of materials of historic nature, avoid
producing "permanent" materials.

Patient Information Programs

Perhaps the term "captive audience" is a bit strong, but once a
person checks into a hospital, the patient may feel that way. Whatever
the length of the stay, there are certain things a person needs to know.

The most popular medium for patient information programs is the
pamphlet or booklet—in a variety of sizes, shapes, colors and designs.
For most, the purpose is straight information—the information the patient, family and friends need to know about the hospital, plus as warm a
welcome as can be offered on the printed page. Pamphlets or booklets
should attempt to answer everything a patient could question—
everything from "admitting procedures to "patient's rights" to "what to
bring." The copy should be brief and to the point, the type should be
large and readable, the sections clearly marked.

Hospitals frequently also develop booklets for special patients,
such as children or maternity patients. The content and design is
modified to suit the special audience. An imaginative maternity information piece was developed by Santa Monica Hospital Medical Center in
California. It's a die-cut replica of a carryall bag printed in pastel colors
that opens to show a realistic four-color photo of a baby's travel kit. Into it
are tucked two small brochures—an information piece and a fee schedule. The whole thing can be carried by its own handle, just like a small
suitcase.

Patient information pamphlets for the family and friends of patients
often contain much of the same information, but the approach is different
because the needs are different. The Baptist Medical Center in Birming-
ham, Alabama, lists motels, restaurants and shopping areas near the hospital in its family and friends brochure.

Patient Information

Your guide to
Phelps Memorial Hospital

Hospital patients have many questions—give them straight information in an easy-to-read manner.

Other Media—Some hospitals use closed-circuit television to tell patients what's happening each day in the hospital and to review some of the information covered in patient booklets in interesting visual ways. Video can supplement, but not replace, the printed materials, for the latter must be available when the patient needs to look up something specific.

Hospitals also use tray liners, tray tents, flyers, daily newsletters and special "hotlines" to communicate with patients. None of these communication tools can replace face-to-face communication during a hospital stay. They may save many questions but there will always be others that need to be answered by a member of the staff. It's therefore important that everyone who comes into contact with patients knows the basic information on hospital procedures and policies. Using the established communication channels to keep the staff up to date on changes and to remind them of existing services will make the patient information program more effective.

For Those Out-of-the-Ordinary Times—Into every hospital communicator's life there usually will fall at least one time when a special patient communication effort is needed. It can be something pleasant like an anniversary, the dedication of a new wing or a special service. It can be something difficult, like construction or remodeling in or near the hospital. It can be something unpleasant, like a labor dispute with disrupted services. Whatever it is, the occasion will take a special communication effort to keep patients, friends, families and staff informed.

The media used are often special or expanded versions of the existing communication channels. As in so many other instances, hospital communicators seem to rise to new heights of skill and creativity when the pressure is on. When leisurely planning a happy event, hospital communicators have produced beautiful communication packages built around a single theme. In times of distress, hospital communicators have produced daily newspapers or news bulletins to keep one of their most important audiences, the patients, well informed.

When the Hospital Stay Is Over—Since one of the main objectives of a hospital information program is to build goodwill with patients, their families and friends—and through them the community—many hospitals follow up with an evaluation. Some have "exit interviews"; others distribute forms when patients leave or with letters sent to patients a few days later. Information gathered from patients can be used to improve services and communication for future patients.

Membership Drives

Most communicators probably spend more time on the receiving than the sending end of membership drives. If you find yourself in charge of a membership drive, the receiving end is not a bad place to start. There's little evidence to indicate that we are not subject to and motivated by the same factors as others.

Variety, creativity, novelty, enthusiasm, originality—all play an important part in membership drives. The competition is keen just to get your message noticed, let alone acted on. A membership drive is often a good time to let your imagination go and dream up new ideas, new slogans, new themes and new designs. Brainstorming can pay off handsomely. Just keep this in mind: whatever you come up with must suit the audience you're after.

Catchy slogans and themes are often handy, especially in campaigns that involve existing membership. It helps to have something to call the drive, something that people can talk about and become involved with. One IABC membership drive was called ProQuest, chosen to reflect the professionalism of the association and the campaign, while stressing the quest required for membership recruitment. "We're proud and we're professional" became the rallying cry used to encourage members to share the benefits of their association. Everything produced for the campaign carried the ProQuest theme and logo. Each recruit and recruiter received one in a series of four ProQuest coasters. Each of these 4¼-inch ceramic tiles sported a communication proverb. Any IABC member who recruited four new members during the campaign received the full set of coasters.

Some of the most successful drives count on the active participation of persons who already are members. Getting members fired up to go out and sign up more people is not always easy. It takes planning, work and creativity. Prizes and other gimmicks may help, but it usually comes down to building a sense of mission and competition.

Many membership drives rely entirely on direct mail, a specialty, indeed a world, all its own. If your organization is considering a direct-mail drive, the best recommendation is to go to a consulting firm that specializes in direct mail.

Rules to Campaign By—The American Society of Association Executives lists twelve "keys" to boosting membership:

1. *Figure out how much a member is really worth to you and how much it costs the organization for each member.* Until you know that, you don't know how much you can spend to attract each new member. ASAE predicts that you'll probably find that members are worth more than you expect and that you therefore can invest more in campaigns to sign up new members.

2. *Set goals.* You cannot adequately evaluate a drive if you have not set realistic goals. You cannot know how to plan to reach your objectives until you know what they are. Sound planning is as important to a membership drive as it is to any other communication effort.

3. *Use a selling theme.* ASAE recommends developing a strong selling message around a single selling idea—and that idea should be the most compelling reason for new members to join. Be careful with your creativity. Whatever theme you develop also must say something about your organization. Once developed, use the theme with everything—visually and verbally.

4. *Simplify.* Find the essence of your message and your appeal—why

should someone join your organization?—then put it across simply and directly. Keep your graphics and your writing on target. Don't make people hunt for the message. They won't.

5. *Sell the benefits.* Identify and promote the one benefit that will be most helpful to new members. It may not be the service that is most used by current members, so don't jump to conclusions. Remember, the prospective member will be asking, "What's in it for me?" Provide that important answer.

6. *Don't bore people.* You're competing for the prospective member's time and attention. Don't waste it. Get to the point as interestingly as you can. Don't assume that a long list of services is necessarily a shortcut. A list can be as dull and as meaningless as long blocks of copy. Look for ways to visualize your organization and its services and then let art and photos tell as much of the story as possible.

7. *Use a letter with your membership package.* People are more likely to read a brochure and act on it if there's a letter with it. Next to face-to-face visits or telephone calls, a letter (even if it's printed) is the most personal form of communication. Use it to "talk" about the benefits of joining. Make it interesting and be specific.

8. *Develop a graphic identity.* For most people, what comes out of the envelope when your membership message arrives is what they'll know about the organization. Start with the logo and make sure that everything carries the visual message and impression you want.

9. *Try new media.* Don't limit your drive to a brochure and a letter. Use displays, your publications, ads, posters, take-one boxes, telephone calls, postage meter messages. . . .

10. *Make it easy to join.* Don't make your membership application an aptitude test for the gifted. Make it easy for the prospective member to jot down the key information and send it back. Take care of small details such as making sure that the paper isn't too glossy to write on.

11. *Use your members.* If the organization is providing good services for members, they should be your best sales people. A member-get-a-member campaign can be very successful and cost effective.

12. *Keep at it.* A single membership drive, even a successful one, is not enough. Organizations need membership development programs and continuity is the key. Don't feel that a rejected membership offer is a rejection forever. Make several contacts.

Have several persons try using the material you send to promote membership. The more complicated the mailing, the greater the need to make sure that every statement and every instruction is clear.

Don't Forget to Evaluate—Because you set goals in the beginning, you have something against which to measure your success and refine future programs. It is not always easy to pinpoint why a particular drive is successful, but try. Keep careful records and look for common elements of successful and unsuccessful drives.

A Penny Saved—If you paraphrase the adage "A penny saved is a penny earned," you could say, "A member retained is a member you don't have to go out and look for." Don't spend so much time looking for new members that you neglect the ones you have. Many new members drop out after the first year. Find out why through sampling and surveys and plan carefully to hold members in the future.

Special-Purpose Communication of One-Time Events, Activities and Disasters

Acquisitions, Mergers and Reorganizations

Few business events require more communication skill and planning than mergers, acquisitions and major reorganizations. What is needed in each case is a communication effort that is complete, honest and impeccably timed. Frequently it must be carried out under soul-trying conditions of secrecy, mistrust and government regulations and restrictions.

The communication effort cannot hope to be successful without some essential factors. Top management must be committed to the communication effort. Most of the important information to be communicated must come from the top management of one or both organizations involved. Management, of course, has a great interest in seeing that the merger, acquisition or reorganization takes place as smoothly as possible. Without a good communication program, thousands of hours can be wasted while employees and others speculate about what is or might be happening. Any delay or gap in communication will be filled immediately by rumors and the grapevine.

Usually in these often delicate, unsettling business maneuvers, it is impossible to answer all questions to everyone's satisfaction, but a well-planned communication effort can anticipate most of the questions and develop answers. Employees want answers that are honest and as complete as possible. Platitudes, sugar coating and false assurances must be avoided. The truth will come out eventually and it's better to have it come in the beginning from management.

The timing of information is crucial and often difficult. If publicly owned companies are involved, in the United States all communication must be done within the rules set forth by the Securities and Exchange Commission. For instance, in the case of an acquisition, there must be a public announcement as soon as negotiations involve more than the chief executives of two organizations. As soon as anyone else enters the picture—lawyers, aides, financial experts—the news must be released to the Dow Jones wire, to a competing wire service and to a New York financial paper. The communication program should swing into action as soon as the public announcement is made. The planning for all of this must be done well in advance.

Ideally, the information about the merger or acquisition should go to employees of both organizations at the same time it is released to the public. At most, the communicator has four or five hours to reach employees after the public announcement. Obviously that's not enough time to develop and implement a plan. Even with advance planning, the communicators must move quickly and efficiently.

When the merger or acquisition involves privately held companies and disclosure is not mandatory, it is obviously easier to plan and carefully implement a communication program. The first announcement to employees should outline the basic facts, give the reasons for the merger or acquisition, and explain honestly how it is likely to affect both companies. The worst thing that can happen is for the employees of one or both companies to learn about a merger from the media.

How to Get the Word Out—The best way to communicate the essential information rapidly and accurately depends on several factors, including the type and size of the organizations, the number of locations involved, and the existing communication programs. After the initial release of information to employees, many organizations follow up with bulletin board announcements; others immediately hold series of meetings for employees. The CNA Financial Corporation used a "hotline" telephone system with trained personnel assigned to take the calls. Where it exists, companies have effectively used closed-circuit television to air taped messages or interviews with top executives.

Keep It Going—The need to communicate does not end when the first flurry of activity dies down. Employees will continue to have important questions. Normal communication programs and channels may be, at least for a time, more complicated. There will be new procedures, new sensitivities, and new people to work with.

It usually makes a difference to employees whether they are in a company that has acquired or has been acquired, but both groups have important communication needs. Although all employees need to know what's happening, the groups usually most seriously affected are supervisors and managers. In the company acquired, the managers and professionals will wonder if they should "wait and see" or if they should start looking for new jobs. In the parent company, managers will wonder what the addition of new, perhaps stronger, departments will do to them.

A company's communication channels can play important roles in the long-range efforts to mold two organizations into one. Articles in publications and newsletters, feedback programs and meetings all have important roles.

An Organization Moves

A move to a new location, whether it is across town or across the country, can be traumatic for organizations and the individuals who work for them. Throughout any relocation, one thing will remain constant— the need for accurate, timely information. Employees will have a seemingly endless supply of questions, concerns and doubts. The organization will have a continuous, developing supply of information that needs to be communicated. The communicator's task: to plan, establish and maintain a timely, honest two-way flow of information.

Start Early—You cannot start planning the communication program for a relocation too soon. The first announcement—whether it's the decision to build a new building, to move to a different building or to relocate to a different part of the country—should be a planned and early part of the overall communication effort.

Surveys of employees will help determine which aspects of the move are causing concern. Once known, these concerns can be faced, solutions found and the information communicated. Tune in to the grapevine and be aware of any misinformation that's flourishing. Everyone will be concerned about a relocation, and everyone will have an opinion. Part of the communicator's job is keeping those opinions positive. Help management find ways to involve employees in the planning process. People are less threatened by things they have a part in and feel more committed to those things they help plan.

The well-planned communication effort will continue to look for

Special-purpose communication requires the honing of basic communication skills to answer specific needs.

and answer the questions that arise at every step along the way. Better yet, it will anticipate and answer questions before they're asked. Where's the cafeteria? Is there parking? Are there restaurants in the area? Where's my desk or office? Where's the department that used to be just down the hall?

The families of employees have an important stake in any relocation, particularly if it is a move to a new city. Much of a well-planned move involves orienting families to the new community and helping them find homes. The communication plan also must address these considerations and do so openly and honestly.

Regular communication channels have a big part to play. The employee publication is a logical place for major articles on a relocation, and many have capitalized on the hassle of the move with amusing photo stories. It's an excellent way to involve numerous people and encourage camaraderie. Many organizations have produced special newsletters to handle the bulk of the communication about a move. Letters, hotlines, meetings, audiovisual presentations and brochures also have been used effectively.

A major part of a relocation that also becomes part of the communication plan is the pre-move tour of the new location. When Sentry Insurance moved 1,600 employees from four locations into one building in July, it started taking busloads of employees to the new building in May and June. Each employee was given the chance to visit the spot where he or she would work.

On a larger scale, when Borden moved from New York to Columbus, Ohio, it arranged weekend trips so that employees and their families could get firsthand knowledge of the new community and take the first steps toward locating homes. Employees already in Columbus were named Borden Hosts and matched, as much as possible, with new employees according to interests. They met with the visitors and gave them personal impressions and information on the community.

The open house is also an important communication tool in a relocation. It gives the employees, their families and community members a chance to take a good look at the facilities. Open houses are usually accompanied by other communication media—brochures, maps, guided tours, lectures, films, slide presentations, letters of invitation and media coverage.

If the relocation is to a new community, it is important to tell both the old and the new community just what the relocation means. To the new community it means new jobs, new people, added income, a market for houses, more people using the services. For the old community it could have a negative economic impact. All these things are newsworthy and will probably attract local media attention. The communicator will have to plan carefully and use a variety of communication techniques to get the story across honestly and positively. A major relocation also is news within the industry so industry publications need to be kept informed.

Name Change

For the purposes of discussion, assume that the decision to change the organization's name already has been made after careful analysis. Unless there are reasons of security or competition, the communication of a name change can begin even before the decision to make the change has been made. When Mutual Service Insurance of St. Paul, Minnesota, was contemplating a name change, the company publication carried a news story quoting the vice president for marketing. The story gave background on the need to consider a change, pointed out that firms specializing in corporate identity were being screened and gave a proposed timetable of events. The story indicated that "employees, agents, key department heads, top management, policyowners—everyone will have the opportunity to express opinions."

A project as all-encompassing as a name change calls on the planning, coordinating, managing and creative abilities of the communicator to think of everyone, everything and every way to get the word out and to generate the cooperation that will be needed at all levels of the organization. One of the first steps is the development of a complete, detailed guide for the use of the new name, logo and colors. Include such things as specific rules for where the name should be positioned on stationery and business cards, the exact ink color of the logo (if there is one), how the name may be abbreviated (if it may be), and so on.

Getting the Word Out—A personal letter from the chief executive officer to all employees is a popular and effective way to announce a name change. The letter should include a concise and positive reason for the change and briefly answer the questions perceived to be most common and important.

The initial letter can be followed up by articles in the company publications, employee meetings, training sessions, bulletin board notices and so on. Many organizations prepare name-change bulletins, which are issued frequently and regularly to cover various aspects of the name change. For instance, when all the banks and subsidiaries in the Midlantic system added or adopted the new name, a weekly newsletter called *name change* was produced for all employees. Each issue covered one aspect of the changeover process—customer orientation, forms, signs, telephones and so on. The issue on stationery described the contemporary design, provided samples of the new format for all letters produced on the new stationery (a stationery and graphics manual with guidelines and instructions was provided later), gave delivery dates for the new paper and told everyone how to dispose of the old stationery.

Letters, brochures or announcement folders can be sent to shareholders, financial audiences, customers and other key audiences. News releases, press conferences, advertising and sales promotion campaigns all become part of the total plan to establish the organization's new name and identity. Special attention should be paid to one of the most important communication tools—the telephone. People who are used to hearing, "Good morning, Amalgamated Buggy Whip," may be startled to hear, "Good morning, Octopus United." A transition message might be, "Good morning, our new name is. . . ."

The changeover to a new name takes place on one given day. It may take a couple of years before the last sign, form and piece of machinery is finally renamed. It also may take a while before the new identity is established in the minds of the organization's many audiences.

Communicating in a Crisis

The crucial test of the effectiveness of the entire communication program and plan comes with crisis—when it's too late to build trust, credibility, lines of communication, recognized media. In any crisis situation—whether it's a strike, a natural disaster, a scandal, or a major industrial accident—the communication effort will be more effective if the important audiences already are either favorably disposed or neutral toward the organization. To go into a crisis and try to communicate with a hostile audience is going in with two strikes against you.

Some basic plans should be ready if and when calamity strikes. To prepare them, do the following:

1. List every crisis that could conceivably happen to your organization. This is a good project for a staff meeting. One-person departments may work in cooperation with a few persons from related departments. List the obvious disasters, then keep going. Life is full of surprises. After a while you'll see that they fall naturally into categories that will make the list easier to manage.

2. Determine the policy that should guide the handling of each major category of potential crisis. Clarify the policies and make sure they're available in concise written form that's readily retrievable.

3. Obtain commitment from top management to honest, open, timely communication during an emergency. Even organizations normally committed to ongoing and candid communications have been known to develop stage-fright in a time of stress. An emergency is not the time to decide "mum's the word." Information openly, honestly and promptly given is infinitely better than that which is pried out or uncovered or told only after the fact.

4. Construct a basic plan for dealing with emergencies. If the major categories of potential crises require different handling, make sure these variations are covered. The plan or plans should be as thorough as possible. Try to foresee all the problems that could possibly develop. Try a "what if—then" approach. What if the plant is hit by a natural disaster? Then we'll have to. . . . What if it knocks out all telephones and power? Then we'll have to. . . . What if there are serious injuries? Then we'll have to. . . . Don't be afraid to in-

clude seemingly small details. The more you prepare in advance, the easier things will go if an emergency arises.

5. Write down your emergency plan and be sure the persons who will need it have copies or can find them. It can be an outline, but it should contain enough detail to be of use to anyone who may need it. Be prepared for an emergency that could happen while you're away.

6. Identify the key spokesperson or spokespersons for each potential crisis. In most cases it is better to have a single source, especially for the external media. The best source may vary with the situation, however, or it may be necessary to include a person or persons with technical expertise. Build the necessary lists.

7. Make sure you can reach this person or these people at all times. Have home telephone numbers of key management people. Know how to reach them if they're away. Have a list of reliable substitutes. If there are key people you'll need to rely on for background information or technical data, add them to the Find Fast list.

8. Vice versa. Make sure that the key people know how and where to reach you if there's an emergency.

9. Brief and coach your spokespersons so that they will have some idea what to expect. Whether it's the glare of television cameras or the heat of an employee meeting, prepare the spokesperson as much as possible in advance, when life is calm. Look for opportunities for the spokespersons to handle difficult situations. Help them develop capability to handle stressful situations.

10. Anticipate that there may be situations when you and the spokespersons will not have the answers. Usually, the best action is to admit it, not to guess or speculate.

11. Develop written background information in advance, especially in highly technical areas. Develop a simple glossary of terms that clearly and briefly explain the terminology and key points of your organization's business.

12. Evaluate and update the plan every six months. Situations and personnel change.

Conclusion

No matter if it's a special-purpose communication that's part of an ongoing program or a special one-time event, the basic ideas that have been stated and restated in each section of this chapter are essential:

1. Every communication effort must be carefully planned. Have written plans with clearly stated goals and objectives and the basic strategies for reaching them.
2. Every communication program or project must have the support of top management.
3. The communication program and the communicator are integral parts of management.
4. Credibility must be established and maintained through honest, open, timely two-way communication throughout the organization.
5. Communication programs should be complete, well rounded, ongoing. They should be proactive, not reactive.
6. Communication plans should carefully identify all the audiences, and select and use the most effective medium or media to reach each of them.

Rae Leaper, ABC, is senior editor in the corporate communication department of Standard Oil Company of California. She is accredited by the International Association of Business Communicators and served as IABC president in 1978–79.

CHAPTER 15

Handling Organizational and Professional Problems

FREDERIC HALPERIN, ABC

You're putting your monthly magazine to press when the boss calls to say

- The company's space-age widget (the feature lead for this issue) has been recalled.
- The company is on the brink of bankruptcy.
- The chief executive officer has been fired and the new one (formerly the comptroller) thinks no news is good news.
- Your budget's been cut in half.

Or you're in charge of communication at a nonprofit organization and the chairman calls to say

- One of your agencies has been accused of squandering funds.
- "Unexpected" expenses have forced an overall reduction of budget.
- The executive director has quit.
- You've got to increase your output at 60 percent of your prior budget.

You've got a "special problem." What do you do?

First, recognize that most special problems are usually not the real problem at all. Rather, they're symptoms of a larger problem—lack of written policy, objectives and an action plan that reflect management's needs. There is a several-step process you can use to solve these special problems until you can tackle the larger issue.

This chapter introduces a problem-solving process, then deals with some specific problems many communicators face. The intent is to pose some questions and offer insights that can help you move past the barriers. That way, you can get back to your primary function—advising management and helping to plan and implement communication programs that move the organization toward its major goals.

The Problem-Solving Process

Describe the problem in detail as you see it. Be sure to cover every aspect—the who, what, where, why, when, and how of it. This will probably require some research on your part. Next, share your analysis with some of your peers and ask for comments and suggestions. If possible, ask your boss to provide some insight. Then, rewrite your description of the problem if necessary, taking into consideration the comments and suggestions you've received. Once you've redefined the problem, you can take steps to solve it.

There are a number of ways you can develop alternative solutions. Past experience always helps. Have you or others had the same or a similar problem that you solved in the past? Many times you can reapply the solution with good results. Are there other ways to solve it? Try the traditional approach of listing likely solutions along with the potential advantages and disadvantages of each. Then narrow the field down to the most likely candidates.

Try brainstorming. Assemble a small group (5 or 6 people) of concerned professionals and let your imaginations fly. No judging. No commenting on one another's suggestions. Each person says everything and anything that comes to mind, and one person lists the ideas. The objective is *quantity*, not quality. The idea is to maintain a high energy level in the group; everyone should be shouting ideas as quickly as they arrive. After 10 or 15 minutes of brainstorming, evaluate the ideas, add to them, reshape them and build on them. Narrow the list down to the best half dozen, then analyze the advantages and disadvantages of each to decide which one or two seem the best.

No matter how you have chosen your one to two proposed solutions, the next step is to write up your recommendation and a plan for implementing it. The plan should state not only what must be accomplished but also the deadline for each step of implementation and the name of the person responsible for that part of the plan.

Have your plan approved before you implement it. If at all possible, obtain management commitment to the plan—not just a signature, but an assumption of responsibility for at least part of the solution. If you can get management to accept ownership of the plan, you can rest assured the job will get done.

How do you get management to assume ownership? It will help if the solution seems to be in the best interests of management. That's obvious. More important is to have management participate not only in solving the problem but in developing the solution. Involve management in the whole problem-solving process. Invite affected members of management to join you in analyzing the problem, in identifying the solution, and in creating the plan. Then it's only natural for them to take responsibility for carrying out the plan.

Inheriting a Mediocre Communication Program

If you take over a less than effective communication program, you will be expected to do some evaluating and changing. That does not mean change for change sake. But no one will be surprised if you study the effectiveness of the program and implement improvements where warranted. In fact, if you are considering a job where a mediocre program exists, you should be sure management understands that you will make changes.

A mediocre program is not necessarily a bad one, so don't hurry to make piecemeal changes that may or may not be viewed as positive. You are too new in your job to assess the reactions to those piecemeal changes—either from management or from others. Some members of management may have helped build that mediocre program; others might resist trading the familiar for something new. Management will be more impressed with a businesslike approach. In other words, set objectives for the program, evaluate the current program to see how well it meets those objectives, and draw up plans to correct any deficiencies. The plan should include specific actions, timetables, budgets and responsibilities.

What happens if you are required to do a quick fix, if you have no time for research and evaluation? Here's where the problem-solving process comes into play. What's the problem? Does it pertain to the communication staff? Are there enough people to do the work? Do they have the proper skills, knowledge and abilities? Are they properly motivated? Do they have the tools or facilities they need to do their jobs? Is the budget insufficient? Is that because it isn't allocated properly, or is it just too small? If there isn't sufficient budget, is that because the organization just doesn't have the funds? Or is it lack of management commitment to communication? Or did your predecessor never ask for sufficient dollars or never justify a larger budget? Is the problem the quality of graphics and printing or production? Is that tied back to budget considerations, or does it have to do with lack of commitment or ability on the part of your suppliers?

Perhaps everything is well written and well produced, yet has no impact on employees, management or both. Why? Is the source of the problem management's communication philosophy? Many mediocre programs stem from a management philosophy of "we'll tell them what we want them to know." If that's the attitude, you've got a major education job ahead of you before you can move forward. Do your communication objectives tie back to organizational goals important to both your employees and your management? Have the goals been explained in such a way that people understand the impact on their jobs and on the organization? Do people know how your communication objectives are tied to those goals? Are your messages sent to a place where your audiences can receive them at a time when they are willing to receive them, and in a form that they are able to receive?

Those are some potential problems that could cause a mediocre or worse communication program. Once you have identified the problem affecting your program, define it carefully and follow the problem-solving process outlined at the beginning of this chapter.

Coping with an Uncooperative Top Management

One of the most difficult problems any communicator can confront is dealing with an uncooperative top management. Not all uncooperative managements are alike. Many can be turned around quickly; some take years to educate; and some are terminal cases—that is, you'll have to put your life on the line first. As in any problem-solving situation, your first step is to define the problem:

What does uncooperative mean? Does it mean they won't give you the time of day; they're truly not interested in communicating nor sure they need a communicator on staff? Do they see your job as putting out the "house organ" and not making any waves? Or does it mean they leave communication up to you; that's what they hired you for? It's not so much that they don't care about communication. They used to enjoy it themselves when the place was smaller and they didn't have so much to do. It's just that they are too busy now and really don't understand about magapapers and video and all the stuff you need to know now.

Who, specifically, is uncooperative? Is it the chief executive officer? the president? the executive director? the vice president of administration? personnel? public relations? marketing? manufacturing? the general counsel or comptroller? the chief surgeon? your boss? Who in top management does cooperate?

Are there particular times when members of top management are uncooperative? Are there times when they cooperate? Are there particular subjects about which members of top management are uncooperative? Are they helpful on others?

Are there particular circumstances under which members of top management are uncooperative? Under what circumstances do they cooperate? Under what circumstances do they provide enthusiastic and wholehearted support?

Once you've identified the problem and defined its parameters, you can build a better working relationship with those members of top management whom you need to educate. In most cases, you have an interpersonal communication problem with a particular audience—that kind of problem is usually curable.

Start with common ground. Perhaps it's with the subjects or circumstances you've identified as being a real turn-on for top management. Can you develop a program that supports this interest? Can you provide other support services for these officers of the organization? The idea is to create some outstanding programs based on mutually agreeable goals, to build personal credibility with top management and demonstrate how well-thought-out communication programs can help management achieve organizational goals.

Your ultimate goal is to have a common understanding about the role of both communication and the communicator in the organization. That doesn't usually happen in a week or a month or even a year when management is uncooperative. It usually takes a series of steps—steps that create trust and credibility for you and for the value of well-planned and executed programs. Here are some other tips you may wish to consider:

- Be cooperative and enthusiastic about management's programs. If you think they're off base, offer some creative, constructive suggestions that will show that you are an important part of the management team.

- Find out about problems in the organization. Where you can, pitch in and help solve them. People you help will be your greatest supporters.
- Don't take on more than you can handle. It's important that you succeed while you are trying to build credibility.
- Use the problem-solving process.

Once you are accepted as part of the management team, you'll find larger and more difficult problems to solve. That is one of the prices of success at problem solving. But you can use the same problem-solving process no matter what the scope of the problem. And if you become good at it, you'll find your services are always in demand.

When Top Management Changes

A new chief executive officer or other top officer can create problems for you. The new boss will have a lot of things on his or her mind, and one of them is the evaluation of current programs and the elimination or improvement or programs where warranted. Your job is to help make the transition smooth and to demonstrate your competence and the value of your programs. In other words, make the evaluation easy and make yourself useful.

If you have based your communication programs on organizational objectives, have evaluated their effectiveness, and have taken steps to keep them on target, you have a good story to tell. Offer to share your objectives with the new boss. Suggest that any changes made in organizational priorities have an effect on your objectives and programs. Certainly you'll want to take the new boss's concerns into account when reshaping your programs.

Figure out a way to demonstrate your competence to the new boss. Introduce the leader of your organization to constituencies. An interview in your publication is a natural vehicle. How about a videotape interview? Or, are meetings in order? It is important that you assess the boss's strengths and weaknesses as a communicator so that you can help present his or her ideas as effectively as possible. Communication training is a possibility—many new chief executive officers find speech and interview training invaluable. What opportunities are there to introduce these ideas? What opportunities are there to assist in this difficult transition period? What helpful information can you provide? Once again, the problem-solving process can be invaluable for coming up with ideas that can ensure a smooth transition and keep you and your communication programs on track.

There is another aspect of your job when there is a change in top management. If it is important to communicate with the new boss, it is of equal importance to communicate with the entire organization. Changes can create havoc in any organization—especially when they are changes at the top. People at all levels become uneasy because new leadership brings uncertainty. You and communication can play a key role in minimizing uncertainty and keeping the organizational ship on course.

You should try to anticipate the questions that will be on people's minds and answer those questions so that the organization can proceed with its normal routine. Your new boss will appreciate your efforts in this, especially if your analysis of the situation is thoughtful and your proposed communication solutions are effective.

Many communicators fail to recognize this as an important—even critical—job. And you probably should involve a number of thoughtful members of management in the process. Given some careful planning, your communication programs at times of top-management transition can contribute greatly to your organization's success.

Handling the Sensitive Story

These days, there are few communicators who do not have to deal with sensitive issues periodically. Strikes, accidents, charges from government agencies or activist groups, controversial legislation, environmental and energy issues, affirmative action, revolutionary products or services, mergers and acquisitions, plant closings—these and many other issues can and will be viewed as sensitive by decision makers at many of our organizations.

How will you deal with them? Will you be able to cover them at all in your internal communication programs? The best way to ensure that top management considers communication essential and that you understand your role in helping the organization to cope is to have a communication policy and a set of objectives. These can help you create a thoughtful position for the organization and share it with employees.

Even so, every situation is different. So it's important to follow a problem-solving process in determining your recommendation. Research the situation completely. Know all sides of the sensitive issue, especially your management's position. If management doesn't have a position, help them agree on one; your research could be invaluable. If management's position cannot be defended, help them see the shortcomings the opposition will point out.

Once you know management's position, decide what to communicate to employees or to your other important publics. Is it just enough information to understand the organization's position? Or is it a program that asks them to take action? The point is, you have to decide what you want people to do with the information. That will help determine the angle of the story.

Should you tell both sides of the story? If you can easily and effectively refute the other side, then a point-by-point rebuttal can be very effective. What if the argument is moot? In that case, it's probably best to recognize that there are two sides to the issue but not to dwell on an explanation of the organization's position. Tell the story in a way that will appeal to employee self-interest or to your other publics' self-interests.

Sometimes, communicating sensitive issues can be detrimental to the organization. If the organization has made an error, it may be best to say nothing rather than risk beginning a dialog that would only cause more harm than good. This can be especially true when there are legal ramifications, and when admitting a problem or a past error could hurt the organization in court.

Many times, there are conflicts between the organization's legal and communication needs. You must recognize both these needs as valid. Then you must do your best to build the case for communication if you feel it is necessary. Top management will have to decide which need is more important.

An excellent example of a conflict between communication and legal needs occurred during the building of a skyscraper in a major metropolitan area. Citizen's groups formed and threatened suit as the construction began to interfere with their television reception. Employees of the company were torn. Some of them were also experiencing "ghosting" on their TV sets. Others were sympathetic to their neighbors whose reception was affected. Still others didn't want the company to stop building their new headquarters. The communicators recommended a complete internal and external communication program detailing what the company was doing to ensure that TV reception would not be adversely affected. Their point was that their employee relations and customer and community relations were too important to risk. The General Counsel, on the other hand, said the suits would likely go to court, and he would have a much stronger case if the information was withheld for presentation to the judge.

Both points of view were valid, and both were based on a concern for what was best for the company. They were presented to a committee of top officers for decision. The officers decided to effect a full-scale communication program, and some citizens changed their positions. The case was later won in court.

Reviews and Censorship

A perennial thorn in the communicator's side is getting approvals. Often the problem arises because we do not have a written communication policy and a set of objectives that management embraces. Sometimes the problem is the result of our own misguided concept of communication's role in the organization.

Few organizations encourage or even tolerate investigative journalists on the payroll. That's not the reason we were hired; we are employed to help management achieve organizational goals through better communication. This means we need to understand management's point of view, and we ought to be willing, even happy, to work with management to decide on the substance of our programs.

To a large degree, you decide whether you and those who review your copy work together constructively or in an adversary relationship. If you are forever trying to sneak sensitive stories past management, you will not be trusted and you will find most of your programs watched carefully and often censored. If you work with management and become recognized as a reliable and credible member of the team, you will find the comments of those who review your stories helpful. In fact, you will begin to get involved in planning stories you might never have heard about were you not a member of the team.

What ought to be reviewed? Most of us know which stories are sensitive. And it's in everybody's self-interest to get a second opinion on those issues. You should voluntarily share your story lines with those in the know and solicit their comments. It's wise to get another opinion even on stories that have a remote chance of causing problems. It is better to know about the problems in advance; if you still feel the story is necessary, build your case knowing both sides of the issue, present it to a higher level, and accept the decision.

Who ought to be the reviewer? Your immediate boss is usually a good sounding board if you trust his or her understanding of the organization. Someone who is an authority on the subject of your story ought to get a chance to share insights with you. Sometimes it's a good idea to set up a working committee that represents the various areas in your organization.

A review committee? Yes, properly selected and used, it can be your best ally for effective communication. And if you ask that a committee be formed, you'll probably have a chance to suggest good representatives to serve on it; so take the initiative. Initially, you'll find the review committee is an excellent group for you to prove your competence to. Once done, they'll not only help you with their advice on sensitive stories, but they'll support you within their various departments. They'll call you with ideas for stories, get you involved with important issues at the planning stage, and help you to meet the organization's communication objectives.

It is important to share your objectives with this committee and entertain their ideas on altering your objectives. You should educate them on how you go about doing your job, and what kinds of steps are involved in producing a communication piece. Finally, you should come to some agreement with them on what their role is. Style is not their concern, for example. Their insight on the facts and the implications of stories is.

That's the ideal situation, but let's say your reviewer is not so understanding or doesn't care about the communication implications of an issue. For some reason beyond your control or understanding, your story or program is censored. What can you do? First, don't take it personally. Anger and frustration are not necessarily your best friends when there's disagreement. Take a walk if you can, or a breather, and think about the situation. Is the issue important enough to argue?

If it is, and if you have a good case for disagreeing with the censor, try reasoning with him or her. If that doesn't work, you have to escalate. Get the support of your boss and ask that the issue be resolved at a higher level. In some cases, your boss may resolve it without consultation. Usually, the boss will attempt to find a compromise that will satisfy both you and the censor. Sometimes the decision will have to be made by top management.

One example of a censorship situation that turned out well: Customer service complaints at a large consumer company were increasing. So the communicator prepared an article to show employees how they could help solve the problem. At the review stage, the vice president of operations (who was responsible for customer service) rewrote the article to indicate there was no great problem—he didn't want his department to look bad. The communicator couldn't convince the vice president that the problem had to be recognized before it could be dealt with, nor that the article would not ring true with employees. The communicator explained the situation to his own boss, who referred the problem to the president of the company. The article was printed in its original form. The president decided that dealing with the problem was more important than saving face for the customer service department.

None of us likes censorship. We can usually avoid it by planning our programs carefully, researching our stories completely, and using review committees to our best advantage. Sometimes compromise is necessary. Sometimes we lose. Losing shouldn't be a problem for you unless you haven't done your best job preparing yourself for the fray.

The review committee can be an excellent problem-solving group. If you use it to develop solutions to your communication problems, you'll find you have a great deal of help in implementing your plans.

Your Budget's Been Slashed

This situation rears its ugly head so often that it's questionable if it should be treated as a special problem. Budget cuts are routine in many organizations when income and expenses fall out of line or it looks like things might get bad.

The budget problem is a fact of life. The solution is one that can be planned for, just like life insurance. If you review past communication budgets, you ought to get a good idea of the extent of budget cuts in the past. If there's no history to rely on, talk to some other communicators in your industry and guess what your typical budget cut might be. Talk to others in your organization. That's how you get a handle on the potential problem.

What if you discover your budget may be cut by as much as 20 percent? Can you accomplish that kind of a cut and still meet your communication objectives? Surely you can meet at least your high-priority objectives.

Review your current program. How much can you cut by using less expensive paper? Making your publications one-color? Changing the format to one that is more cost efficient? Reducing the number of pages in publications or the length of some A/V shows? Delivering publications at work instead of mailing them home? Delaying the beginning of a new communication endeavor? Doing some of the work yourself that's normally done by suppliers?

Have you saved enough to continue your current programs, even though somewhat altered? If you cannot meet your budget cut through these choices, you will probably have to reduce your program. This may be your opportunity to kill that publication you feel is ineffective, but which management keeps holding on to. At least you may be able to alter it in the name of good management. What are some other alternatives? Can you cut the number of issues of some of your publications, or the number of A/V shows scheduled for this year? Combine two publications into one and take advantage of some printing and distribution economies? Eliminate a part of your program? Eliminate staff? Require departments you are doing programs for to finance their own endeavors?

You will have to choose carefully from among these alternatives. The idea is to do as little damage as possible to your program so that you can continue to meet your high-priority communication objectives for the year. Also remember that when budgets are being slashed and layoffs are being considered, your employees need to know more than ever what is happening and how it will affect them. In the interest of keeping the organization from panic or depression, you may need to scrap your fancy magapaper and substitute a newsletter you can write and issue within a workday.

Talk to your suppliers and get their help and recommendations. They've been through this hundreds of times and may know "the answer" that will work for you. Get your advisory board involved. Consider your objectives. Consider current communication needs. Consider the future. And make your decisions logically, using the problem-solving process. Don't wait until you receive formal notice that a cut is required. Make your contingency plans now so that when it happens, you have a good idea of possible choices.

Deadlines and Crisis Projects

Two other areas that often cause problems for communicators are meeting regular deadlines and responding to crisis projects in a timely fashion. Many times, it's the crisis project we blame for missing other deadlines.

Let's think about deadlines first. Why do we have them? Obviously, there are a couple of reasons. Without a deadline, many of us would never finish our projects on a timely basis. But that's not the primary reason for deadlines. The reason for deadlines is to ensure a regular and timely flow of information to your audience. That's an important part of effective communication. And it is even recognized by laymen as such.

Recently, the communicator at a major U.S. manufacturing company that has sophisticated communication capability surveyed employees on the effectiveness of his programs. Most employees said they thought the programs were weak. Some were unaware of the programs. Why? The bimonthly newsletter, besides carrying little in the way of real news, was published only twice last year. The quarterly video report from top management came out three times. The communicator and his staff had problems meeting their deadlines, what with clearances and crisis projects.

How do you avoid that pitfall? It all goes back to your policy and objectives. If you have management's firm commitment to effective communication, you don't have to miss deadlines to wait for clearances or get a late-breaking story out. Your communication plan must include ways to get fast-breaking news to employees without holding up regular media.

What do you do about the hole in your program created when a story is held up? You plan ahead. If you are on top of what's happening in the company, you know what issues are likely to cause problems; you've got a back-up story ready just in case. In fact, there is no excuse for not having a current file of back-up material always at hand. I'm not talking about filler. Your publication and your video news programs are not made up entirely of news. There are some stories that are timeless. Features on employees, historical information on some part of the organization, reprints of material from your archives with some new perspective—all of these are candidates for filling the hole that periodically appears in your publication or A/V show.

The other aspect of meeting deadlines has to do with educating management on the importance of meeting schedules and the cost—both in dollars and in communication effectiveness—of missing your deadlines. Also, be sure you have given those who need to review your materials sufficient time to do so. If you aren't taking this into account, you may be the cause of the problem. If you don't show respect for others' time, they'll feel no obligation to respect your apparently arbitrary deadlines.

Crisis projects by their very nature will upset your office routine. And many times they require inordinate amounts of your time. There are two important aspects of crisis projects to consider: the first is how to organize to get the job done; the second is how to avoid or minimize crisis in the future.

The most important aspect of crisis management is the manner in which you react. Obviously, crisis is upsetting, and the first reaction is to do something about it. Many skip the analysis and planning steps and forge ahead, many times with the wrong tools and the wrong approach. If you can, slow the tempo down. Take the time to get a firm understanding of the problem and execute the problem-solving process. It is the only way you can be sure you have considered alternative solutions and the pros and cons of each. Take the time to write a plan so that everyone knows what has to happen, where it should happen, and who is responsible for which part of the plan. In the long run, this will save you time and ensure a better chance of success.

A written plan will do even more for you: It will put management on notice about the deadlines necessary for successful completion of the project. It will help management set some priorities and choose the parts of the plan they can accomplish successfully within the given time frames. It will show your ability to respond thoughtfully in crisis.

If you are really thoughtful, you will create a plan that anticipates crisis and minimizes it in your organization. (We spend far too much time reacting, and far too little anticipating and correcting to avoid crisis.) How does one anticipate and avoid crisis? By listening and planning. Listening can take many forms. Informally, get plugged into the grapevine and take the time to talk with people. That way, you can stay on top of employee concerns and bring them to management's attention before they reach crisis proportions.

Formal listening programs can also help. Most companies today have at least considered or even experimented with them. Regular, ongoing attitude studies help you identify concerns and spot trends before they become crises. It is important to review this kind of information regularly. Upward communication programs ranging from "letters to the editor" to "telephone hotlines" and "speak-up" systems should be charted and analyzed to the same ends.

As the organizational communicator, your role is to keep management informed of the trends and encourage action to alleviate concerns. Your job also entails using your media to tell employees that management hears them and is taking action based on what it's hearing. With dialog taking place between employees and management, you create trust and credibility that alleviates the need for much crisis communication. The problem-solving process is useful here in deciding how to deal with employee concerns constructively and keep the dialog flowing.

Working with a Highly Decentralized Staff

Managing creative people can be difficult, especially for communicators who have little or no management training or experience. The problem can reach critical proportions if you are relying on a staff that is highly decentralized. When you're not in daily touch with those who report to you, you have to rely on their ability to do the job and their motivation to do it well. Given the right environment, you can rely on most people to do a job to the best of their abilities. The manager's job, then, is to create the proper environment and help them develop as communicators.

Start by telling people what their responsibilities are. Most managers of decentralized operations find their staffs need a written guide that explains what management's expectations are, what policies and procedures apply in that job, what general information people in that job ought to know, and who to go to for more information. Call that your communicator's guidebook and supplement it with other regular communications that show ideas, approaches and changes in corporate direction.

Most managers of decentralized staffs find it important to conduct periodic workshops with their staffs. This ensures a common understanding of policies, objectives and plans; helps to keep the staff up to date on new and emerging communication theory and techniques; provides an opportunity for counseling on skills improvement; and creates an esprit de corps among the far-flung staff.

Finally, most managers of decentralized staffs find it necessary to deal with their staff's communication products on an exception basis. That is, the manager discusses products that are below expectations with the staff person involved, and they agree on recommendations for improvement. Similarly, the manager recognizes outstanding work by phone and letter.

Evaluate how well your staff works to achieve its goals by using the problem-solving process to identify problem areas and develop solutions. Start with a list of questions. Who are the members of the staff? What are their responsibilities? How well do they carry them out? For each staff person:

- Are skills up to par? Where is remedial work necessary?
- Is his or her knowledge of the organization and the job satisfactory? What are the apparent weak areas?
- Does the person have the tools and facilities to do the job well?
- Are the resources (time and budgets) available to support this staff person?
- Does local management support the effort, or is it uncooperative?
- Is the person enthusiastic and supportive of communication policies and objectives?

Based on the analysis, determine who needs what kind of help. Build that into your workshop agenda or deal with it on an individual basis. In some cases, you may be able to provide assistance directly by supplying information that has been missing or by interceding with local management for better support or more resources. In any case, you should communicate your concerns to your staff and let them know your plan of action. You should poll your staff periodically to discover their concerns and recommendations. Once they see that you're supportive in their efforts, they'll support you in yours.

The Problem Is You

We cannot take all the blame for the problems that face us as communicators, but we often *are* a part of the problem. We should be aware of ourselves and the part we play in making communication happen in our organization—or keeping it from happening.

Many of us build boxes for ourselves and never venture outside the boundaries of our box. We limit ourselves, our capabilities and our potential for growth. Think about it. How many times have you stopped yourself from doing something that would help your organization either because you thought you couldn't get support for it or because it wasn't in your job description? If any of the following apply to you, you should consider the problem and understand its effect on you and your organization:

1. Do you limit your contacts in the organization to those you receive permission to see? An effective communicator must have access to all the sources of news. If you're limiting yourself, you're limiting the effectiveness of your program.
2. Do you believe you've seen it all or read it all so that you don't need

to continue your education about how people and organizations work and what's happening in our field? If that's the case, time is probably passing you by while you are putting out the publication.

3. Is it your attitude that organizations generally take advantage of people, and so your role is to represent the downtrodden masses with the unfeeling captains of industry? You're probably not very happy in your job, aren't trusted by management, and know from experience that every organization is that way—at least it's been that way everywhere you've worked.

4. Are you frightened by the phenomenal technological advances that have taken place in our field and not confident you can master them or manage some smart aleck who can? You probably have managed, then, to convince your management that video is a fad and feedback will just cause people to get upset. How long will you be able to hold out?

Ideally, each of us knows areas where we can do better. It is our responsibility to develop a plan to improve in those areas. Our profession is not an easy one. We need to know so much about how people think, how they interact, what various media can do at what cost, how to build surveys and select representative samples, how to train supervisors in interpersonal communication, and on and on and on. So it is important for us to keep learning and keep talking with one another, both in our organizations and in our professional associations. The key is knowing what we know, knowing what we don't know, and knowing how or where to find the information.

The communicator's role in an organization has to do with helping management achieve organizational goals through communication. If you have a communication policy and objectives and a plan to meet those objectives, you are far ahead of many of your peers. You'll avoid many of the problems they'll face. If you can find a problem-solving process that works for you and use that process in your work, you'll be still farther ahead. Finally, if you can identify some other successful communicators and share your experiences and problems with them periodically, you'll find help in solving even the insurmountable problem.

Frederic Halperin, ABC, is a communication consultant at Hewitt Associates in Rowayton, Connecticut. He is accredited by the International Association of Business Communicators.

CHAPTER 16

Legal Considerations

FRANK WALSH, JD, APR

Now and in the foreseeable future, communication law will continue to change frequently and expand into new areas. The once stable laws of libel and privacy continue in extremely uncertain patterns as communicators strive to sort different standards of malice and fault. The significantly improved U.S. copyright code awaits judicial interpretation. Canadian officials say their 56-year-old copyright law needs updating. The impact of legal guidelines into the fields of discriminatory language and practices, as well as restrictions on the use of political information in employee publications, need the 1980s for clarification.

Although general mass communication law sets the patterns, the courts have seen a significant difference between the primary purpose of the "commercial press" and organizational communication. The primary purpose of the organizational communicator's tools, according to the courts, is to serve the business and commercial needs of the sponsor. Some courts have even classified the use of these tools as a form of institutional advertising. The law in the United States does not give advertising the full measure of First Amendment protections, as it does "commercial press" news.

While the relationship of communicator and attorney will grow closer in the coming years, communicators will need to exercise sound legal judgment based on their personal knowledge. In areas like financial reporting, they should always seek advice before publishing.

Libel *

Organizational communicators and their organizations are as open to claims of libel as mass media reporters and their publishers or owners

---

* *Libel* as used in this chapter concerns itself with civil libel. Any consideration of criminal libel would have little or no application to organizational communicators.

are. In fact, such claims are increasingly more frequent. The cost of a libel suit can be high, including damage awards, loss of company and personal reputation, and legal costs. Defamation consists of both slander and libel. Slander is limited to verbal communications; libel includes broadcast materials as well as other fixed forms of communication.

Legislatures and courts have defined libel in a variety of ways, but they all focus on a person's or organization's reputation. An acceptable definition is "a *publication* which tends to impugn the honesty, virtue or reputation, alleges mental or physical defects of a *person* and thereby exposes him to public hatred, contempt or ridicule." The primary elements in any libel are publication, identification (person), and defamation or damage (e.g., impugn honesty). A discussion of these elements should give you a clearer understanding of the "dangerous words" concept.

Publication, the first element in any libel, occurs at the time a third party—a single person or many—is exposed to the libelous material. Thus the dictation of a letter to a secretary, or an employee bulletin that is called back from the mailroom, completes the publication element. Communicators must think more broadly than the news columns of their newspapers or broadcasts. Advertisements, editorials, letters to the editor, headlines, cutlines, photos and cartoons may all contain libelous material. Perhaps more extreme, but still well within the context of publication, are posters, statues or other three-dimensional forms, and physical acts such as hanging a person in effigy.

Little protection is offered the communicator who libels by mistake. Take, for example, the caption identifying four employees that ends up under a photo of four horses. The amount of damages might be limited, but the libel would probably stand.

The "one publication rule," simply stated, means that a person is libeled only once, even though the particular edition of the publication may have a distribution of thousands. If a communicator picks up a story from another publication and runs it in his own, however, the new publication constitutes a new libel.

Identification is the second of the three elements of libel. Generally, identification means that a particular individual (in contrast to a large group) feels the loss of reputation, public hatred, comtempt or ridicule. Generally an individual or small group may succeed in a libel suit, but groups larger than fifty persons cannot. Persons in the larger groups have not been able to convince the court that as individuals they have suffered a loss of reputation.

In some instances involving libel, a full identification is necessary so that no more than the single individual can claim injury. For example, an employee was killed in an automobile accident and you run a story about it in a company publication, saying, "According to police officers at the scene of the accident, John Williams was at fault in the accident which killed Peter Alexander, a 15-year employee of ——— company." You may well have complete defense for any suit by John Williams, the driver of the car, but what about any other John Williams who may be injured by the story? In cases such as this, make complete identification in the story—name, age and address—to remove any chance of others being damaged by the story.

Somewhat more unusual, but still sufficient to constitute identification, is the identification of persons by personal characteristics, job position or responsibilities, or other circumstances or traits. The following quote provides circumstance for identification: "One of our employees had seven accidents in the past year. We surely . . ." More than likely, some other employees know the identification of this person.

On the other side of the identification element lies the possibility that a story is written so broadly that a wide range of persons might be included. If this is the case, the group may be too large for any one person to succeed in a libel action.

While individuals bring the majority of libel suits, corporations, products, partnerships, nonprofits and charitable and community institutions may bring libel suits on behalf of injured reputations. As competition between corporations and products becomes more intense, this form of libel may become more common.

Defamation or *damages* means the word or words that cause loss of reputation are interpreted into an amount of money (damages). It is impossible to list all the words, actions or graphics which may constitute a loss of reputation, but some general categories are:

- Word(s) suggesting professional incompetency, such as "quack" in referring to a medical person, "idea-stealer" referring to a supervisor, or "should be pushing a broom rather than sitting behind a drafting board" in referring to an engineer.
- Word(s) suggesting dishonesty, such as "hustler," "on the take," "buys his way to the top," or "writes his best fiction while filling out his tax return."
- Word(s) suggesting sexual impropriety, such as "affair," "homosexual," "loose," "keeps her job with off-duty favors" or the "office camp follower."

- Word(s) suggesting mental or physical condition, such as "mental breakdown" or alcoholism, or suggesting a venereal disease such as gonorrhea.

Any of these defamatory words or phrases can result in damages that are translated in monetary awards. The three most common classifications of damages are

1. *General or compensatory damages:* relating to loss of reputation, shame, hurt feelings, embarrassment and pain and suffering, all intangible claims. General damage awards are often high, sometimes hundreds of thousands of dollars.
2. *Special or actual damages:* relating to tangible loss such as hospital bills or loss of salary of clients. These damages must be proven to the court and usually are out-of-pocket expenses only.
3. *Punitive damages:* the additional damages assessed by the court as punishment for the libel. They may be extremely high and are assessed by the court for intentional libel or libeling with malice. While "mistake" is not a defense to libel in some states, a full retraction often prevents recovery of punitive damages.

The defenses for libel are broad and changing, so communicators need to keep current on the changes. The defenses are truth, privilege, fair comment and the *New York Times* rule.

Truth provides a complete defense against libel in most states. Truth is a significant defense for communicators, but also contains some limitations. First, truth must be shown by the defendant—the communicator. This is not always easy to do, especially if the libel is in the area of such loosely used words or phrases as "near bankruptcy," "rips off customers" or "is close to a nervous breakdown." The second limitation is that "truth" is not the same as "accuracy." The communicator may accurately quote a source. If the statement is libelous, the accuracy of the quote does not relieve the communicator. What often takes place is that the communicator and the source become joint defendants.

Privilege gives the communicator an increasingly important defense. Communicators have the defense of "qualified privilege." It is based on accurately and without malice reporting statements and activities of officials who, because of their public positions, have "absolute privilege." Absolute privilege is the right, regardless of the nature, to be free from claim of libel. It is ordinarily limited to such persons or situations as judges and judicial proceedings, counsel, litigating parties and witnesses, legislators and legislative proceedings and members of the executive branch of government while acting in their official capacities.

This defense becomes increasingly important to communicators as government involvement with business increases. The defense is "qualified" to the communicator to the extent that reports on the "absolute privilege" situations are substantially accurate and without malice. The substantially accurate qualification sometimes creates a problem for communicators because often the testimony, court orders or decrees, or bills and resolutions are stated in legal jargon and are not easily understood by the communicator. The communicator has the responsibility to seek clarification of the material before writing the story.

Fair comment gives the communicator the right to make fair and reasonable comments upon matters of legitimate interest to the public. While the natural targets for fair comment are entertainers (e.g., actors, singers, athletes), politicians, community leaders and various public and private institutions whose activities have an impact on the community may be included within fair comment. The comment may be cruel but may still be fair, according to court cases. The communicator should limit comment to those areas of the activity or person that are public, however. If a communicator is reviewing a play at a theater to which the company ordinarily offers discount tickets, the writer may comment on an actor's acting, his physical characteristics, and even past performances. If the reviewer strays into the personal life of the actor, which is out of the public interest, the reviewer may lose the fair comment defense.

The *New York Times* or *malice rule* provides the communicator with the broadest of libel defenses. It states that the First Amendment

> prohibits a public official from recovering damages for a defamatory falsehood relating to his official conduct unless he proves that the statement was made with "actual malice"—that is, with knowledge that it was false or with reckless disregard of whether it was false or not.

While the rule originally applied to public officials, subsequent rulings expanded the "public" category to include persons classified as public figures or involved in public issues. The rule is currently applied differently for public and private individuals. An understanding of the current application begins with a more specific definition of public and private individuals:

A public may be (1) the kind of individual who achieves persuasive fame or notoriety, or may occupy a position of such persuasive power and influence that he is deemed a public figure for all purposes and in all contexts, or (2) the kind of person who assumes some special prominence in the resolution of public questions. The person may voluntary inject himself into a particular issue or involuntarily is "drawn into" the issue.

Examples of persons declared to be public by court cases include an urban real estate developer who was negotiating with city officials to obtain zoning variances, a former professional basketball player who was engaged in coaching basketball, the author of a bestselling book, a famous baseball player, a renowned chemistry professor, a doctor involved in planning a space flight involving a monkey, and a minister and his church. The court appears to be tightening the public category. A university professor researching the behavior of monkeys under a government grant and an individual convicted of criminal contempt and sentenced to a jail term have been deemed "private individuals."

Persons deemed public must show actual malice on the part of the communicator before they can collect damages. As stated, malice is the knowledge of falsity or the reckless disregard of whether it is false. In additional rulings the court has interpreted malice to mean "extreme departure" from acceptable reporting standards. An important consideration for the courts has been the time the publication has to check the factualness of the material.

Private individuals are, for the most part, exempted from the actual malice test. The court has left it to the states to set a standard of fault to use in libel cases involving private persons. Three primary standards have been adopted by several states:

1. *Reckless disregard test.* This is the same as the "actual malice" standard first provided in the *New York Times* cases and applies to public persons as well as private persons. Only Indiana and Colorado have adopted this standard.

2. *Gross negligence test.* Basically it means the plaintiff must establish by a preponderance of the evidence that the publisher acted in a grossly irresponsible manner without due consideration for the standards of information gathering and dissemination followed by responsible parties. To date, this standard has been adopted only in New York.

3. *Ordinary negligence tests.* This is the standard most frequently

adopted by the states. Ordinarily this standard means the failure of a communicator to exercise reasonable or due care in ascertaining the truth. The states not listed above have either adopted the ordinary negligence test or have not yet made a recent ruling on the subject.

Privacy

Privacy is particularly relevant to organizational communicators, and applications of the law do not always parallel those of the commercial media. Privacy is a catchall civil remedy consisting of four actions that are often confused with, and overlap with, defamation, contract rights, property rights, copyright interests and right of publicity. However, this does not leave the business communicator without some ground rules.

The starting place for the organizational communicator is his own state. Only a few states—New York, California, Oklahoma, Utah, Virginia and Wisconsin—have statutes recognizing privacy. Currently, thirty-five states and the District of Columbia have recognized some kind of privacy rights through court decisions. The U.S. federal courts have also recognized an action for the invasion of a person's privacy. An overview of statutes and court decisions generally shows four activities that can lead to an action for invasion of privacy:

1. *Intrusion into a person's solitude,* including the use of microphones or cameras, has been held to be actionable. A person's home, office, desk and file cabinets are some of the physical locations held to be private. Intrusion by means of wiretaps, telephoto lenses or microphones also have been held to be actionable.

2. *Public disclosure of embarrassing private facts* about a person has been held to be accountable. A publication may win a defamation case based on the defense of "truth," but lose on grounds that truth may not be a defense for a privacy action based on public disclosure of embarrassing private facts. However, if the material is part of a privileged public record, the publication is generally protected regardless of invasion of privacy. Health matters such as sicknesses or disease, financial condition, family matters and criminal activity that may not have resulted in any official action are examples of embarrassing private facts.

3. *Publicity that places a person in a false light* in the public's eye is also actionable. Photos that give, or are used in such a way that they

give, a misleading impression of a person's character are especially vulnerable to false light actions. False light also has the concept of "fictionalization" contained within it, the deliberate or reckless addition of untrue materials, perhaps for entertainment purposes or to make a good story better. Beware when "jazzing up" or "sensationalizing" a story.

4. *Appropriation of a person's name or likeness* has led to many privacy lawsuits and presents the organizational communicator with the greatest privacy danger. An extension of the appropriation action is the "right of publicity." Both these actions simply mean that a person's name, likeness or photograph has value to the individual, and before it can be used commercially, the individual must agree to the use. The balancing factors to these invasions of privacy are the generally accepted defenses. The most frequently stated offenses are

 a. *The newsworthiness of the event* or activity, which makes it of public interest. The courts have defined "news" in a variety of ways, but perhaps the best for organizational communicators is the definition that states: "news is whatever interests the public."

 b. *Consent by the person* to use the information.

 c. *The public figure concept*, which is the application of the "actual malice" rule to privacy.

This overview of privacy applies primarily to the commercial press. The law most often sees the organizational communicator's tools—the organization's media—in somewhat different light. Of the four recognized privacy actions, appropriation presents a far greater threat to the organizational communicator than the other three. Rarely would an organizational communicator invade a person's solitude, publicize private facts or place a person in a false light.

The same is true of the privacy defenses. Because the organizational communicator's tools do not generally fall within the protection of the First Amendment, the actual malice rule does not often apply and newsworthiness has only limited application. So, the greatest protection is the concept of consent.

Canadian law also provides for personal privacy but in a significantly different manner than in the United States. Invasion of privacy at the federal level in Canada is a criminal offense. The statute makes it a criminal act to possess or use eavesdropping equipment without the consent of the police.

Only at the province level is a civil action available to the citizen. And as with most Canadian laws, the law will vary from province to province. There are some parallels at the province level to United States privacy law. For example, the Manitoba statute provides for an invasion of privacy for either audio or visual surveillance with or without trespass, for the appropriation of a person's name or image for commercial purpose and for the use of a person's personal documents. These are similar to intrusion, use of personal facts and appropriation in the United States.

Canadian law provides for either implied or written consent as a defense. However, news is not as strong a defense and there has not been any special protection given to the publications in their coverage of "public" persons as there has been in the United States.

While the general protection of privacy in Canada is by federal and provincial statutes, there is a possibility of a common law privacy action. According to Canadian officials, this possibility rests on the belief that there is an increasing need for the protection of personal privacy and the courts may well move to provide the additional protection.

Organizational communicators should use a story-by-story approach to determine if there are any privacy problems. While this may seem a rather burdensome task, remember that as long as an organizational communicator does not go beyond the limits of normal reporting and interest and is generally accurate (these eliminate physical intrusion, publication of private matters and falsification), the only concern is appropriation.

Consider these examples of stories in an employee publication distributed internally, and assume that for some reason the employee considered them to be an invasion of his or her privacy:

- A photo and name of an employee demonstrating the safe way to operate a particular machine
- A photo of the three top bowlers of a company's bowling league
- A story naming an employee as the winner of a company contest

More than likely, these stories would qualify for the defense of "news" because of the general interest in the information. However, if the same employee publication ran a story promoting a specific product of the company (or the company in general) that used an employee's name or photo, it probably would be appropriation because the information would be considered commerce, trade or advertising. If an article could be used as a direct mail piece for a product or company, or added to a salesperson's portfolio, the article falls into the appropriation category.

Because so much of what an organizational communicator produces falls close to or into the appropriation area, consent is the most important defense.

Implied consent has limited value but has been effective when a written release was not used. An implied consent exists when circumstances exist that make the employee (or member or volunteer) aware of the probable use of the material, and he or she does not object at the time. For instance, if an employee took part in a company skit, during which the company photographer took photos and asked for the correct spelling of names for use in a caption, the employee has given implied consent to use the photo and name. The employee has the right to revoke consent at any time, however.

Consent to use a person's name or likeness needs several requirements to be valid. Among the requirements are the following:

1. *It must be written.* Several court cases and all states having privacy statutes require that consent to use information or likenesses be in writing.

2. *Proper parties.* The organization's representative and the person whose name, photo or other information is going to be used must be included in the consent form. If the person is a minor, the parents or guardian are considered one of the proper parties, along with the name of the minor. While states vary between 18 and 21 years as the age of consent, the use of 21 will make your consent form safe. In rare instances, agents are authorized to give consent for the subject involved. For the organizational communicator's protection, ask for a copy of the agreement showing that the agent has such authority.

3. *Consideration* is the legal term used to describe value given for something received. If a person gives you the use of his or her name, photo or other information, the organization has the legal obligation to give the person something of value in return. The courts are not concerned whether the exchange is fair, but they do require an exchange to make the consent irrevocable. Without consideration, the party permitting the use of his or her name or photo may revoke consent even if the organization has spent a considerable amount of money for the use of the information. Consideration may be $1 at the time of signing the consent release. Another form of consideration is to include other interests as part of the consent release. This is the preferred form when consent is part of an employment form.

4. *Scope* describes the intended use of the information. For organi-

zational uses, the description of the intended use should be broad both in terms of actual use and who may use the information. It is not unusual for a company to want to release a photo to the National Safety Council or to an industrial association. In order to do this safely, the release should give the organization the right to release the material to assignees, transferees, subsidiaries or licensees.

5. *Duration of release* indicates that there should be a length of time during which the content is valid—a specific term of years or a terminal date. Five years is not an unreasonable term, although courts have upheld much longer terms. In the case of an employee, the term is usually the length of employment or shorter if stated in the release. It is generally accepted that consent given by an employee terminates with the conclusion of employment.

6. *Words binding on personal representatives* should be part of the release to make the release binding on the heirs or on any other persons who may succeed to the rights of the person, though this particular element has limited application for the business communicator. If an employee dies, employment is terminated and so is the consent to use the information. Such words are appropriate for a celebrity hired to help the organization for a promotion.

7. *If possible, tie the release to parts of a broader agreement.* This is not unusual in contracts of employment where the employee agrees to several terms and salary or wages act as "consideration." Some nonprofit organizations use this method when registering patients or clients or participants. The following is a part of a contract by an organization sponsoring a golf tournament:

> Sponsor may use golf pro's name and picture for the reasonable promotion of the golf event and for no other purposes whatsoever. It is specifically understood that Sponsor shall make no use of the name or likeness of golf pro which would constitute or amount to an endorsement of any particular company, product, product category or service. It is further understood by Sponsor that nothing continued herein shall be deemed to authorize the granting of any radio or television rights, nor shall Sponsor have the right to sell any photograph, motion picture file or illustration involving golf pro.

8. Another consideration is that the organizational communicator should state in the release that no other *inducements, statements or promises* were made to the person permitting the use of the information. Such a statement prevents the person from saying additional promises were made that were not included in the release.

The model consent form shown in figure 16.1 fulfills the requirements of consent being in writing, including the proper parties, consideration, scope, duration and no other inducements, and makes it binding on representatives. The form applies to an employee but could be adjusted to others by leaving the reference to employee off the form. It could be modified to be part of a broader agreement.

FIGURE 16.1 Model Consent Release

In consideration of the sum of _____ dollar(s) and other valuable considerations, the receipt of which is hereby acknowledged, I certify I am twenty-one years of age and hereby give [organization's name], its successors and assigns and those acting under its permission or upon its authority, the unqualified right and permission to reproduce, copyright, publish, circulate or otherwise use photographic reproductions or likenesses of me and/or my name. This authorization and release covers the use of said material in any published form, and any medium of advertising, publicity or trade in any part of the world for an unlimited period of time or as long as I am an employee of said organization.

Furthermore, for the consideration above-mentioned, I, for myself, my heirs, executors, administrators or assigns, transfer to the organization, its successors and assigns, all my rights, title, and interests in and to all reproductions taken of me by representatives of the organization. This agreement represents in full all terms and considerations and no other inducements, statements or promises have been made to me.

Signature _____

Date _____

While this model consent release provides most of the requirements of a valid release form, each person and organization should consider circumstances special to the particular organization before designing a consent form. As written, this model consent release may or may not provide adequate protection.

Copyright Law

The U.S. copyright law of January 1, 1978, now parallels the Berne Copyright Union, an international agreement followed by most of the leading countries of the world. Under it, American and foreign authors receive substantially the same protection regardless of the country of publication.

Copyright Protection

The law provides statutory copyright protection as soon as a work is created in fixed form. For example, as soon as a story leaves the typewriter it has copyright protection. Nevertheless, formal steps have to be completed before the author has judicial remedies for infringement.

The duration of copyright protection is 50 years plus the life of the author. As a general rule, the life-plus-50-year term applies to unpublished works, to works published during the author's lifetime and to works published posthumously. For the organizational communicator, there is an important exception to the life-plus-50-year rule. "Works made for hire" have copyright protection for 75 years from the first year of publication or 100 years from the year of creation, whichever is shorter. If an organizational communicator writes an article for the company magazine as part of his or her job, the copyright is vested in the company. If the article is written in 1980 but not published in the company magazine until 1981, the copyright protection extends to 2056, or 75 years from the year of publication. When a person works full-time for an organization, the law is clear that the copyright on material created for the organization belongs to the organization, whether the employee is a writer, photographer, artist or in any other creative position.

Problems sometimes occur when a person works for an organization on a freelance basis. When an organizational communicator hires a photographer or other creative person on a freelance basis, it should be made clear from the beginning to whom the copyright belongs. In the case of freelance work, ownership of the copyright is negotiable. A letter of agreement should state clearly the intent of the organization: simply to buy the first use of the material or all uses.

Informal protection of works extends only to the time of publication. As defined in the statute, publication means

> the distribution of copies or phonorecords of a work to the public or sale or other transfer of ownership. Or by rental, lease, or lending. The offering to distribute copies or phonorecords to a group of persons for purposes of further distribution, public performance, or public display constitutes publication.

Once publication has occurred, formal steps must be taken to maintain copyright protection. The initial formal step is copyright notice, though there is a five-year grace period after publication before the copyright notice is required. If the material does not display the usual elements of copyright by the end of the five-year grace period after publication, it becomes part of the public domain, available for use by anyone without recourse by the author. Notice of copyright simply means that three traditional elements of copyright must appear in an obvious position on the work:

> The letter "c" in a circle, or the word "Copyright" or the abbreviation "Copr."; the year of the first publication of the work; and the name of the owner of the copyright

The other two formal steps are deposit of material and registration. In the United States, the owner of a copyrighted work that has been published and that displays notice should deposit two copies of the publication with the Copyright Office, Library of Congress, Washington, D.C. 20559, within three months of the date of publication. Registration is not a condition of copyright protection but it is a prerequisite to an infringement action. There is copyright protection from the time of a work's creation, but the work must be registered before the infringement action can be pursued in the courts. Only one copy is needed to register an unpublished work or two complete copies of a published work. Application forms are free and available through the Copyright Office. The fee is $10.

Fair Use Versus Infringement

The copyright law gives guidelines to help decide whether a specific use of a work is a copyright infringement or "fair use." A general statement in the statute defines infringement as anything that "violates any of the exclusive rights of the copyright owner." The courts have the power to issue injunctions, impound and dispose of infringement articles and award monetary damages as means of enforcement of the statute. A person who infringes a copyright willfully and for "purposes of commercial advantage or private financial gain" risks a fine of $10,000 or imprisonment for not more than a year, or both.

Fair use, including such reproduction of records, may be made for "purposes such as criticism, comment, news reporting, teaching (including multiple copies for classroom use), scholarship or research." To determine whether the use of a work in any particular case is fair use, the statute offers four guidelines: (1) the purpose and character of the use, including whether such is of a commercial nature; (2) the nature of the copyright work; (3) the amount and substantiality of a portion used in relation to the copyrighted work as a whole; (4) and the effect of the use on potential market for, or value of, the copyrighted work. The House of Representatives report on the copyright law indicates that more words may be used from a novel than from a poem and that the scope of the fair use doctrine should be "narrower in the case of newsletters than in that of either mass-circulation periodicals or scientific journals."

Permission to use copyrighted material is usually easy to obtain. Write the owner of the material and indicate exactly what you would like to use, how it will be used, and what credit line will be included. The letter should indicate whether the organization is profit or not for profit. The holder of the copyright can then respond, indicating permission or requesting a certain amount of payment for the use intended.

Organizational communicators should not confuse copyright with the protection of "patent" or with the concept of plagiarism. Patent is the legal protection provided to a process or method rather than something in a fixed form, a requirement of copyright. Plagiarism is an ethical rather than legal concept. If a piece of material is within the "public domain," a communicator has the legal right to use it. If he or she does not attribute the source of the material, however, the ethical concept of plagiarism is violated. Most often, attribution of the source of the material is sufficient to remove any consideration of plagiarism.

The 1924 Canadian copyright act has strong parallels with the copyright code of the United States. The parallels stem from both countries following the international Berne Copyright Union provisions. As in the United States, there is only one federal Canadian copyright law. Officials indicate that the half-century-old copyright law is outdated in several aspects and has been under study for statutory updating. The need for updating comes from new and advanced technology, which the current law does not take into consideration. Two such obvious advances not covered by the current law are the copying machine and cable television.

Government Regulations

The reach of government into organizations of every kind continues to grow. Statutes, executive orders, commissions and regulations have proliferated and the communicator's office has not been missed. Three specific areas are of increasing concern for the organizational communicator: labor relations, discriminatory language and political information.

Labor Relations

The provisions of the 1935 National Labor Relations Act (Wagner Act) and the 1947 Labor Management Relations Act (Taft-Hartley Act), together with the decisions of the National Labor Relations Board (NLRB) and the courts enforcing, interpreting or implementing these statutes, provide the organizational communicator with guidelines for employer-employee communication relating to labor issues.

The labor laws and court decisions restrict an employer from engaging in a free dialog with employees and the public during a time of labor stress. The restrictions are aimed at preventing coercion of employees in the exercise of their rights. The basic law applying to employer communication is Section 8(c) of the Labor Management Relations Act:

> The expressing of any view, argument, or opinion or the dissemination thereof, whether in written, printed graphic or visual form, shall not constitute or be evidence of an unfair labor practice under any of the provision of this Act, if such expression contains no threat of reprisal or force or promise of benefit.

While the section is written in the context of "free speech," the tendency of the NLRB and the courts has been to interpret and apply the exceptions, "threat of reprisal or force" and "promise of benefit" phrases. Communications are not to be judged in isolation but are looked at in the "totality of conduct" of the employer toward employees. The "totality of conduct" concept means that the NLRB will look at the overall relationship of labor and management to see the context of the communication for interpretations. Specific cases provide examples to help organizational communicators know what is and is not a communication that would be judged an unfair labor practice under the act. The unfair labor practice singled out in one case was management's communicating offers directly to workers independently of the union. The company also issued a statement indicating its best and final offer with a deadline for acceptance suggesting that negotiation with the union was not needed. Other company statements held illegal under the act are an attempt to discredit the representatives of a certified union; letters to employees denying a union's authority as bargaining representatives; a clear statement that employees will not bargain with the union even if it wins the election; a statement that a plant would be closed before the employer would bargain with a union; a firm statement that working hours will be reduced (resulting in less weekly pay) if the plant is unionized; and an implication that continued employment was dependent upon rejection of the union.

The following examples indicate what an employer may communicate, although it may lose the right if joined with other matters which, combined, would make the communication unfair under the "totality of conduct" concept. An employer may generally issue public statements, make speeches or circulate printed materials about the company's wage policies, fringe benefits or other practices. It may answer union arguments or charges against the company, point out that union membership is not a requirement for continued employment, justify company action against specific employees in the union, explain to employees or the public generally the effect of a strike, explain the price structure of the employer and its inability to make a higher wage offer, and indicate company preference for one union rather than another.

Canadian law also provides regulations in the area of management-union communication with employees. The Canadian law provides for a Canadian Labour Relations Board that deals with federal organizations such as banking, airlines and railroads. The provinces provide labor relations boards to cover the vast amount of the workforce.

At either level of Canadian government, the labor relations boards may find circumstances which amount to an "unfair labour practice." If such a practice is established, the board may issue a restraining order to stop the activity and suggest specific remedial steps. Activities which have been found to be "unfair labour practices" include coercion, interference with the formation or administration of a union, or the interference of the representation of employees by a union.

The use of organizational publications by management may help establish an "unfair labour practice" in any one of these areas, according to Canadian officials.

Discriminatory Language

Government has become increasingly involved in efforts to eliminate discrimination on the basis of sex, race, color or national origin and in the areas of salaries, fringe benefits and promotion. Statutes, executive orders and commissions provide the basis for nondiscriminatory practices. Some that the organizational communicator should become aware of are the U.S. Equal Pay Act of 1963, Title VII (the Civil Rights Act of 1964, amended in 1972), the U.S. Equal Employment Opportunity Commission, the U.S. Fair Employment Practices Commission and the U.S. Department of Labor. While these are not all the statutes or commissions that may affect the organizational communicator, they are the trend-setters.

Typical of the language being enforced by the various commissions is that of Section 704(*b*) of Title VII:

> It shall be unlawful employment practice for an employer . . . to print or publish or cause to be printed or published any notice or advertisement relating to employment . . . indicating any preference, limitation, specification, or discrimination, based on race, color, religion, sex, or national origin, except that such a notice or advertisement may indicate a preference, limitation, specification or discrimination based on religion, sex, or national origin when religion, sex, or national origin is a bona fide occupational qualification for employment.

While a complaint may be based on discriminatory language contained in an organization's literature, more than likely an organization's literature will be only a part of the commission's or court's review of a complaint. The organizational communicator should know that his or her publication may well be one part of the evidence considered in a hearing on discriminatory complaint.

An excellent source to help organizational communicators write nondiscriminatory copy is IABC's *Without Bias: A Guidebook for Nondiscriminatory Communication*. It contains numerous examples of writing that shows bias and ways to rewrite them without bias. A communicator following this guide should not have to worry about organizational publications being used as evidence of discrimination.

Canada provides both federal and provincial protection from discriminatory language. As with most Canadian law, the federal level handles only those organizations such as banking, airlines and railroads. In these instances, the Federal Human Rights Commission hears complaints. The federal commission covers about 15 percent of the workforce. Provincial Human Rights Commissions cover the remainder of the workforce.

While provincial commissions vary in their statutory authority, they all seek to provide equal opportunity for Canadian citizens, according to Canadian authorities. They also say that while there has not been as much attention about discriminatory language in Canada as in the United States, it is important. As an example of importance, one official indicates that references to sexual or racial bias in organizational publications would become part of a human rights violation investigation.

Political Information

Organizational communicators have established a rich tradition of providing employees and others with information about election candidates and issues. They must know and follow the Federal Election Commission (FEC) and FEC Regulations, and the guidelines provided by the Federal Election Campaign Act as amended in 1976. In general, the act and regulations apply only to federal elections and to profit-making organizations. Partisan communications to the general employee body are prohibited. Nonpartisan communication, in both corporations and labor organizations, is permitted under certain conditions.

Corporations may permit presidential and congressional candidates, their representatives or representatives of political parties on corporate premises to address or meet employees as long as other candidates for the same offices and representatives of all political parties are given the same opportunity. There can be no effort, either oral or written, to solicit or direct control of contributions by members of the audience in conjunction with the appearance, and there can be no endorsement or support of one particular candidate, group of candidates or particular party.

Posters, newsletters or other communication can be published by a corporation to urge employees to register and vote or otherwise participate in the political process if

- The communication is restricted to urging such acts as contributing, voting and registering and describing the hours and places of registration and voting.
- The communication gives the entire list of names and political affiliations of candidates on the official ballot, not one particular candidate or party.
- Voter guides or other brochures describing the candidates and their positions do not favor one candidate or political party over another, and the materials obtained from civic or other nonprofit organiza-

tions cannot endorse or support or have affiliation with any candidate or political party.

- Nonpartisan distribution of reprints of any registration or voting information, such as instructional materials, are produced by the official election administrators for distribution to the general public.

Corporations may support nonpartisan registration and get-out-the-vote drives and even transport persons to the polls if the services are made available without regard to the voter's political preference. A corporation may also donate funds for nonpartisan registration and get-out-the-vote drives to civic and other nonprofit organizations that do not endorse candidates or political parties, and a civic or nonprofit organization in conducting such political activities may utilize the employees and facilities of corporations.

The laws involving business and organizational communication are complex and ever-changing. Communicators cannot afford to be complacent about them. They should know and confer with attorneys versed in the nuances of communication and law.

Frank Walsh, JD, APR, is associate professor of journalism at Ball State University, Muncie, Indiana. He is accredited by the Public Relations Society and is a member of the Montana Bar Association.

CHAPTER 17

Feedback for Evaluation and Information

ROGER FEATHER, ABC

Organizations, particularly in their formal communication systems, often think of feedback as a program to allow an upward communication flow and, in that sense, to provide a monitoring system for organizational attitudes. But feedback in organizations is really much more than a program. It is a concept rooted in an organization's attitude—and primarily in the attitude of its senior management. When the concerns and feelings of each individual within an organization are important, the concept is positive. Effective feedback is the result when that attitude prevails.

Feedback is at the heart of humane, sophisticated management systems. It is also at the heart of the new demands by persons in the workplace and society in general. That demand is for individuals to be heard and recognized. This may well be the central issue in effective communication in the 1980s and beyond.

There are a number of ways to stimulate and improve the quality of feedback; but no method, however well launched and executed, can overcome a management or organizational attitude that gives the impression, "We don't care what they say or feel, we'll still do it our way." Feedback requires an open atmosphere and action resulting from the openness. When people within an organization participate, and have expectations that their participation will be meaningful, they want things to happen. And when things do not happen as a result of their efforts and participation, positive feedback quickly dries up. The efforts to promote involvement become counterproductive and damaging.

Candor depends on an organization's having a strong sense of itself, its direction, and the parts that come together to make it work. With the knowledge of roles firmly in place, and the will to talk openly about

Effective communication involves give and take. Management may use a variety of techniques to get a message to employees, who in turn may take advantage of other programs to send messages back.

those roles, organizations can come to grips with some of the real and important issues that involve people. They can talk about "why" things happen, rather than just "what" and "how."

The nature of the communicator's job should provide access to all parts of the organization. That is an asset and a privilege few others in the organization have. It should be used to advantage. To do an effective communication job, and particularly a valid job on feedback, the communicator must study the organization. The communicator must become an expert on its style, its audiences, its key personalities and their relationships with every segment of the organization. The communicator must ask some hard questions and find the answers. What does top management really believe in? How do they back up, or act out, the beliefs? Do they really want to know what's happening? How will they use the information? How much change, and what kind of change, is possible? Although the data are ever new and changing, when enough data have been digested, objectives and programs can be set or refined.

In building a plan for the communication function within an organization, the feedback element should be an integral part. It is not something that can be tagged on afterward. Sophisticated, detailed planning is not an easy or a fast task. The plan is something that is built up slowly and is constantly fine-tuned.

Feedback, by its nature, produces some surprises. It can surface issues and attitudes that were not known to exist. Some of these surprises can be difficult and even frightening. Generally, however, feedback merely confirms what you already know. If you know, for instance, that things are bad on a specific issue or in a general area, feedback is not going to tell you things are good. It can document and detail speculation, and that information can act as a valuable lever for producing meaningful change.

Feedback is often threatening to managers. Those who tend to be isolated are usually skeptical of negative feedback. Some are concerned that they will be blamed for the attitudes of their subordinates. The value of feedback, like the value of just about everything else, must be sold to management on the basis of, What's in it for me?

Feedback can surface problems and help solve them, but the results come slowly. It takes time to get an effective, two-way flow of communication in operation—and if it is starting in a neutral or negative climate, it takes more time. Feedback is a concept, not a program. This chapter describes ways to obtain feedback.

The Opinion Survey

Opinion surveys are the key method for getting feedback in organizations. They come in a variety of shapes and sizes, but all are designed to find out what people feel or think; to find out their perceptions of the organization. Other surveys measure behavior, or what a person does, but they do not deal with attitudes. The opinion survey is the way to get the best kind of information and, if it is collected, analyzed and used properly, the results can provide a solid base for far-reaching decisions in an organization.

Many people in charge of managing the communication function believe opinion surveys deserve the number-one priority in effort and budget considerations in a communication plan. Before a well-managed organization acts, it seeks out the best available information. In many areas of organizational operation, opinion surveys provide that information. These surveys can delve into the total workplace environment or be restricted to more specific areas but all, it seems, touch on communication within the organization.

FOR THE PEOPLE OF RAINIER BANCORPORATION   JANUARY 1980

Was anybody listening?

EMPLOYEE OPINION SURVEY

It was a year ago this month that 65 Rainier employees sat down to sift through the results of the Employee Opinion Survey and make their recommendations to senior managers.

It was a big job. More than 90 percent of Rainier people — 3,923 of them from every corner of the company — had voiced their opinions on everything from supervisors to safety. The responses were generally favorable — in fact, Rainier stacked up well as a place to work in the minds of most. But there were concerns, too, and employees said so.

Was anybody listening? ECHO polled each of Rainier's companies and divisions to find out what actions they have taken as a result of the survey.

See page 6 for our report.

Sue Schoeff
Editor

Survey results must be communicated fully as they can represent the most important communication effort of the year.

Who Does It and How

Although opinion surveys are a major communication tool, rarely should they be done by in-house communicators. The communicator should be involved at all stages—heavily involved in the latter stages of analyzing and circulating the results—but surveys should be done by people outside the organization or at least by a department not aligned with communication. An outside consultant brings a level and range of experience and expertise to the job that most communicators do not possess. Conducting surveys requires a sound knowledge of scientific research methodology, workplace psychology and computer technology.

The key asset an outsider brings to the job, though, is objectivity, the prime element in surveys. Potential survey respondents must be assured that their feedback is going through an independent and objective channel.

Because managements increasingly recognize the need to listen to employees, selling the idea of an opinion survey is not as difficult as it was a few years ago. In some organizations, however, there is still resistance. Some managements are afraid of surveys. Their objections are standard: we have trouble dealing successfully with the information already on hand; the cost is too high; it's just another toy; there's no beginning, middle or end to them; surveys raise expectations that cannot be fulfilled; management already knows what's going on "down there." In an organization where management doesn't care what employees think, there's hardly any point in even considering a list of objections.

In most organizations, both the communicator and the managers know the information is vital. But on a first survey, even when the management is inclined to see the value, it can take a long period of educating and selling—up to a year or two—to get the final go-ahead. When the green light flashes, many decisions must be made or confirmed before a survey can be conducted. A general purpose or theme has to be determined and, from that, a type of survey chosen.

Surveys can be custom-tailored for an organization or come off-the-shelf. Specially tailored surveys are becoming more popular, particulaly in mid-size or small organizations. They usually include some questions that normally appear in packaged surveys and that can be judged against established norms. Most questions, however, are developed from meetings with both employees or members and management. A group of employees might be asked, for instance, what they feel management should know about. Managers will be asked what they feel employees are concerned about. Survey questions are developed after these discussions or after these persons respond to the open-ended questions.

A survey targeted to a specific subject, such as communication or benefits, may have as few as 30 questions. For a broader-based survey, there may be 150 or more. After the questions are developed, they should be pretested for clarity and to ensure that management can act on them. This usually takes two to three weeks.

Packaged surveys sometimes allow space for questions of specific interest to the organization. Although the trend is away from long surveys, some packaged surveys covering broad areas have as many as 300 questions. It has been noted that long surveys can produce fatigue and loss of concentration long before they are completed.

An advantage of packaged surveys is that an organization can make judgments against a substantial normative data base. Norms can be misleading, however. For instance, general norms might indicate that 70 percent of the respondents feel an organization's communication is credible most of the time. If your rating comes in at 65 percent, some managers may feel that since it is only 5 percent below normal, it is acceptable.

Most survey questions are multiple-choice, offering four or five options. The choices range from "most" to "least," or some similar variation, and an "I don't know" option. Although the order in which questions are asked should have some rhythm, with easier questions generally at the beginning, the flow should not be obvious. Most questions are asked in a positive manner, but a few should be in a negative style to break the routine. Brief demographic information is usually asked at the beginning of the survey.

There should be questions at the end of the survey asking respondents whether they think the survey process is of value and whether they believe change will result from it. There should also be space for write-in comments. While these comments tend to be negative, they can be of great value.

In small organizations, the general practice is to survey everyone. Larger organizations usually survey only a randomly selected sample. However, those not sampled often feel left out, so everyone should be offered the opportunity to respond whenever possible. Random selection can be made by the last digits of social security numbers, or by having the computer select every third or sixth or "nth" person on the list, or by some other means. At the analysis stage, random selections have to be judged against the organization's basic demographics. Attempts to code survey forms will reduce the level or the honesty of responses dramatically unless the purpose of the coding is explained. The mere hint of an attempt to make personnel identification can invalidate survey data.

Surveys can either be mailed or filled out at work on company time or at meetings. The latter two, of course, will give close to 100 percent response, but they are extremely difficult to handle if there are more than 2,000 people in the organization or if the people are in a variety of locations. If surveys are completed on-site in the organization, the arrangements should be conducted by someone outside the organization. The response to surveys mailed to the home can vary widely. If proper explanations are given and good promotion is done in advance, responses can be as high as 70 percent or 80 percent. If the response is less than 50 percent, the quality of the results is usually suspect.

There should be advance promotion for any survey, and some of it should spell out very clearly why the survey is being conducted, what the benefits might be, how the results will be used and how they will be fed back to the respondents.

Making Survey Results Useful

Even with relatively small numbers of respondents, information from survey forms should be processed by a computer to save time and to easily and accurately obtain cross-reference data. Although questions are "scrambled" on survey forms to obtain more spontaneous answers, at the analysis stage they should be grouped under a few specific areas for analysis. The information should also be broken down by individual groups of respondents so that the groups can be compared against the overall response.

It takes time to get even initial results back—inevitably, more time than was estimated. Initial raw results can be misleading, but they are sometimes helpful for deciding how to feed back results. The time it takes to get full results plus an outside analysis varies greatly. It can take from three to six months or even longer from the time of the questionnaire for larger samples.

Both management and participants should be informed of the progress of the survey periodically. Reminders keep the idea of the survey in people's minds and let them know that their efforts are not being ignored.

Surveys produce vast amounts of material so long, intensive hours of analysis are needed to digest the material and put it into perspective. It must be compiled and selected so that the information can be presented in an easily understandable form. The selection should be honest and open, with back-up information available if requested. While one or two people from the organization may work with the outside person to prepare the results, the same basic results should go to everyone in the organization. Withholding information from participants, a common practice in many organizations until recently, runs counter to the concept of surveys as open feedback methods and can damage the credibility of an organization. Results must be communicated as fully as possible. A story in the organization's publication, however detailed, is not enough; a special edition, or insert, is only slightly better. Results should be communicated with special booklets, A/V programs, group meetings and any other methods available. Survey results can be the most important communication effort of the year.

Overall results from a survey may reveal that things are generally fine, with only one or two problem areas to deal with. Then again, the results may indicate a lot of negatives. They may be broad-based or as specific as pinpointing an incompetent individual manager. Before approving an attitude survey, the senior management of an organization must commit itself to back changes if the results required them. Where problems are indicated and changes aren't possible, management must explain why.

Sometimes, action can be taken quickly; sometimes, it's a slow process. But before any action is taken after the results are released, it is best to recheck the results with various levels of employees or members in small group meetings, in themselves feedback sessions that may also provide new interpretations of the results or indicate a lack of understanding about what the results mean.

Changes should not be made on the basis of survey results before some discussions are held. If changes are required, they should be explained fully, and it should be indicated that they are based on the survey. In fact, if changes are required at any time during the months of the survey process, reference should be made to the survey in the explanation. Without the direct reference, participants may imply that the organization disregards their feedback efforts.

Modern management sees attitude survey results as a legitimate form of upward communication requiring appropriate feedback downward. They are not for management's use only. Some organizations set up employee or member task forces to find solutions to problems identified in survey results.

Obviously, both big and little changes may seem to be required in the results. Don't get caught up in the big ones and ignore the little ones, as often happens. By making the little changes quickly, an organization indicates it is responding to the questions it poses.

Mini-Surveys

Mini-surveys on attitudes toward specific issues, or the behavior regarding a single event, can be very useful. They may not hold up to scientific scrutiny, however, and thus should be treated with some caution. They can bring in a lot of information at little expense.

A communicator should be able to get answers to two or three simple, brief questions from at least 100 people a week during the normal course of the job. If that sample is not broad enough, a half hour a day on the phone by the communicator or a support person can increase it.

Mini-surveys can be done regularly or only on special occasions. Either way, the idea of them and the reasons for them should be publicized in advance, and the results should be fed back to everyone in the organization. Treating the information as secret or not important can seriously affect the candor and participation of respondents in subsequent mini-surveys.

Readership Surveys

Readership surveys should generally attempt to measure only what people do or don't do when they approach a publication or other communication effort. While readership surveys can be simple or sophisticated, they must be as objective as opinion surveys. Many readership surveys backfire, or are invalid because they are not objective. Communicators who include surveys as inserts or tear-out sheets in publications, or are involved closely in conducting their own surveys, do a disservice to the organization and their readers because it is a conflict of interest to attempt to do an objective survey on yourself. Usually these kinds of surveys have such a low rate response that they are invalid.

Independent readership surveys guaranteeing anonymity can, of course, be valuable. A short, simple survey sent on a postcard with a return address that has no direct connection to the communicator can provide very useful information. Just the question "Did you read the following articles in the last issue of ———" and a list of the article titles can indicate what interests readers and what does not. The question asks only what a reader did, not what he or she thinks.

Many communicators expect too much from readership surveys. Generally they cannot provide valid, in-depth information to prompt major changes. More than one organization has had readership survey results showing positive reactions and opinion survey results showing communication as a major negative aspect of an organization's operation.

Communicators can also expect too much from "Letters to the Editor" columns. Unless the organization is large and, more important, has a hard-earned tradition of openness, letters columns can be an embarrassment. They are often promoted strongly and when no letters appear, or none express other than mundane sentiments, the credibility of the whole communication operation can be damaged. Certainly people should have opportunities to comment, but expectations should not be high that they will. Question-and-answer columns in publications sometimes fare a little better than "Letters" if they are set up with controls on them similar to formal question-and-answer programs. But again, the expectations often are greater than the results.

Other Techniques

Formal question-and-answer programs in organizations, often called "speak-up" programs because the best-known and longest-running one is IBM's "Speak-Up," provide a direct, two-way communication flow from bottom to top. They all share some characteristics. They are based on confidentiality, have an independent coordinator, send questions and answers through the mails, and have access to and the support of the top person in the organization.

The perception that employees have of openness through all levels of the organization through these programs is often very important. The programs say clearly to all employees that senior management is listening to you and wants to know your opinions and your concerns. One danger in these programs, however, is that people at all levels can think of them as the beginning and end of feedback. In fact, they should be a reflection of an attitude that welcomes openness and candor.

Although all the programs strongly endorse and promote the idea that the prime way to get answers to questions is to talk to immediate supervisors, they recognize that supervisors do not always have all the answers. They also recognize that some employees have trouble talking to their supervisors.

Even when the purposes of the program have been fully explained, some managers still see them as a threat to their responsibility and authority. They must be thought of as a parallel channel for communication, not a substitute. For senior management, the programs are a system of checks on managerial behavior and performance. An appraisal of the concerns raised points out problem areas and provides a broader reading of the organization's climate. The number of people represented by one question, or even two or three, on a specific issue is always a concern.

Programs of this kind are usually instigated by people at the top, unlike most communication programs, which are planned and sold by people handling the communication function. And while question-and-answer programs certainly are communication programs, they generally operate outside the formal communication systems. Since they start at the top, there is usually no question about top-level support. One problem that can develop is that after the first flush of enthusiasm and success, senior-level people can become bored with the program. That, of course, diminishes its value and effectiveness quickly. The programs need continuous support. They also need lots of planning and supporting policies. It is very difficult to change programs of this nature once they are operating.

While the main measure of the programs is in the quality and quantity of the questions, many people judge their success by being able to say, through the program, "You're right, we're wrong, here's the action we've taken to fix it." The key to the program is anonymity, and the key to that is an independent, credible coordinator. Both the safety factors of the program and the coordinator must have a high visibility. People must see, and be constantly reminded, that there is no chance for them to be identified. Because one of the advantages of the programs is that they skirt the immediate supervisor, they often deal in questions concerning the immediate supervisor. There can be a very real fear of retaliation, so any indication that a name has been revealed will damage the program irremediably.

The coordinator must have the trust of the employees. A good part of the job is spent talking to employees, individually and in groups, to build trust and promote confidentiality. Most coordinators widely advertise the fact that they open mail sent to the program, that they alone know who has asked a question. They generally point out that after the question has been answered, the name is destroyed and no records are kept.

In many real ways, the coordinator is the organization's ombudsman with the power to investigate issues at all levels. Normally, the coordinator does not have to accept answers to the question regardless of who the answer is from. He or she can go back and request a better answer. The coordinator should be the emissary of the chief executive officer, accountable only to that person. To be independent, the coordinator should be seen as not aligned to any department in the organization, though some programs work out of personnel or administration offices, which makes the job of promoting freedom of action more difficult.

Normally, coordinators have not had communication training or worked in the communication area. The job does not really require that background. In fact, many say that a generalist who has worked in a variety of jobs and levels in the organization has the best training.

Before that first question arrives, senior management and the chief executive officer must sit down and contemplate how to answer the most difficult, nastiest, embarrassing questions they can think of because while most people are basically positive, the program is an invitation to the negative side. The program must anticipate the worst—and it will usually come. In fact, in the beginning the program will probably be tested with loaded disagreeable, vexatious questions. The basic commitment is to answer all questions from whatever source, to surface whatever perceived problems there are in the organization.

A negative answer is completely acceptable if it is clear and candid and provides the answer to "Why?" The asker may not like the answer, and it may not be in his or her best interest, but the point is that there was an opportunity to ask it and to get an answer. Most questions, however, are rather ordinary. About 65 percent of them deal with straightforward personnel administration or benefit issues, working environment, personnel policies, safety and customer or community relations.

Although the tone can vary from program to program, and certain specific, topical issues can prompt a spate of queries, about 55 percent of submissions are complaints, about 40 percent straight questions, and about 5 percent opinions. Occasionally, a suggestion will come in that can, with the sender's permission, be routed to the suggestion plan if there is one.

The programs are open to all employees, but since they tend to do end runs around managers, the assumption is often made that managers will not use the program. In most cases, in fact, managers submit questions at a higher frequency than lower-level employees. All questions should be acknowledged as received; when the answer is going to take longer than the normal time, the sender should be notified. Most programs supply answers in eight to ten working days.

The replies must come from the top, the small group of senior people in the organization. Although these people may delegate someone to do the investigation and prepare a draft answer, if must be reviewed and signed by someone at the top. If the question is directed by the sender to a specific person, that person must sign the answer. Usually the coordinator directs the question to the most likely person and that person is responsible for getting the answer back and on time. Some coordinators estimate that they send close to 30 percent of the answers back for a better response. The first answer might have had faulty facts or been unresponsive to the question or patronizing or too curt. The number of answers prepared in a month varies from two to six per 1,000 employees. A specific controversial issue can raise the average momentarily.

To submit questions to the program, employees use a brightly designed question form that folds up into a self-mailer. Although interoffice mail can be used, most forms are designed with a postage paid business reply stamp. Since questions can be long and involved, there are 15 to 25 lines of space left for them. The forms usually include a statement that supervisors should be a person's best source of information and a notice

HOTLINE REPORT

Caller: I just received the most recent issue of Weyerhaeuser Today from Tacoma. On the front page was an article boasting of Weyerhaeuser's 1979 record earnings. At the same time there are 1,400 people in the Eastern Oregon Region that have been curtailed due to market and economic conditions. What gives?

HOTLINE: It is easy—but incorrect—to think of Weyerhaeuser Company operations as just those that exist in the Klamath Basin. In fact, Weyerhaeuser Company consists of more than 50,000 employees involved in fourteen different operating regions throughout the United States, Canada and overseas, along with a variety of subsidiary company interests. Each of these regions or subsidiaries produces a different product mix, serves different markets and experiences different operating profits and losses. Recently, sales of pulp and paper products along with export trade have been strong areas for Weyerhaeuser Company while the housing industry has been softening at a serious rate. The Eastern Oregon Region, of course, is not involved in any of the pulp, paper or export markets which are currently strong. Also, our Region is not alone in reacting to the effects of a general slump in the housing market. Curtailments, layoffs and shutdowns have been in the news for the last several months wherever mills are closely linked to housing industry markets. It's not all gloom and doom for Eastern Oregon either. Of Weyerhaeuser's three Hardboard

facing. As early as last July our employee newsletter, Growth Rings began carrying notices, statements and feature stories indicating that curtailments were indeed possible if industry conditions continued to worsen. Similar warnings have appeared in almost every issue since July, as well as on Hotline. We didn't know how bad it would get, and we can't tell you what we don't know, but we have done our best to inform people about the possibilities. Some people were listening.

Caller: We've made it through poor markets before without drastic curtailments. What is so different now?

HOTLINE: For one thing, the current expected level of U.S. housing starts has dropped to the lowest point since July 1976, and is still declining. Some folks are speculating that it will turn out to be the worst period since 1946. Add to that our nation's current rate of inflation, declining levels of productivity and record high mortgage interest rates and you've got a number of factors that are different than they have ever been in the past.

Caller: We keep hearing how bad the lumber market is and yet turn around and work overtime to process lumber that the Merchandiser sends to the Sawmill. This could easily be run at the same time that the mill runs.

HOTLINE: Byron Dahlen told Hotline that when Mill #1 is cutting pine, the introduction of Douglas-fir flitches has created sorting prob-

Caller: Why can't Weyerhaeuser Company use profits made in other regions and businesses to keep the Eastern Oregon Region running?

HOTLINE: It's not a matter of funds, rather, markets and prices. Currently, demand and prices for local products are low. It is a fact of life that if you are running any kind of manufacturing business, at some point you simply must stop producing a product if there is no demand for it, or if the customers are not willing to pay what it costs to produce your products.

Caller: I'm concerned with the main crossing on Route "A." It's getting a lot of potholes and rough spots. I was wondering if it would be possible to get it repaired. Same thing goes for the road to the Truck Shop.

HOTLINE: Dave Wilson, Plant Engineer, said that the "A" Route crossing is an item that requires regular and frequent maintenance due to the heavy traffic of Sort Yark log movement, log trucks, and plant use vehicles. Wilson said that just prior to receiving the Hotline comment the area had just been graveled and graded again. Wilson said they'll try to increase the frequency of repair to eliminate the really serious problems of road roughness and potholes.

Caller: I've seen several Weyerhaeuser Company pickups on the highway that have been exceeding the speed limit. I have been passed by Company pickups while I was driving 55 m.p.h. I'm not perfect,

Publication of employee questions and the organization's responses strengthens the perception of openness and candor while protecting the anonymity of the employee.

that only the coordinator will see the question. A tear-off piece at the bottom with space for the sender's name and address can be coded and locked away by the coordinator.

Questions are generally retyped so that anything that might reveal the sender's identity or specific job location is removed. Some forms provide an option of sending the answer to the job location, others send them only to the home; some ask for permission to publish the letter without identification, others indicate that if it is of sufficient interest, it will be published. Forms should be made available in open racks in all areas of the organization. Because some employees fear being seen picking up a form, programs often advertise that forms can be sent directly to the home on request.

Programs are generally regularly promoted through bulletin board notices, posters, stories in employee publications and at general or special meetings. These programs need high visibility and consistent, lively promotion gives it to them. Question-and-answer programs are operating mostly in nonindustrial, nonunion organizations such as banks, insurance companies and utilities. Nevertheless, there are some in industrial, unionized organizations that operate successfully in cooperation with the union. In most cases, the normal union grievance procedure and the program work side by side. Some programs are part of a larger package, which can include an "open door" program, skip-level meetings with managers and face-to-face group meetings. Most programs provide material for columns in regular employee publications. Some publish their own bulletins of selected questions and answers.

Direct costs for a program are usually not high, but when indirect costs such as the time senior managers use to get answers are included, the costs can multiply.

Anne Kelley, coordinator of Feedback for Illinois Bell Telephone, sums up her feelings about the program this way: "Personal points of view is what Feedback is all about. It is a serious business because the integrity of the company is on the line. It is a two-way pipeline through which inquiring, angry, hostile, sometimes bitter employees receive sane, reasoned, level replies giving the whys and wherefores of policies and decisions."

While formal programs and surveys are the major ways to obtain reliable in-depth feedback, there are numerous other methods available to communicators. It is a key part of the communicator's job to know what's happening throughout the organization. The day-to-day work usually includes checking out changes and new developments, talking to people at all levels of the organization, and collecting facts and feelings on just about everything. But that's not enough. Communicators need to develop special programs and make specific efforts to get feedback. Sifting through information, categorizing it, assessing it, and reporting on it in an understandable way can have a positive, direct impact in the organization.

Listening Posts

The communicator cannot be in all places at the same time. He or she must use other ears and eyes. Choosing a few people in strategic places in the organization, and explaining to them in some detail what kind of information is needed and why, can provide a steady stream of valuable reports. The people chosen should be the informal leaders in the organization, the ones who are at the center of making things happen in an informal way—an organizer of recreation events, the person who always seems to plan the office get-together, or the one people go to in order to get the supposed latest inside information.

The contacts have to be made, built up, and used carefully. These people are useful information sources, not spies. They should have public recognition, and their supervisor should acknowledge their role. In the best sense, they should be one section of the communicator's "beat."

There are people who can be useful in this way but may have conflicting roles. If they do not undermine their integrity, they are good sources of regular information. For instance, the person handling benefit claims in personnel can tell what issues are confusing people by the number of questions received; the plant nurse can indicate areas of stress or unrest resulting in increased activity in health services. Even in a large organization, a weekly check with ten or twelve people can produce valid feedback information.

The Grapevine

The designated listening posts can be key people on the grapevine, but the grapevine is much broader than that. Many managements abhor the grapevine, but it is a normal, natural information channel in all organizations. And it reflects the climate, good or bad.

The grapevine is tricky in that it moves irregularly, outside normal reporting relationships—and it moves fast. Tests show that about 80 percent of information on the grapevine is accurate, at least in part. It usually has a high emotional content that reveals attitudes more than facts, and it is particularly useful for a reading on the "climate" in an organization.

The communicator should treat the grapevine as a legitimate feedback source, get attuned to it, collect the information in purposeful ways—and, of course, correct the misinformation that sometimes flows through it. The worst thing to do is to ignore the grapevine or attempt to stamp it out with retaliation or censure.

Various areas in organizations collect information for reasons not related to communication. Sometimes, with a little research, these can provide good feedback information. A regular check on the union grievance system, for instance, can tell you what issues are being raised, and whether they are single instances or part of a larger problem. These systems are generally confidential and must be used with discretion, but with the trend toward labor-management joint committees centered around Quality of Work Life issues, the channels should become more accessible to communicators.

Suggestion systems are closely aligned with the communication

function, even though most of them deal in manufacturing or safety issues. Getting involved in the plan as a communication adviser can yield
considerable information. Some suggestion systems are broadly based
and have, as one of their prime functions, general feedback. Most, however, are award systems designed to bring in practical, workable ideas.

Individual personnel files are confidential, of course, but statistics
gleaned from them can be valuable. If an organization has a computer-
based personnel data system, specific information such as turnover
levels and absenteeism rates can be gathered easily.

Feedback can also be collected regularly from sales figures, newspaper comments, community reactions and public requests for information. All this material has a direct impact on the organization and communicators should assess it, report on it and develop programs, where
necessary, to respond to it.

Meetings

The communicator can also arrange meetings to gather feedback at little
or no cost. For instance, getting a randomly selected group of people
together for an hour and using the last issue of the employee publication
as a talking point can bring in valuable information. Because of the time
off the job, these meetings usually have to be cleared through supervisors. They can also be run, however, in off hours on a volunteer basis.
Many employees will jump at the opportunity to express opinions in
small-group settings.

Telephone information systems with fast news output have been
discussed elsewhere, but other systems designed to allow people to ask
questions or offer opinions on tape are being used in a number of organizations to gather feedback. If a question is asked and a name given, the
answer is sent directly back to the individual. Since these systems do not
include the checks and balances of more formal systems, the questions
are usually rather routine. The anonymous comments that are sometimes
offered, though, can pinpoint a serious problem area.

Since people feel the need to talk to the top person, some organizations are putting their chief executive officer or other senior people on
the end of a phone or direct calls on a specific few hours in a day. These
programs are heavily promoted, and if the senior people can be convinced to handle some potential hot questions on-the-spot, the programs
can be very effective. Providing the direct channel with no interference

can show that the organization is open and wants to listen. The persons answering the phone should have a reasonable manner and be candid. A few curt or less than honest answers can make the program counterproductive.

Action from Reaction

Managing change in a busy, competitive, technological world is the prime task of organizations today. And effective management has to be based on good information. Managements want results; to get them they need to know what's happening. If the planning is done properly, feedback programs can usually be sold in organizations. Ongoing education programs in attitudes will be necessary, but organizations want to listen. Sperry, for instance, is running a major internal and external program on listening. They feel it is the most important aspect of communication, and the one communication skill that no one is taught.

All communication is really a response to upward communication or feedback. But that idea seems to be just recently gaining a foothold in most organizations. The key to organizational communication is good information. Feedback is a way to get that information. It is needed, wanted and demanded in organizations today.

Roger Feather, ABC, is head of Feather Communication Services, an independent communication consulting firm in Toronto, Ontario. He is accredited by the International Association of Business Communicators and has served on the association's executive board.

PART **V**

ORGANIZATIONAL COMMUNICATION ODAY AND TOMORROW

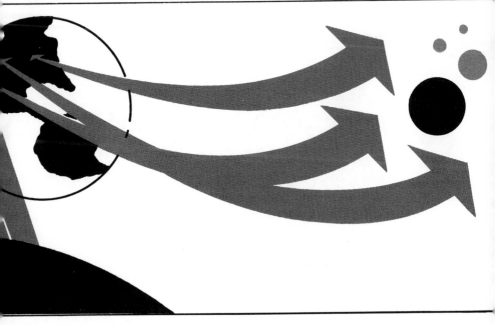

The future is something everyone reaches at the rate of 60 minutes an hour—no more, no less. Professional communicators should anticipate the movements of the future and be ready to cope with them *if* they occur. Look at history, social issues, geopolitical shifts, technological advances and individual professional development as preparation for the future.

CHAPTER 18

Trends and Issues: Challenges Ahead

LOUIS C. WILLIAMS Jr., ABC, APR

An executive recruiter was asked what qualities he looked for when interviewing candidates for senior jobs in organizational communication. After detailing the expected points—experience, personality, skills—he said, "But those are really only superficial kinds of measurements. What I, and my clients, want to see is an individual who understands the world around him. Is that person able to relate to historical perspective and, more important, to make decisions that will show that the long view has been considered as an integral part of the problem-solution process? I want to know what kinds of books he or she reads, what he or she does in spare time, and how he or she places all that into the scheme of everyday living and working."

At first glance, that statement almost seems to be at odds with the fact that today's organizational communicator is being asked to initiate change rather than respond to it. Yet it's true. A person cannot initiate change unless he or she understands where the problems came from. For example, the union movement in the United States has gone through several stages of development. In the beginning, there was the need for survival. The robber barons, and what passed at the turn of the century as big business, were exploiting labor. Security was nonexistent. Pay was abysmal. Chances of being injured on the job were double or triple today's record. The union movement arose to combat all that. It did, most successfully.

Then things began to change. People began to look at work and the workplace as a place for individuals to develop as human beings. They began to talk about sharing goals. Union chiefs began to talk of participatory management—the worker should have a say in how an organization is run.

Today, most union movements and the strife exhibited in strikes or walkouts are not over basic issues of wages and benefits, but rather over basic management ingredients: Should workers be forced into overtime against their will? How should we overcome the dulling drudgery of automation? How can we handle the displacement of workers caused by technology? What rights does an individual have to dignity on the job?

Unions continue to be strong and integral parts of the management process. They still can paralyze a city or region, even a country, in certain circumstances. But the why of their existence is so different from what it used to be that to attempt to communicate with today's workers in the terminology and issues of the past is to court failure. Instead, the communication expert of today and tomorrow should be looking introspectively at the organization, understanding the needs and frustrations of today's workers and balancing them against the needs of the organization, walking a very fine line to obtain a meshing of those needs so that both can be satisfied.

The day when the editor of a publication could be concerned only with recording the life of an organization is gone. John Bailey, executive director of the International Association of Business Communicators, puts it most succinctly: "The specialist (the disseminator of news) still is in demand and will continue to be so, but those managing communication will be the generalists. This appears to be contrary to what is happening in society as a whole but it already is occurring. Even Little Sisters of the Poor Hospital uses a bulletin board, paycheck stuffer and an orientation slide show. The pure editorial positions are at the AT&Ts and Exxons.

"Specialization will be most obvious in the type of audience with which a communicator is involved: external, internal, investors, government, etc. They will use multiple media with specific audiences. . . . The communicator of 1990 will need a thorough knowledge of the organization and the industry of which it is a part because that knowledge will be the basis for their communication programs."

Harold Burson of Burson-Marsteller adds another perspective: "Today, we can no longer afford pat answers to difficult problems. The whole area of employee relations is studded with untapped possibilities for . . . practitioners who really understand the role of communication in an industrial society."

If you add to the informational need the explosion in access technology, you can be overwhelmed with choices. Educator Gerald M. Goldhaber calls it "information shock." He says, "A computer makes it possible for us to read immediately any book stored in the major libraries. A word-processing machine makes possible the revision of a book in less than a day. Within five minutes, we can talk by telephone to almost any part of the world. Satellite networks enable us to be eyewitnesses at the impeachment of a president, of the landing of a spaceship on the moon and even of a full-scale war—without ever leaving our living rooms."

The challenge is clear. The communicator of the future will have to manage information and assemble programs and media to meet objectives that solve the problems organizations face.

Looking Ahead

Historians and newspaper people are wont to label a period of history with some sort of label that describes the era succinctly. For example, the decade just ended has been called the "me" decade—with good reason. The 1970s produced eight trillion, one hundred sixty thousand self-help books! We learned how to be more aggressive. How to be less aggressive. How to be thinner. How to live with our fat. We learned how to say no. We learned when to say yes. We bought self-help therapy books to "get it together." And then we went to therapy to pull ourselves apart—all to become the "new woman" or the "new man." All in all, it was a roller-coaster ride with lots of ups and downs and lots of buzz phrases: "I've got to get my act together." "I've got to discover the real me." "I'm OK, you're OK." "We've got an open marriage."

Throughout the '70s, we kept getting hit over the head with facts. We found that people in our governments lied to us, that the glories of war weren't, that our gas tanks were empty.

Out of the glaring disappointment and disillusionment comes a new decade, perhaps the most important in this century—not for what it promises, but for what is not being promised. We seem to be on the threshold of a decade that will see the replacement of the "me" with the "we."

There are many examples: First, the family. Psychologists and others have been bemoaning the demise of the family for years, and they have been right. The splintering of the family unit has been a dominating force in our society. To say the least, it is a phenomenon with far-reaching consequences. But, deep down, the need for family remains, and today it appears that need is on the verge of a comeback. The tremendous growth of worldwide religious cults is one outpouring of this movement. People want to be part of an identifiable group, especially one that will offer psychological reinforcement and love.

Of course, divorce rates are still high. In some places in the United States the odds of getting a divorce now are greater than the odds of a marriage lasting. Nevertheless, there is an increasing trend toward marriage. Yes, people still live together first. They may also enter into marriage with a contract and a different view of the marriage's potential success than their parents did; yet marriage still remains a stable and viable alternative.

Consider the television series "Roots." That story struck a vital nerve in much of the world. These weren't rich people checking out a genealogy because they had nothing better to do. "Roots" symbolized a deep-seated belief that most of us feel, namely, the need to know where we come from. A chance to discover *our* family. That's an emphasis on "we," not "me." It has almost become a justification of our person, our existence.

North America has been called a land of joiners. Studies indicate that the average American adult belongs to three associations, and it is estimated the same holds true for Canada. It takes a book seven inches thick to list the hundreds of thousands of them. The reason for these associations goes beyond the need to promote an idea or belief. People want to "prove" they belong. We want to have reinforcement for convincing others about a point of view or a profession or, even, ourselves. Part of it, of course, has to do with trying to bring society down to a more manageable size. We find it difficult to identify with millions of brothers and sisters in a nation. An association or a club can make us very important within a specific group.

I mentioned earlier our proclivity for buying trillions of self-help books. What's the aim of those books? They are designed to make us more acceptable to our peers. *We* need to feel that *we* are able to make and keep friends. And the more governments create a numerical society, the more we will rebel against it with our own means of survival.

Governments of many countries are more socialistic than ever. Like it or not, we are headed toward an even more paternal point of view about our lives. In the United States, income taxes were nonexistent a hundred years ago. Social security didn't exist fifty years ago. Regardless of political beliefs, you have to admit that most countries have more social programs today than they did a few years back. The budget for the U.S. Department of Health, Education, and Welfare alone is larger than the gross national product of all but a handful of countries in the world. One could certainly make a case against the quality of programs we get from social agencies, but one certainly can't deny the "we" of them. Does anybody seriously believe that trend is going to change?

Consider what's happening to the subways and buses of the world's great cities. They're packed. Car pooling has become a national pastime. Freeways, motorways and autobahns around most major cities may be jammed, but imagine how much worse it would be without the impetus to find friends to share costs or an alternative means of transportation. We—that's "we"—are sharing our transportation. And the funny thing is that we have only begun.

Finally, look at the world of business. We discussed earlier the psyche of the labor movement and its modification in objectives. From gut-level problems of safety and money, big labor has moved to declare war on the "how" of business. How decisions are made. How people are motivated. And how profits are distributed. Unions want a piece of the decision-making pie. In Germany and other European countries this attitude has advanced to the point where management and labor literally share the decision-making process. Unions are often represented on the boards of directors and viewed as legitimate partners in the management of the company.

Governments, too, want to share in the management of business. They tell business the rules of safety and regulate the engineering of products; they tell us how we can compete with each other, the amount of money that can be made, what kinds of people must be hired; they protect pensions and profit-sharing plans from disaster and insinuate themselves into the management process in thousands of other ways. Yet many people are firmly convinced that governments need to do more. If that isn't a "we" attitude, what is?

Even today's shareholder wants to be part of the decision making. There was a time when a stockholders' annual meeting was a dull affair attended by people with time on their hands. They drank tea and munched cookies, congratulating the officers on how nice they looked. No more. The Evelyn Davises and Lewis Gilberts of the world have changed all that. To be sure, a couple of scandalous affairs like the Penn Central bankruptcy of a few years back helped mightily. Directors of large corporations have even found they are being sued by shareholders when things don't go right. What is the world coming to? It's coming to "we," that's what.

Those are some of the societal factors that are affecting the atmosphere inside the organization. Now, switch the scene to a single individual in an organization—the chief executive officer. He or she is the key element in the great "we" equation, because the CEO is the person who is converting all the philosophy into a reality-laden chain of events.

Look at a typical scenario. The chief executive officer, hero of hometown and leader of the masses, goes to Washington, fully expecting to be shown the respect he gets at home. Is he in for a surprise.

First, he hops on his private plane and heads for Washington to do battle with the politicians. But the *Washington Post* is waiting at his hotel and wants him to respond to the senator who has accused him of exploiting migrant labor. "No comment," he cries and harrumphs his way across the lobby and up to his room. Standing at the door is a representative from U.S. Immigration with a subpoena forcing him to testify on the matter of migrants who are illegal aliens, working in his plant.

That's only a beginning. Before the chief executive officer leaves Washington, he may be attacked by consumer activists who want to know why his products aren't safe, government regulators who say his plants aren't safe, and union representatives who berate him because his parking lots aren't safe.

Needless to say, he's glad when his business is completed in Washington so he can go back home to the safety of *his* plant and *his* people. What does he find there? The constituency he thought existed doesn't. He finds his plant is on strike, and National Labor Relations Board representatives are waiting at the door to his office. "Unfair labor practices," they scream at him.

Enough of that scenario: chief executive officers around the world are reacting to a variety of pressures and pains inflicted by sources both within and without the organization. They need help. Just as the employees discussed earlier need help.

To obtain that help, the senior managers of our businesses are calling on communication experts. Communicators are working to build a bridge of trust that will carry ideas and joint objectives from the Land of Chaos to the Land of Accomplishment. That trust is based on a foundation of candor, credibility, and "we"—the sharing of the burden, the mutual solving of problems and the willingness to address the issues that most concern employees as human beings.

Issues of Concern

A look at one issue most experts believe will be paramount in the years ahead should give some feeling for the extent and depth of the problems facing communicators: Productivity. In the first half of the twentieth century, the backbone of industrial success was the ongoing, seemingly forever rising levels of productivity. Wages and benefits skyrocketed and so did productivity, until the mid-1960s. Then things began to change. Technology slowed.

Add to that the impact of inflation, and one has the vicious dynamic duo that seems destined to plague the world of the 1980s. "How can I stay even with prices? If my company doesn't supply me with wage increases to match inflation, I and my family are the losers. Why should I work harder for less?"

How does this impinge on the communicator of tomorrow? The answer becomes clear when we begin to convert the need into the reality of problem-solving communication. A. Robert Abboud, former chairman of the First National Bank of Chicago, said it best when he pointed an accusatory finger at both workers and management, saying: "There's a tendency to equate the terrible situation with productivity in this country with taking a smoke or going to the washroom too often. Well, that's not what it's about at all. I think everyone, including the unemployed, wants to put in a good day's work. We have highly educated, energetic, conscientious people. What we have to do is put the tools in their hands and give them enough leverage to get the job done. Licking inflation and helping productivity are the same thing. The average man is interested in stopping price increases. He understands that. At work, management must construct ways to improve productivity and convince him of their validity. He has to believe in their necessity. Then there won't be any problem."

If ever there was a call for the services of the broad-based communicator, this would seem to be it. The communicator is not going to design wide-scale systems for improving productivity, but he or she can assure that the message of why productivity must be improved is communicated in ways that will assure it will happen. It means understanding, for example, that productivity improvements mean working smarter, not harder. It means understanding the issues that effect how the people feel about their jobs, and why. The communicator must appeal to the emotions and minds to help bring about the necessary changes.

The IABC recently conducted a survey of fifty chief executive officers, asking them to list the concerns and issues they thought would be most important over the next several years. Table 18.1 gives a pretty good overview of the kinds of issues ahead. CEOs were also asked if a communication program could have an impact in these five specific areas. Table 18.2 shows their response.

TABLE 18.1. MAJOR PUBLIC ISSUES AND CONCERNS

ISSUES	TIMES MENTIONED
Inflation and compensation	14
Government issues, including regulation	8
Equal opportunity employment and job opportunities	6
Technology	5
Economic education	5
Energy and environmental concerns	5
Retirement and pensions	4
Consumerism	4
Productivity	3
Quality of work life	3
Credibility	2
Health care	2

TABLE 18.2 CAN COMMUNICATION HAVE AN IMPACT ON THESE PROBLEMS?

	YES	NO	POSSIBLY	UNABLE TO ANSWER
Labor relations	44	3	2	1
Productivity	47	1	1	1
Safety	46	—	2	2
Absenteeism	42	1	5	2
Quality control	44	2	3	1

Career Preparation

The task is gigantic. The process of filling an information vacuum with thoughts, words and deeds is mind-boggling. But it must be done, and there are any number of ways that a communicator—young or old, experienced or inexperienced—can help assure the process will take place.

Formal education. There are basic attributes of a communicator that can be learned best and most efficiently in a classroom. Study history and its role in the scheme of things; study writing and the technological aspects of communication; study the basic principles of business— economics, research techniques, psychology and so forth; study the learning process.

Informal education. This is the kind of learning that people talk about but don't always factor into the total educative process. Everything from the way we decide to take a vacation to the books we read, the movies and plays we see, the clubs we join, will affect our learning patterns.

Professional involvement. Every profession has associations that can assist in the process of learning. The opportunity to lead in an organization can help to sharpen leadership skills for the job back home. Seminars and the opportunities to test ideas against peers and persons who may be farther along the career track can be highly valuable.

Good reading habits. Another basic, necessary ingredient to the learning process that needs to be expanded is our reading habits. Most of us tend to read materials for areas of narrow interest, especially those with which we agree. We need to broaden ourselves beyond what we already know, to look into areas of the unknown. We may not agree with the philosophy espoused, but if we do not study it, how can we understand why others *do* support a particular point of view? As any debator knows, know your opponent's case as well or better than your own to argue a point successfully.

The mentor. Most people find role idols valuable, whether they recognize it or not. It is common to hear about them in relation to sports or theater or television or movies. Communicators also have need to find some person or persons on whom to depend for guidance. That individual may be local—in your organization—or from afar. What is important is to search for the clues that helped him or her gain that success. What should you emulate? And what mistakes should you avoid?

Conclusion

The communications business is in flux. Technological and societal changes have an impact on us that is being felt with ever increasing force and complexity. The demands being placed on organizations have never been more challenging or difficult—or potentially more rewarding.

We truly are at the dawn of a new communication age. Pretty pictures, beautifully printed brochures and publications, and articulate narratives, more than ever before, will need to be supplemented by substantive dialogue that considers the empirical needs of audiences of all sizes and kinds.

There is an additional, but just as important, thought to be considered: The "compleat" communicator of tomorrow will recognize and be able to factor in the universality of problems that face other organizations. And by so doing, will further the cause of understanding between people in countries everywhere. That may sound grandiose but, in fact, our achievements will only match our objectives. If we plan small, we will achieve small.

Louis C. Williams Jr., ABC, APR, is a vice president of Hill & Knowlton in Chicago. He is accredited by both the International Association of Business Communicators and the Public Relations Society of America and served as IABC president in 1979–80.

APPENDIX A
Further Reading

Part I

D'Aprix, Roger. *The Believable Corporation.* New York: AMACOM, 1977.

D'Aprix, Roger. *Corporate Truth . . . and How to Tell It.* San Francisco: Harper & Row, 1981.

de Mare, George. *Communicating at the Top.* New York: Wiley, 1979.

Foltz, Roy G. *Management By Communication.* Radnor, PA: Chilton, 1973.

Garnett, John. *The Work Challenge.* London, UK: Industrial Society, 1978.

Goldhaber, Gerald. *Organizational Communication.* Dubuque, IA: Brown, 1979.

O'Connell, Sandra. *The Manager as Communicator.* San Francisco: Harper & Row, 1979.

Wilson, Ian. *Corporate Environments of the Future.* New York: American Management Association, 1976.

Part II

Albert, Kenneth J., ed. *Handbook of Business Problem-Solving.* New York: McGraw-Hill, 1980.

Berdie, Douglas P., and John F. Anderson. *Questionnaires: Design and Use.* Metuchen, NJ: Scarecrow Press, 1974.

Burger, Chester. *The Chief Executive: Realities of Corporate Leadership.* CBI Publishing, 1978.

Cutlip, Scott M., and Allen H. Center. *Effective Public Relations.* Englewood Cliffs, NJ: Prentice-Hall, 1978.

Dartnell Public Relations Handbook. Chicago: Dartnell, 1980.

Davidson, William L. *How to Develop and Conduct Successful Employee Attitude Surveys.* Chicago: Dartnell, 1978.

de Mare, George. *Communicating at the Top.* New York: Wiley, 1979.

de Mare, George. *Communicating for Leadership.* New York: Ronald Press, 1978.

Derriman, James. *Public Relations in Business Management.* New York: International Publications Service, 1972.

Drucker, Peter F. *Management: Tasks, Responsibilities, Practices.* New York: Harper & Row, 1974.

Dunham, Randall B., and Frank J. Smith. *Organizational Surveys: An Internal Assessment of Organizational Health.* Glenview, IL: Scott, Foresman, 1979.

Foltz, Roy G. *Management by Communication.* Radnor, PA: Chilton, 1973.

Lesly, Philip. *Public Relations Handbook.* Englewood Cliffs, NJ: Prentice-Hall, 1978.

Newsom, Douglas Ann, and Alan Scott. *This is PR: Realities of Public Relations.* Belmont, CA: Wadsworth, 1976.

Odiorne, George S. *Management by Objectives.* New York: Pitman, 1965.

Oppenheim, A. N. *Questionnaire Design and Attitude Measurement.* New York: Basic Books, 1966.

Robinson, John P.; Robert Athanasiou; and Kendra B. Head. *Measures of Occupational Attitudes and Occupational Characteristics.* Ann Arbor: Institute for Social Research, University of Michigan, 1969.

Ross, R. D. *Management of Public Relations.* New York: Wiley, 1978.

Steele, Fritz, and Stephen Jenks. *The Feel of the Work Place: Understanding and Improving Organizational Climate.* Reading, MA: Addison-Wesley, 1977.

Part III

Alexander, Louis. *Beyond the Facts: A Guide to the Art of Feature Writing.* Houston: Gulf Publishing, 1975.

Annual of Advertising, Editorial and Television Art and Design. New York: Art Direction Book, annually since 1922.

Arnold, William E., and Robert O. Hirsch. *Communicating Through Behavior.* Englewood Cliffs, NJ: Prentice-Hall, 1977.

Baird, Russell N. *Industrial and Business Journalism.* Philadelphia: Chilton, 1961.

Ballinger, Raymond. *Art and Reproduction.* New York: Van Nostrand Reinhold, 1977.

Barker, Larry L., et al. *Groups in Process: An Introduction to Small Group Communication.* Englewood Cliffs, NJ: Prentice-Hall, 1979.

Baskette, Floyd K., and Jack Z. Scissors. *The Art of Editing*. New York: Macmillan, 1977.

Booth, James L., et al. *Basic Public Speaking: Principles and Practices*. Winston-Salem: Hunter Publishing, 1977.

Bradford, Leland P. *Making Meetings Work: A Guide for Leaders and Group Members*. La Jolla, CA: University Associates, 1976.

Brady, John. *The Craft of Interviewing*. Cincinnati: Writer's Digest, 1976.

Brennan, John. *The Conscious Communicator*. Reading, MA: Addison-Wesley, 1974.

Brillhart, John K. *Effective Group Discussion*. 3rd ed. Dubuque, IA: Brown, 1978.

Callihan, E. L. *Grammar for Journalists*. Radnor, PA: Chilton, 1969.

Charnley, Mitchell V. *Reporting*. New York: Holt, Rinehart and Winston, 1966.

Click, J. W., and Russell Baird. *Magazine Editing and Production*. Dubuque, IA: Brown, 1979.

Clynes, Manfred. *Sentics: The Touch of Emotions*. Garden City, NY: Doubleday, 1978.

Craig, James. *Designing with Type*. New York: Watson Guptill Publications, 1971.

Craig, James. *Production for the Graphic Designer*. New York: Watson Guptill Publications, 1974.

Creativity Annual. New York: Art Direction Book, 1971.

Cronkhite, Gary. *Public Speaking and Critical Listening*. Menlo Park, CA: Cummings, 1978.

D'Aprix, Roger. *The Believable Corporation*. New York: AMACOM, 1977.

de Mare, George. *Communicating for Leadership*. New York: Ronald Press, 1968.

de Mare, George. *Corporate Lives: A Journey into the Corporate World*. New York: Van Nostrand Reinhold Co., 1976.

Efrein, J. O. *Video Tape Production and Communication Techniques*. Blue Ridge Summit, PA: Tab Books, 1971.

Egan, Gerald. *You and Me: The Skills of Communicating and Relating to Others*. Belmont, CA: Brooks-Cole, 1977.

Ferguson, Rowena. *Editing the Small Magazine*. New York: Columbia University Press, 1976.

Fletcher, Alan; Colin Forbes; and Bob Gill. *Graphic Design: Visual Comparisons*. New York: Reinhold Publishing, 1963.

Foltz, Roy G. *Management by Communication*. Radnor, PA: Chilton, 1973.

Fontaine, Andre. *The Art of Writing Non-Fiction.* New York: Crowell, 1974.

Frank, Ted, and David Ray. *Basic Business and Professional Speech Communication.* Englewood Cliffs, NJ: Prentice-Hall, 1979.

Friant, Ray J., Jr. *Preparing Effective Presentations.* New York: Pilot Books, 1978.

Gifford, F. *Tape: A Radio News Handbook.* New York: Communication Arts Books, Hastings House, 1977.

Gray, Bill. *More Studio Tips.* New York: Van Nostrand Reinhold, 1978.

Gray, Bill. *Studio Tips.* New York: Van Nostrand Reinhold, 1976.

Gronbeck, Bruce E. *The Articulate Person: A Guide to Everyday Public Speaking.* Glenview, IL: Scott, Foresman, 1979.

Harriss, Julian; Kelly Leiter; and Stanley Johnson. *The Complete Reporter.* New York: Macmillan, 1979.

Herdeg, Walter, ed. *Graphis Annual.* Zurich, Switzerland: Graphis Press, annually since 1952.

Herdeg, Walter, ed. *Graphis/Diagrams.* Zurich, Switzerland: Graphis Press, 1979.

Hibbitt, George W. *How to Speak Effectively on All Occasions.* Philadelphia: West, 1979.

Hilliard, Robert L. *Writing for Television and Radio.* New York: Communication Arts Books, Hastings House, 1976.

Hofmann, Armin. *Graphic Design Manual.* New York: Van Nostrand Reinhold, 1965.

Hurlburt, Allen. *The Grid.* New York: Van Nostrand Reinhold, 1978.

Hurlburt, Allen. *Layout.* New York: Van Nostrand Reinhold, 1977.

Hurlburt, Allen. *Publication Design.* New York: Van Nostrand Reinhold, 1976.

Itten, Johannes, *Design and Form.* New York: Van Nostrand Reinhold, 1975.

Izard, Ralph S.; Hugh M. Culbertson; and Donald A. Lambert. *Fundamentals of News Reporting.* Dubuque: IA: Kendall/Hunt, 1973.

Jackson, Peter C. *House Journal Handbook.* London, UK: Industrial Society, 1977.

Karo, Jerzy. *Graphic Design: Problems, Methods, Solutions.* New York: Van Nostrand Reinhold, 1975.

Kelly, Eugene W., Jr. *Effective Interpersonal Communication: A Manual for Skill Development.* Washington, DC: University Press of America, 1977.

Kemp, Jerrold E. *Planning and Producing Audiovisual Materials.* San Francisco: Chandler, 1968.

Kirsch, Donald. *Financial and Economic Journalism.* New York: New York University Press, 1978.

Lem, Dean Phillip. *Graphics Master 2*. Los Angeles: Dean Lem Associates, 1977.

Lewis, John. *Typography: Basic Principles*. New York: Reinhold, 1963.

Mabry, Edward, and Richard Barnes. *The Dynamics of Small Group Communication*. Boston: Houghton Mifflin, 1979.

MacRae, Donald L., et al. *You and Others: An Introduction to Interpersonal Communication*. New York: McGraw-Hill, 1976.

Mascelli, Joseph V. *The Five C's of Cinematography*. Hollywood: Cina/Grafic, 1977.

McLeod, Elizabeth. *Producing an Employee Handbook*. London, UK: Industrial Society, 1976.

Metzler, Ken. *Creative Interviewing*. Englewood Cliffs, NJ: Prentice-Hall, 1977.

Minor, Ed, and Harvey R. Frye. *Techniques for Producing Visual Instructional Media*. New York: McGraw-Hill, 1977.

Murray, Michael. *The Videotape Book*. New York: Bantam Books, 1975.

Nelson, Roy Paul. *Articles and Features*. Boston: Houghton Mifflin, 1978.

Nelson, Roy Paul. *The Design of Advertising*. Dubuque, IA: Brown, 1977.

Nothdurft, K. H. *The Complete Guide to Successful Business Negotiation*. Edison, NJ: Leviathan House, 1972.

Olmsted, Michael S., and A. Paul Hare. *The Small Group*. New York: Random House, 1978.

Parsons, Edgar. *Audio-Visual Communication for Associations*. Washington, DC: Chamber of Commerce of the United States, 1974.

Phillips, Gerald M., et al. *Group Discussion: A Practical Guide to Participation and Leadership*. Boston: Houghton Mifflin, 1978.

Pocket Pal. New York: International Paper, 1979.

Potter, David, and Martin P. Anderson. *Discussion in Small Groups*. Belmont, CA: Wadsworth, 1976.

Prochnow, Herbert V. *The Successful Speaker's Handbook*. Englewood Cliffs, NJ: Prentice-Hall, 1977.

Publications Index. Rochester, NY: Eastman Kodak, 1979.

The Push Pin Style. Palo Alto, CA: Communication Arts, 1970.

Rehe, Rolf F. *Typography: How to Make It Most Legible*. Carmel, IN: Design Research International, 1974.

Rivers, William L. *Free-Lancer and Staff Writer*. Belmont, CA: Wadsworth, 1976.

Rivers, William L. *Finding Facts: Interviewing, Observing, Using Reference Sources*. Englewood Cliffs, NJ: Prentice-Hall, 1975.

Rivers, William L. *Writing: Craft and Art.* Englewood Cliffs, NJ: Prentice-Hall, 1975.

Roberts, Kenneth H. *Primer for Film-Making: A Complete Guide to 16 and 35mm Film Production.* Indianapolis: Pegasus, Bobbs-Merrill, 1971.

Robinson, J. R., and P. H. Beards. *Using Videotape.* New York: Communication Arts, Hastings House, 1967.

Robinson, Richard. *The Video Primer.* New York: Links Books, 1974.

Rosen, Ben. *Type and Typography.* New York: Van Nostrand Reinhold, 1976.

Rosenfeld, Lawrence. *Now That We're All Here . . . Relations in Small Groups.* Chappaqua, NY: Merrill Analysis, 1976.

Rowe, Mack R., and David Curl, Harvey R. Frye, Jerrold Kemp, and Wilfred Veenendaal. *The Message Is You: Guidelines for Preparing Presentations.* Washington, DC: Association for Educational Communications & Technology, 1976.

Saltman, David. *Paper Basics.* New York: Van Nostrand Reinhold, 1978.

Shutter, Robert M. *Understanding Misunderstanding: Exploring Interpersonal Communication.* New York: Harper & Row, 1978.

Smith, Dennis R., and L. Keith Williamson. *Interpersonal Communication: Roles, Rules, Strategies and Games.* Dubuque, IA: Brown, 1977.

Souto, Mario Raimondo. *The Technique of the Motion Picture Camera.* New York: Communication Arts, Hastings House, 1969.

Stone, Janet, and Jane Bachner. *Speaking Up: A Book for Every Woman Who Talks.* New York: McGraw-Hill, 1977.

Strunk, William, Jr., and E. B. White. *The Elements of Style.* New York: Macmillan, 1979.

Swain, Dwight V. *Film Scriptwriting.* New York: Communication Arts, Hastings House, 1976.

Toothman, John M. *Conducting the Small Group Experience.* Washington, DC: University Press of America, 1978.

Turnbull, Arthur T., and Russel N. Baird. *The Graphics of Communication.* New York; Holt, Reinhart and Winston, 1980.

Umphrey, Majorie A. *Getting to Know You: A Guide to Communicating.* Irvine, CA: Harvest House, 1976.

van Uchelen, Rod. *Paste-Up.* New York: Van Nostrand Reinhold, 1976.

Verderber and Verderber. *Inter-Act: Using Interpersonal Communication.* Belmont, CA: Wadsworth, 1977.

Wells, Theodora. *Keeping Your Cool Under Fire: Communicating Non-Defensively.* New York: McGraw-Hill, 1980.

Westley, Bruce. *News Editing.* Boston: Houghton Mifflin, 1972.

White, Jan. *Designing for Magazines.* New York: Bowker, 1976.

White, Jan. *Editing by Design*. New York: Bowker, 1974.

Whyte, William H., Jr., and the Editors of Fortune. *Is Anybody Listening?* New York: Simon and Schuster, 1952.

Wilkie, Bernard. *Creating Special Effects for TV and Films*. New York: Communication Arts, Hastings House, 1977.

Williamson, Daniel R. *Feature Writing for Newspapers*. New York: Hastings House, 1975.

Zelko, Harold P., and Frank E. Dance. *Business and Professional Speech Communication*. New York: Holt, Rinehart and Winston, 1978.

Zettle, Herbert. *Television Production Handbook*. Belmont, CA: Wadsworth, 1976.

Zinsser, William. *On Writing Well*. New York: Harper & Row, 1976.

Part IV

Ackoff, R. L. *Concept of Corporate Planning*. New York: Wiley, 1970.

Bassett, Glenn A. *The New Face of Communication*. New York: AMACOM, 1968.

Blake, Robert R., and Jane S. Mouton. *Making Experience Work: The Grid Approach to Critique*. New York: McGraw-Hill, 1977.

Cutlip, Scott M., and Allen H. Center. *Effective Public Relations*. Englewood Cliffs, NJ: Prentice-Hall, 1978.

Davis, Keith. *Human Behavior at Work: Organizational Behavior*. New York: McGraw-Hill, 1977.

Drucker, Peter F. *The Effective Executive*. New York: Harper & Row, 1967.

Drucker, Peter F. *Managing for Results*. New York: Harper & Row, 1964.

Drucker, Peter F. *The Practice of Management*. New York: Harper & Row, 1954.

Ewing, David W. *Long-Range Planning for Management*. New York: Harper & Row, 1972.

Federal Election Commission. *Federal Election Commission Regulations*. Washington, DC, 1977.

Francois, William E. *Mass Media Law and Regulation*. Columbus, OH: Grid, 1978.

Goldhaber, Gerald, and Don Rogers. *Auditing Organizational Communication Systems; The ICA Communication Audit*. Dubuque, IA: Kendall-Hunt, 1979.

Hasling, J. *Group Discussion and Decision Making*. New York: Harper & Row, 1975.

Jones, J. Morgan. *Introduction to Decision Theory*. Homewood, IL: Irwin, 1977.

Kepner, Charles H., and B. B. Tregoe. *Rational Manager: A Systematic Approach to Problem Solving and Decision Making*. New York: McGraw-Hill, 1965.

McGregor, Douglas. *The Human Side of Enterprise*. New York: McGraw-Hill, 1960.

Maier, Norman R. *Problem Solving and Creativity in Individuals and Groups*. Monterey, CA: Brooks/Cole, 1970.

Managerial Decision Making. New York: AMACOM, 1975.

Miller, Gordon. *Decision Making: A Look at the Process*. New York: AMACOM, 1974.

Nelson, Harold L., and Dwight L. Teeter, Jr. *Law of Mass Communications*. Mineola, NY: Foundation Press, 1978.

Odione, George. *Management Decisions by Objectives*. Englewood Cliffs, NJ: Prentice-Hall, 1968.

Rogers, Everett M., and Rehka Agarwala-Rogers. *Communication in Organizations*. New York: Free Press (Macmillan), 1976.

Roodman, Herman, and Zelda Roodman. *Management by Communication*. Methuen, 1973.

Sayles, Leonard R., and George Strauss. *Managing Human Resources*. Englewood Cliffs, NJ: Prentice-Hall, 1977.

Simon, Morton J. *Public Relations Law*. New York: Appleton-Century-Crofts, 1969.

Steele, Fritz. *Consulting for Organizational Change*. Amherst: University of Massachusetts Press, 1975.

Vroom, Victor H., and Phillip Yetton. *Leadership and Decision Making*. Pittsburgh: University of Pittsburgh Press, 1973.

Without Bias: A Guidebook for Nondiscriminatory Communication. San Francisco: International Association of Business Communicators, 1977.

Trade Magazines and Journals

Communication Management and Public Relations

Channels
Public Relations Society of
America
845 Third Avenue
New York, NY 10022

Communications & Management
Towers, Perrin, Forster & Crosby,
Inc.
600 Third Avenue
New York, NY 10016

Communication Management
National Communication Services
Inc.
875 Sixth Avenue, Suite 1001
New York, NY 10001

Communication Notes
Council of Communication
Societies
P.O. Box 1074
Silver Spring, MD 20910

Editor's Newsletter
The Anderson Press
P.O. Box 774
Madison Square Station
New York, NY 10010

Hollis Public Relations
Hollis Directories
Contact House, Sunbury-on-
Thames
Middlesex UK TW16 5HG

IABC News
International Association of Business Communicators
870 Market Street, Suite 940
San Francisco, CA 94102

ICC Newsletter
Industrial Communication
Council
P.O. Box 3970
Grand Central Post Office
New York, NY 10017

IPRA Review
International Public Relations Association
50 Pine Grove
London, England N20 8LA

Jack O'Dwyer's Newsletter
J. R. O'Dwyer Co. Inc.
271 Madison Avenue
New York, NY 10016

*Journal of Organizational Com-
munication*
International Association of Business Communicators
870 Market Street, Suite 940
San Francisco, CA 94102

PR Reporter
PR Publishing Co. Inc.
Dudley House
P.O. Box 600
Exeter, NH 03833

Public Relations Journal
Public Relations Society of
America
845 Third Avenue
New York, NY 10022

Public Relations News
127 East 80th Street
New York, NY 10021

Public Relations Quarterly
44 West Market Street
Rhinebeck, NY 12572

Public Relations Review
Foundation for Public Relations
Research & Education
Communication Research
Associates, Inc.
7338 Baltimore Boulevard, Suite
101A
College Park, MD 20740

*The Corporate Communications
Report*
Corpcom Services, Inc.
112 East 31st Street
New York, NY 10016

*The Journal of Business Com-
munication*
American Business Communication Association
911 South Sixth Street
University of Illinois
Champaign, IL 61820

The Ragan Report
Lawrence Ragan Communications
Inc.
407 South Dearborn Street
Chicago, IL 60605

Graphic Design and Photography

American Photographer
111 Eighth Avenue
New York, NY 10011

Art Direction
19 West 44th Street
New York, NY 10036

Communication Arts Magazine
Coyne & Blanchard, Inc.
410 Sherman Avenue
P.O. Box 10300
Palo Alto, CA 94303

Design Commentary
Britt Stewart Communication
Designs
Suite 222, 3166 Maple Drive N.E.
Atlanta, GA 30305

Graphics Today
25 West 45th Street
New York, NY 10036

Impact
203 North Wabash Avenue, Suite
1804
Chicago, IL 60601

Industrial Photography
United Business Publications, Inc.
750 Third Avenue
New York, NY 10017

Photography
United Business Publications, Inc.
475 Park Avenue
New York, NY 10016

Photomethods
Ziff-Davis Publishing Co.
1 Park Avenue
New York, NY 10016

Print
355 Lexington Avenue
New York, NY 10017

The Editorial Eye
Editorial Experts, Inc.
5905 Pratt Street
Alexandria, VA 22310

U & lc
216 East 45th Street
New York, NY 10017

Association Communication

Association & Society Manager
Barrington Publications Inc.
825 South Barrington Avenue
Los Angeles, CA 90049

Association Management
American Society of Association
    Executives
1575 Eye Street N.W.
Washington, DC 20005

Association Trends
Martineau Corp.
7204 Clarendon Road
Washington, DC 20014

Editors' News
American Society of Association
    Executives
1575 Eye Street N.W.
Washington, DC 20005

Miscellaneous

Administrative Management
Geyer-McAllister Publications,
    Inc.
51 Madison Avenue
New York, NY 10010

Audio-Visual Communications
United Business Publications, Inc.
475 Park Avenue South
New York, NY 10016

Business Notebook
P.O. Box 4111
Grand Central Station
New York, NY 10017

Business Screen
Harcourt Brace Jovanovich
757 Third Avenue
New York, NY 10017

Folio
125 Elm Street
P.O. Box 697
New Canaan, CT 06840

Harvard Business Review
Harvard University Graduate
    School of Business Adminis-
    tration
Boston, MA 02163

Labor Law Journal
Commerce Clearinghouse
4025 West Peterson Avenue
Chicago, IL 60646

Management Review
American Management
    Association
Trudeau Road
Saranac Lake, NY 12983

Marketing Communications
United Business Publications, Inc.
475 Park Avenue
New York, NY 10016

Meetings & Convention Planning
Meetings & Conventions
Ziff-Davis Publishing Co.
One Park Avenue
New York, NY 10010

Personnel Administrator
American Society for Personnel
    Administration
30 Park Drive
Berea, OH 44017

Personnel Journal
A. C. Croft Inc.
866 West 18th Street
Costa Mesa, CA 92627

Successful Meetings
Bill Communications Inc.
1422 Chestnut Street
Philadelphia, PA 19102

Video News
Phillips Publishing
8401 Connecticut Avenue
Washington, DC 20015

Some IABC Gold Quill Award Winners

The Gold Quill award of the International Association of Business Communicators cites superior achievement and innovation in organizational communication. These recent recipients, who won the awards on behalf of the organizations and departments listed, are excellent sources of additional information about business and organizational communication.

Design

Magazines

Margi A. Schulz
Margi Schulz Design, Inc.
2500 Wilshire Boulevard
Suite 900
Los Angeles, CA 90057

Charles E. Petty
Singer Co.
30 Rockefeller Plaza
New York, NY 10020

Claudia B. Flisi
American Express
125 Broad Street
New York, NY 10004

James F. Ellis
Texas Gas Transmission Corp.
P.O. Box 1160
Owensboro, KY 42301

Nicolas Sidjakov, for Foremost-McKesson, Inc.
Crocker Plaza
1 Post Street
San Francisco, CA 94104

Donald L. Dunnington
National Alliance of Businessmen
1730 K Street, NW
Washington, DC 20006

Michael Tripoli
Winston Gifford
Harriet Blickenstaff
Ralston Purina Co.
Checkerboard Square
St. Louis, MO 63188

Ralph Shiftlet
Jim Brooks
Hughes Aircraft Co.
Building 100 MS C-680
P.O. Box 90515
Los Angeles, CA 90009

Jack Sherin
Sherin & Matejka Inc.
800 Second Avenue
New York, NY 10017

Alexander C. Suczek
Ceco Publishing Co.
30400 Van Dyke
Warren, MI 48093

Nicolas Sidjakov, for Crown Zel-
    lerbach
One Bush Street
San Francisco, CA 94119

Newspapers, Magapapers, Newsletters

Treva M. Davis
New York Life Insurance Co.
51 Madison Avenue
New York, NY 10010

Lana Oppenheim
Iowa State Education Assn.
4025 Tonawanda Drive
Des Moines, IA 50312

Andrew Molnar
George Watson
Ceco Publishing Co.
30400 Van Dyke Avenue
Warren, MI 48093

MTA Publications Div.
Massachusetts Teachers Assn.
20 Ashburton Place
Boston, MA 02108

Alfred Chiesa
Mobil Oil Corp.
150 East 42nd Street
New York, NY 10017

Irene Hannon
Anheuser-Busch
721 Pestalozzi
St. Louis, MO 62118

Lee C. Bright
Eastern Airlines
Bldg. 16, Room 118
Miami International Airport
Miami, FL 33148

Joseph Maranto
Mobil Oil Corp.
150 East 42nd Street
New York, NY 10017

Walter Giersbach
Dun & Bradstreet Corp.
299 Park Avenue
New York, NY 10017

Jack Sherin
Sherin & Matejka Inc.
800 Second Avenue
New York, NY 10017

Patricia Wilson
Patricia O'Brien
Exxon Company, USA
Box 2180
Houston, TX 77001

Walter Greenwood
Pacific Northwest Bell
1600 Bell Plaza
Seattle, WA 98191

W. F. Taft
Southern Company Services
P.O. Box 720071
Atlanta, GA 30346

Special Publications, Print Media and Annual Reports

Andrew Molnar
Ceco Publishing Co.
30400 Van Dyke Avenue
Warren, MI 48093

Russ Tatro
Pepsi-Cola Co.
Anderson Hill Road
Purchase, NY 10577

Charles Wills
RJ Reynolds Industries Inc.
World Headquarters
Reynolds Boulevard
Winston-Salem, NC 27102

Susan Dornblaser
Parker Drilling Co.
8 East Third Street
Tulsa, OK 74103

Joel Sarrett
Paul Broadhead & Associates
2212 B Street
Meridian, MS 39301

Peter Allan
RJ Reynolds Industries Inc.
RJR World Headquarters
Winston-Salem, NC 27102

Joe Williams
TRW Reda Pump Div.
P.O. Box 1181
Bartlesville, OK 74003

Connie Eckard
Getty Refining & Marketing Co.
P.O. Box 1650
Tulsa, OK 74102

Lee Heidel
RJ Reynolds Industries Inc.
World Headquarters
Reynolds Boulevard
Winston-Salem, NC 27102

Sam Smart
Smart & Associates Ltd.
Toronto, Ont. M5A 2Y8

Ronald S. Humiston
Anheuser-Busch Cos. Inc.
721 Pestalozzi Street
St. Louis, MO 63118

Shayna Loeffler
Walter Young
Sweetheart Plastics, Inc.
1 Burlington Avenue
Wilmington, MA 01887

William Schechter
Public Relations Department
Avis, Inc.
1114 Avenue of the Americas
New York, NY 10036

Newspapers/Magapapers/Newsletters

Candace Pearson
Southern California Gas Co.
P.O. Box 3249 T/A
Los Angeles, CA 90051

Kathleen M. Law
Alcan Smelters and Chemicals
    Ltd.
Box 1800
Kitimat, B.C. V8C 2H2

Betty Lynn Sprinkle
Baylor College of Medicine
Texas Medical Center
Houston, TX 77030

Patricia Groer
Mountain Bell
1005 17th Street
Denver, CO 80202

Hugh E. Flaherty
The Pittston Company
One Pickwick Plaza
Greenwich, CT 06830

Susan Curry
Hermann Hospital
1203 Ross Sterling Boulevard
Houston, TX 77030

Alma Flocke
New England Telephone
185 Franklin Street, Room 1607
Boston, MA 02110

Jon Healy
SCM Corporation
299 Park Ave.
New York, NY 10017

Ben Wheatley
Conoco Chemicals Co.
Suite 2136
P.O. Box 2197
Houston, TX 77001

Al Repato
Pacific Telephone
140 New Montgomery, Room 628
San Francisco, CA 94105

Ken Estes
Atlantic Richfield Co.
515 South Flower
Los Angeles, CA 90071

Roland Russow
Miami Valley Hospital
One Wyoming Street
Dayton, OH 45459

Sue Schoeff
Rainier National Bank
P.O. Box 3966
Seattle, WA 98124

Jerry Singer
Burger King Corporation
P.O. Box 520783 (MS 1441)
Miami, FL 33152

Susan C. Richards
Continental Bank
231 South LaSalle Street
Chicago, IL 60693

Jack Sherin
Sherin & Matejka Inc.
800 Second Avenue
New York, NY 10017

Stephen Coury
US Jaycees
P.O. Box 7
Tulsa, OK 74121

Bruce Reisman
Long Island Public Relations
New York Telephone Company
100 Garden City Plaza, Room 203
Garden City, NY 11530

Deborah K. Lewis
Security Pacific Bank
H8-7, Box 2097 T.A.
Los Angeles, CA 90051

John Hines
Anheuser-Busch, Inc.
721 Pestalozzi Street
St. Louis, MO 63118

Michael J. Jenkins
Wyandotte General Hospital
2333 Biddle Avenue
Wyandotte, MI 48192

Leslie Lynch
Gulf Oil Canada Limited
800 Bay Street
Toronto, Ont. M5S 1Y8

Llewellyn Ligocki
Municipality of Metropolitan
  Seattle
821 Second Avenue
Seattle, WA 98104

Marilyn J. Adams
Pacific Northwest Bell Telephone
  Co.
1600 Bell Plaza #3211
Seattle, WA 98191

Deborah Garrett
Patricia Wilson
Exxon Company USA
P.O. Box 2180
Houston, TX 77001

Robert L. Chandler
Methodist Hospital
506 Sixth Street
Brooklyn, NY 11215

Irene Hannon
Anheuser-Busch
721 Pestalozzi Street
St. Louis, MO 63118

Publications Section
Joseph V. Maranto
Mobil Oil Corporation
150 East 42nd Street
New York, NY 10017

Arline Datu Kane
Michael Reese Medical Center
2929 South Ellis Avenue
Chicago, IL 60616

Dorothy Wolf
AT&T Long Lines
Box 3288
San Francisco, CA 94119

Jack Frank
Kathleen Donnelly
Forbes Health System
500 Finley Street
Pittsburgh, PA 15206

Neil Field
Pacific Telephone & Telegraph
  Company
1010 Wilshire Boulevard, Room
  501
Los Angeles, CA 90071

Highlights
Indiana Bell Telephone & Telegraph Company
240 Meridian St.
Indianapolis, IN 46204

Camille Emig
Anheuser-Busch
721 Pestalozzi
St. Louis, MO 63118

Jean Rover
State Accident Insurance Fund
400 High Street, SE
Salem, OR 97312

William M. Powers
The Port of San Diego
P.O. Box 488
San Diego, CA 92112

Annual Reports (including Employee Reports)

Michael Watras
Corporate Graphics Inc.
343 East 30th Street
New York, NY 10016

Dong Kingman Jr.
Marsh & McLennan Co. Inc.
1221 Avenue of the Americas
New York, NY 10020

Russell R. Pate
Hill & Knowlton, Inc.
2500 One Dallas Center
Dallas, TX 75201

John Ziegmann
Baxter + Korge Inc.
8328 Westglen
Houston, TX 77063

David Lock
Lock/Pettersen Ltd.
56 Greek Street
London W1V 5LR England

Mary Ewalt
Mary Jane Muysenberg
Children's Hospital of Michigan
3901 Beaubien
Detroit, MI 48201

David Koonce
Omark Industries
2100 SE Milport Rd.
Portland, OR 97222

Larry Newell
Wisconsin Power & Light
    Company
Box 192
Madison, WI 53701

Jeanette Nelson
Trinity University
715 Stadium Drive
San Antonio, TX 78284

Melissa Brown
Herman Miller Inc.
8500 Byron Road
Zeeland, MI 49464

Graham L. Allen
California Canners & Growers
3100 Ferry Building
San Francisco, CA 94106

Steve Barnhill
Bozell & Jacobs
2000 Two Allen Center
Houston, TX 77002

Lic. Bruno J. Newman
Anderson Clayton & Co. S.A.
Blvd. M. Avila Camacho No. 1
5° Piso
Mexico 10 D.F.

Los Angeles Junior Chamber of
    Commerce
Dave Orman
Marilyn Haese
Atlantic Richfield Co.
515 South Flower
Los Angeles, CA 90071

Phyllis McIntyre
Syntex Corporation
3401 Hillview Avenue
Palo Alto, CA 94304

Barry Nelson
Public Relations Department
Borg-Warner Corporation
200 South Michigan Avenue
Chicago, IL 60604

Patrick H. Bowers
James P. VanEyck
Communication Services
Employers Insurance of Wausau
200 Westwood Drive
Wausau, WI 54401

Christine Ann Craft
Albany General Hospital
1046 West Sixth Avenue
Albany, OR 97321

Susann T. Studz
Peterson, Howell & Heather, Inc.
Box 2174
Hunt Valley, MD 21203

Jeff Lightburn
Harriet Blickenstaff
Ralston Purina Company
Checkerboard Square
St. Louis, MO 63188

Special Communication Programs—All Media

Alan J. Williams
Metropolitan Water District
Box 54153
Los Angeles, CA 90054

John Lomoro
National Museum of Man
Ottawa, Ont. K1A OM8

Publications Division
Public & Emp. Comm. Dept.
US Postal Service
475 L'Enfant Plaza, SW
Washington, DC 20260

Kirk E. Howard
Communications Services
Employers Insurance of Wausau
2000 Westwood Drive
Wausau, WI 54401

Pat Walker
PA Institute of CPAs
1100 Lewis Tower Bldg.
225 South Fifteenth Street
Philadelphia, PA 19102

Elizabeth D. Howe
Sweetheart Plastics, Inc.
1 Burlington Avenue
Wilmington, MA 01887

J. Richard Johnson
Donald P. Durocher
Nat. Bank of Detroit
611 Woodward Avenue
Detroit, MI 48226

Susan Milhoan
Florida Medical Assoc.
801 Riverside Avenue
P.O. Box 2411
Jacksonville, FL 32205

Edward M. Romanoff
Public Affairs
Standard Oil Co.
Cleveland, OH 44115

Alvie L. Smith
Corporate Communications
General Motors Corp.
3044 West Grand Boulevard
Detroit, MI 48202

Communication Auditing and Surveys

Tom Christensen
David F. Felten
Synectics, Inc.
207 Dixie Way North
South Bend, IN 46637

Sunny Spurgeon
Ball Memorial Hospital
2401 University Avenue
Muncie, IN 47303

Sheri Rosen
Shell Oil Company
Box 576
Houston, TX 77001

Alvie L. Smith
Donald A. Weber
General Motors
3044 West Grand Boulevard
Detroit, MI 48202

Roger D'Aprix
Xerox Corporation
Xerox Square
Rochester, NY 14644

Llewellyn Ligocki
Municipality of Metropolitan
   Seattle
821 Second Avenue
Seattle, WA 98104

External Magazines

Bettina Haugaard
Main Lafrentz & Co.
280 Park Avenue
New York, NY 10017

Debra Wierenga
Linda Powell
Herman Miller, Inc.
Zeeland, MI 49464

Janet Laible
Ingalls Mem. Hospital
One Ingalls Drive
Harvey, IL 60426

Doug Fritzsche
Fluor Magazine
333 Michelson Drive
Irvine, CA 92730

David L. Ringler
Foremost McKesson, Inc.
One Post Street
San Francisco, CA 94101

Dave Weiss
Iowa Power & Light
666 Grand/Box 657
Des Moines, IA 50303

Stephen D. Gelineau
Union Hospital
500 Lynnfield Street
Lynn, MA 01904

Alexander Suczek
Ceco Publishing Co.
30400 Van Dyke
Warren, MI 48093

Jane Spangenberg
American Forest Institute
1619 Massachusetts Avenue NW
Washington, DC 20036

Tibor Taraba
R. H. Donnelley Corp.
825 Third Avenue
New York, NY 10022

Susan Pescar
Memorial Hospital Med. Center,
 Long Beach
2801 Atlantic Avenue
Long Beach, CA 90801

Joyce Cole
Publications Staff
WR Grace & Co.
114 Avenue of the Americas
New York, NY 10036

Robert Ostermann
Marathon Oil Co.
539 South Main Street
Findlay, OH 45840

Millie Ward
Arkansas Industrial Development
 Commission
205 State Capitol Building
Little Rock, AR 72201

Robert Danielenko
International Periodical
 Distributors Association
350 Madison Avenue
New York, NY 10017

Jo Hunter
Wachovia Bank
P.O. Box 3099
Winston-Salem, NC 27102

C. Michael Dabney
Cleveland Clinic
9500 Euclid Avenue
Cleveland, OH 44106

United Computing Systems, Inc.
Benita Hoover
2525 Washington
Kansas City, MO 64108

Roger Morris
Public Affairs Department
EI du Pont de Nemours & Com-
 pany
1007 Market Street
Wilmington, DE 19898

Merrilee Gerew
Public Relations
Pacific Health Resources
1423 South Grand Avenue
Los Angeles, CA 90015

JoAnn Lundgren
Metropolitan Water District
Box 54153
Los Angeles, CA 90054

Downs Matthews
Exxon Company, USA
Box 2180
Houston, TX 77001

The Review
Kenneth Bagnell
Imperial Oil Limited
111 St. Clair Avenue West
Toronto, Ont. M5W 1K3

Dan Mullis
Panhandle   Eastern   Pipe   Line
     Company
Box 1642
Houston, TX 77001

Internal Magazines

Lorrie Temple
AT&T Long Lines
Room 3B240
Bedminster, NJ 07921

Joan M. Kampe
Foremost-McKesson, Inc.
One Post Street
San Francisco, CA 94101

Stuart Greenbaum
California District
Attorneys Association
555 Capitol Mall, Ste. 1545
Sacramento, CA 95814

Kenneth Pitt
New Jersey Bell
540 Broad Street, Room 1705
Newark, NJ 07101

Carl Kelly
AT&T Long Lines
Room 3B240
Bedminster, NJ 07921

Beverly Freeman
Transco Companies Inc.
P.O. Box 1396
Houston, TX 77001

Joy Hart
Liquid Paper Corp.
P.O. Box 225909
Dallas, TX 75265

Polli Howard
Future Homemakers of America
2010 Massachusetts Avenue NW
Washington, DC 20036

John Gerstner
Deere & Company
John Deere Road
Moline, IL 61265

C. Anne Prescott
Illinois Bell Tel. Co.
225 West Randolph
Chicago, IL 60606

Harriet Blickenstaff
Ralston Purina Co.
Checkerboard Square
St. Louis, MO 63188

David S. Jones
Texas Real Estate Research Center
Texas A&M University
College Station, TX 77843

Diane C. Creel
CH2M Hill
1500 114th Avenue SE
Bellevue, WA 98004

Graham Allen
California Canners & Growers
3100 Ferry Building
San Francisco, CA 94106

Harriet Blickenstaff
Winston Gifford
Karen Kozal
Ralston Purina Co.
Checkerboard Square
St. Louis, MO 63188

Publications Division
Public & Emp. Comm. Dept.
US Postal Service
475 L'Enfant Plaza, SW
Washington, DC 20260

Rick Moss
Georgia-Pacific Corp.
900 SW Fifth Avenue
Portland, OR 97204

David S. Jones
JoAnn Armke
Texas A&M University
College Station, TX 77840

Linda Hunter
Pennex Ltd.
107 Paramount Road
Winnipeg, Man. R2X 2W6

Linda L. Althar
St. Francis Hospital of Lynwood
3630 Imperial Highway
Lynwood, CA 90262

Publications Section
Joseph V. Maranto
Mobil Oil Corporation
150 East 42nd Street
New York, NY 10017

Kathy Mackay
Levi Strauss Co.
Two Embarcadero Center
San Francisco, CA 94106

Charles E. Petty
The Singer Company
8 Stamford Forum
Stamford, CT 06904

Milt Simpson
Continental Oil Co.
High Ridge Park
Stamford, CT 06904

Special Print Communication

Bulletins and News Sheets

Vicci L. Rodgers
Lynchburg Foundry
Drawer 411
Lynchburg, VA 24505

David O. Weber
Port of Oakland
66 Jack London Square
Oakland, CA 94607

Public Relations Department
J.C. Penney Company
1301 Avenue of the Americas
New York, NY 10019

Don Walsh
Dairyland Power Coop
Box 817
La Crosse, WI 54601

E. Jane Beckwith
St. Francis General Hospital
45th Street off Penn Avenue
Pittsburgh, PA 15201

Public Relations Department
Good Samaritan Hospital and
    Health Center
2222 Philadelphia Drive
Dayton, OH 45406

Employee Handbooks and Benefits Brochures

Nanci A. Healy
Frank B. Hall & Co.
261 Madison Avenue
New York, NY 10016

Karen Bondy
Wells Fargo Bank
Personnel Communications #992
475 Sansome Street
San Francisco, CA 94111

Transco Companies, Inc.
Ethan Hirsh
Box 1396
Houston, TX 77001

Philip Freud
Roy G. Foltz
TPF&C
600 Third Avenue
New York, NY 10016

Ronald Winans
JR Simplot Company
One Capital Center
999 Main Street
Boise, ID 83707

James T. Darcy
Southwest General Hospital
18697 East Bagley Road
Middleburg Heights, OH 44130

Recruiting Brochures

Steve Barnhill
Rice University
P.O. Box 1892
Houston, TX 77001

William O. Shearer
James E. Hunter
Communications Res.
Lawrence Livermore Lab.
P.O. Box 808, Mail Code L-447
Livermore, CA 94550

Nancy Rodrigues
Medical Center Hospitals
600 Gresham Drive
Norfolk, VA 23507

Daisy Kramer
Barnes Hospital
Barnes Hospital Plaza
St. Louis, MO 63110

Lester F. Van Dyke
Pennzoil Company
Box 2967
Houston, TX 77001

Corporate Identity Communication

Susan D. Jones
Riggs National Bank
Box 1912
Washington, DC 20074

John Ziegmann
Baxter + Korge, Inc.
8323 Westglen
Houston, TX 77063

Special Events
Jerald M. Yaris
Rockwell Mem. Hospital
2400 North Rockton Avenue
Rockford, IL 61101

Bill Paull
Mica McCutchen
Houston Natural Gas Corporation
Box 1188
Houston, TX 77001

Laura Stein
Albert Einstein Medical Center
York and Tabor Roads
Philadelphia, PA 19141

Sales Promotion Material
Barbara Loveland
Herman Miller Inc.
8500 Byron Road
Zeeland, MI 49464

Montgomery Area
Chamber of Commerce
P.O. Box 69
Montgomery, AL 26101

Marilyn Smith
Carnation Company
5045 Wilshire Boulevard
Los Angeles, CA 90036

Other
Ann M. Kelchburg
Continental Corporation
80 Maiden Lane
New York, NY 10038

Douglas G. Evans
BC Forest Products
1050 W. Pender
Vancouver, BC V6E 2X3

Jeff Lightburn
Harriet Blickenstaff
Ralston Purina Company
Checkerboard Square
St. Louis, MO 63188

Harold Bordwell
IBM
555 Bailey Avenue
San Jose, CA 95150

Jeanne Klemm
Credit Union Executives Society
6320 Monona Drive
Suite 300
Madison, WI 53716

Susan P. Krough
Palmquist Creative Services
1300 South Green Bay Road
Racine, WI 53405

Timothy L. Bigelow
Booz-Allen & Hamilton
245 Park Avenue
New York, NY 10017

Public Relations Department
Newport News Shipbuilding
4101 Washington Avenue
Newport News, VA 23607

Ceco Publishing Co.
30400 Van Dyke Avenue
Warren, MI 48093

Gary J. Osland
AT&T
195 Broadway, Room 418B
New York, NY 10007

Irene Hannon
Anheuser-Busch Cos. Inc.
721 Pestalozzi Street
St. Louis, MO 63118

Peter F. Gross
T.B. Wood's Sons Company
440 North Fifth Avenue
Chambersburg, PA 17201

Lester F. Van Dyke
Pennzoil
Box 2967
Houston, TX 77001

Special Visual Communication

Displays and Bulletin Boards

Randy Braaksma
Terry Vande Water
Herman Miller, Inc.
8500 Byron Road
Zeeland, MI 49464

Exhibit Group
Southern New England Telephone
   Co.
227 Church Street
New Haven, CT 06506

Laurie Himmelman
Varian Associates
611 Hansen Way
Palo Alto, CA 94303

Nicholas G. Biro
Holiday Inns, Inc.
3742 Lamar Street
Memphis, TN 38195

Lee Hill
Lawrence Livermore Laboratory
Box 808
Livermore, CA 94550

Case Information Center
JI Case Company
700 State Street
Racine, WI 53404

Posters and Other Special Visual Projects

Jeanne O'Neill
US Postal Service
475 L'Enfant Plaza SW
Washington, DC 20260

Craig Westover
Adhouse Corporation
1275 University Avenue
St. Paul, MN 55104

Peter Allan
RJ Reynolds Industries Inc.
RJR World Headquarters
Winston-Salem, NC 27102

Barry Lachter
Louisiana-Pacific Corp.
1300 SW Fifth Avenue
Portland, OR 97201

Jane McCallum
Arkansas Industrial Development
   Commission
205 State Capitol
Little Rock, AR 72201

Publications Staff
Lighting Business Group
General Electric
1644.01 Nela Park
East Cleveland, OH 44112

J.A.C. Struthers & Associates
3100 Dewdney Avenue
Regina, Sask, S4T OY4

Jan Collier
Fluor Corporation
3333 Michelson Drive
Irvine, CA 92730

Graphics Prod. Div.
Public & Emp. Comm.
US Postal Service
475 L'Enfant Plaza SW
Washington, DC 20260

Communications Dept.
Martin Marietta
Aerospace—Orlando
P.O. Box 5837, MP101
Orlando, FL 32855

Leatrice H. Higa
Dillingham Corp.
P.O. Box 3468
Honolulu, HI 96801

Debbie Murphy
Lincoln General Hosp.
2300 South 16th Street
Lincoln, NE 68502

Writing—All Media

Editorial Writing

Dave Weiss
Iowa Power & Light
666 Grand/Box 657
Des Moines, IA 50303

J. L. Baird
NJ Bell Telephone
540 Broad Street, Room 1506
Newark, NJ 07101

Gerald L. Wykoff
Association of the Wall and Ceiling
    Industries–International
1711 Connecticut Avenue, NW
Washington, DC 20009

Charles L. Smith, III
Jersey Central Power & Light
    Company
Madison Avenue at Punch Bowl
    Road
Morristown, NJ 07960

Charlotte Taylor
Georgia Power Co.
P.O. Box 4545
Atlanta, GA 30302

John C. Warren
Saint Mary's Hosp.
1216 Second Street, SW
Rochester, MN 55901

Interpretive and Feature Writing, Personality Profiles, and Miscellaneous

David O. Weber
Port of Oakland
66 Jack London Square
Oakland, CA 94607

Martin Szostek
C&P Telephone Co.
800 17th Street NW
Washington, DC 20006

Robert T. Allen
Imperial Oil Ltd.
111 St. Clair Avenue W.
Toronto, Ont. M5W 1K3

Lawrence F. Lindgren
The Kroger Company
1014 Vine Street
Cincinnati, OH 45201

Lester F. Van Dyke
Pennzoil Co.
Box 2967
Houston, TX 77001

William Childress
Ceco Publishing Co.
30400 Van Dyke Avenue
Warren, MI 48093

Sammye Johnson
San Antonio Magazine
P.O. Box 1628
San Antonio, TX 78396

Kathy Mitchell
Georgia Power Co.
P.O. Box 4545
Atlanta, GA 30302

Jean M. Jarvis
AVCO Financial Serv.
620 Newport Center Drive
Newport Beach, CA 92660

A. John Adams
John Adams Associates Inc.
1825 K Street NW
Washington, DC 20006

W. Russel Savage
Southwestern Bell
1010 Pine, Room 1229
St. Louis, MO 63101

The Review
Imperial Oil Limited
111 St. Clair Avenue West
Toronto, Ont. M5W 1K3

Lester Brooks
Exxon Company, USA
Box 2180
Houston, TX 77001

Diny E. Dalby
London Free Press
Employees' Association
P.O. Box 2280
London, Ont. N6A 4G1

Alvie L. Smith
GM Corporation
3044 West Grand Boulevard
Detroit, MI 48202

Gaynell Doehne Adams
Shell Oil Company
Box 2463
Houston, TX 77001

Jerome F. Collins
Public Affairs
The Irvine Company
550 Newport Center Drive
Newport Beach, CA 92663

Robert Cornet
Miller Brewing Co.
P.O. Box 482
Milwaukee, WI 53201

Dick Mendenhall
Bell of Pennsylvania
One Parkway
Philadelphia, PA 19102

Public Relations Department
J. C. Penney Company
1301 Avenue of the Americas
New York, NY 10019

Kenneth L. Gold
Thomas J. Lipton, Inc.
800 Sylvan Avenue
Englewood Cliffs, NJ 07632

C. V. Glines
Air Line Pilots Association
1625 Massachusetts Avenue NW
Washington, DC 20036

Deborah B. Garrett
Exxon USA
P.O. Box 2180
Houston, TX 77001

Jeanne O'Neill
US Postal Service
475 L'Enfant Plaza, SW
Washington, DC 20260

Kathy Hamilton
Kaiser Aluminum & Chemical
   Corp.
300 Lakeside Drive
Oakland, CA 94643

Anthony M. Schettino
Impressions—ABA Industries, Inc.
200 Powerhouse Road
Roslyn Heights, NY 11577

Audiovisuals

Video Programs

Georgia Power Co.
Training Services
#11 LaVista Perimeter Office Park
Tucker, GA 30084

Robert M. Wendlinger
Bank of America
Box 37000
San Francisco, CA 94137

Doug Shryock
AT&T Long Lines
795 Folsom
San Francisco, CA 94107

Jacqueline Hook
Getty Oil Company
3810 Wilshire Boulevard
Los Angeles, CA 90010

Ralph Winter
Broadway Dept. Stores
3380 North Mission Road
Los Angeles, CA 90254

Monica Frakes
General Mills, Inc.
P.O. Box 1113
Minneapolis, MN 55440

Public Affairs Department
Canadian National Railways
935 La Gauchetière Street West
Montreal, PQ H3C 3N4

Michael Keady
AT&T Long Lines
Room 2B-260
Bedminster, NJ 07921

Karen Schwartz
Ohio Bell Telephone Co.
100 Erieview Plaza
Cleveland, OH 44114

Connie Tegge
AT&T Long Lines
Room 2B-260
Bedminster, NJ 07921

Sound-Only Programs

Regen Dennis
John Kvasnosky
Boeing Aerospace
Mail Stop 85-19, P.O. Box 3999
Seattle, WA 98124

Boeing Aerospace Company
James R. Douglas
M/S 85-19 Box 3999
Seattle, WA 98124

Dean Borg
University of Iowa
Hospitals & Clinic
Iowa City, IA 52242

Ron Wilson
Southern Company Services
64 Perimeter Center East
Box 720071
Atlanta, GA 30346

Still Illustration Programs

Corp. News Bureau
Monsanto Company
800 North Lindbergh Blvd.
St. Louis, MO 63166

Joseph G. Lambert
Tupperware Home Parties
P.O. Box 2353
Orlando, FL 32802

Albert B. Wann
C&P Telephone Company of
   Virginia
609 East Grace Street
Richmond, VA 23261

William Kerr-Gray
Hay Associates
229 South 18th Street
Philadelphia, PA 19103

Judith A. Sprankle
Jon H. Wells
Industrial Indemnity Company
255 California Street
San Francisco, CA 94111

Fred Halperin
Hewitt Associates
666 Glenbrook Road
Stamford, CT 06906

Films

Pennsylvania   Power   &   Light
    Company
Two North Ninth Street
Allentown, PA 18101

Phyllis Stephenson
Newport News Shipbuilding
4101 Washington Avenue
Newport News, VA 23607

Otto W. Glade
Exxon Company USA
P.O. Box 2180
Houston, TX 77001

Russell Moser
Centron Films
1621 West 9th Street
Lawrence, KS 66044

Marlys Taege
Bethesda Lutheran Home
700 Hoffman Drive
Watertown, WI 53094

Robert Tribble
US Forest Service
630 Sansome Street, Room 519
San Francisco, CA 94111

Multimedia Programs

Mattel Employee Benefit Changes
TPF&C
600 Third Avenue
New York, NY 10016

Howard Charbeneau
John Walters
Monsanto Res. Corp.
Mound Facility
P.O. Box 32
Miamisburg, OH 45342

Patricia L. Quolke
Equibank N.A.
Oliver Plaza
Pittsburgh, PA 15222

John Ziegmann
Baxter + Korge, Inc.
8323 Westglen
Houston, TX 77063

J. Daniel Hines
Banquet Foods Corporation
100 North Broadway
St. Louis, MO 63102

Michael Palmer
Teleglobe Canada
680 Sherbrooke Street W.
Montreal, PQ H3A 2S4

Ongoing Communication Programs—All Media

*Ongoing Internal Communication
Programs*

Dave Orman
Atlantic Richfield Co.
515 South Flower Street
Los Angeles, CA 90071

Dennis Wigent
Michigan Bell Telephone Com-
    pany
Room No. 1804
1364 Cass Avenue
Detroit, MI 48226

John Otter
Saginaw Steering Gear
3900 Holland
Saginaw, MI 48605

Loretta Harriss
John DeSilva
AT&T Long Lines
440 Hamilton Avenue
White Plains, NY 10601

Pat Hogan
Sherin & Matejka, Inc.
800 Second Avenue
New York, NY 10017

Brian Klimkowsky
Juan Penna
P.O. Box 808
Mail Code L-447
Lawrence Livermore Lab.
Livermore, CA 94550

Alvie L. Smith
General Motors
3044 West Grand Boulevard
Detroit, MI 48202

Gene Hill
Phillips Petroleum Company
4-D-4 Phillips Building
Bartlesville, OK 74004

Elaine Michalak
Owens-Corning
Fiberglas Corp.
Fiberglas Tower
Toledo, OH 43659

Francis P. Frost
Dept. of Communications
US Catholic Conference
1312 Massachusetts Avenue NW
Washington, DC 20005

Corporate Communications Dept.
Great-West Life
60 Osborne Street, North
Winnipeg, Man. R3C 3A5

David G. Gosler
General Motors Corp.
11-24 General Motors Building
Detroit, MI 48202

Pamela Jackson
The Sheraton Centre
123 Queen Street W.
Toronto, Ont. M5H 2M9

Roger M. D'Aprix
Information Systems Group
Xerox Corporation
Xerox Square
Rochester, NY 14644

Employee Information Section
Florida Power & Light Company
Box 529100
9250 West Flagler Street
Miami, FL 33152

Robert Neubert
Elaine Jones
Atlantic Richfield Company
515 South Flower Street
Los Angeles, CA 90071

Ongoing External Communication Programs

Kathy A. Scott
Florida Federal Savings & Loan
P.O. Box 1509
St. Petersburg, FL 33731

Hank Smith
Rose Batson
Neal Spelce Assoc.
P.O. Box 1905
Austin, TX 78767

Charles D. Connor
Navy Recruiting Dist.
1220 SW Third Avenue
Portland, OR 97204

Hutchins/Young and Rubicam
For Rochester Gas & Electric
89 East Avenue
Rochester, NY 14649

Joyce Hergenhan
Consolidated Edison Company
4 Irving Place
New York, NY 10003

Ruth F. Hammond
Ontario College of Art
100 McCaul Street
Toronto, Ont. M5T 1W1

Steve Beckham, Scott Grunden,
    Mike Melby
State Accident Insurance Fund
400 High Street SE
Salem, OR 97312

Richard W. Schulze
Harnischfeger Corporation
Box 554
Milwaukee, WI 53201

Helen Vollmer
Mark Schumann
Glenn, Bozell & Jacobs
One Allen Center, #710
Houston, TX 77002

Doyle Mote
Southern Bell Tel. Co.
288-125 Perimeter Center, West
Atlanta, GA 30346

Thomas   Gorman,   Ann   Tretter,
    Mary Phelan
Aaron D. Cushman & Associates,
    Inc.
130 South Bemiston, #710
St. Louis, MO 63105

Steve Barnhill
Bozell & Jacobs
2000 Two Allen Center
Houston, TX 77002

John E. Guiniven
News Services Dept.
International Paper Co.
220 East 42nd Street, Room 1805
New York, NY 10017

Ronald L. Scott
JI Case Company
700 State Street
Racine, WI 53404

University Publications
Nancy S. Brod, Director
Northern Illinois University
DeKalb, IL 60015

Photography-Illustration—All Media

Karen Kozal
Ralston Purina Co.
Checkerboard Square
St. Louis, MO 63188

Alvie L. Smith
GM Corporation
3044 West Grand Boulevard
Detroit, MI 48202

Joseph Frassetta
Bell of Pennsylvania
One Parkway, 15th Floor
Philadelphia, PA 19120

Dennis E. Harding
Gulf Oil Corp.
P.O. Box 116
Pittsburgh, PA 15230

Candace Pearson
Southern California Gas Company
P.O. Box 3249 T/A
Los Angeles, CA 90051

Kathleen L. Pendleton
Realtors National Marketing
    Institute
430 North Michigan Avenue
Chicago, IL 60611

R. T. Whitman
Kwasha Lipton
429 Sylvan Avenue
Englewood Cliffs, NJ 97632

Joseph Maranto
Mobil Oil Corporation
150 East 42nd Street
New York, NY 10017

J. Worth Wilderson
Tennessee Valley Authority
400 Commerce Avenue
Knoxville, TN 37901

J. Bruce Baumann
Cummins Engine Co., Inc.
1000 Fifth Street
Columbus, IN 47201

Paul Kutz Jr.
Carolina Telephone and Telegraph
    Co.
720 Western Boulevard
Tarboro, NC 27886

W. K. Haynie
Gulf States Utilities Co.
P.O. Box 2951
Beaumont, TX 77704

Joyce Cole
W. R. Grace & Co.
1114 Avenue of the Americas
New York, NY 10036

USF&G Bulletin
USF&G Companies
P.O. Box 1138
Baltimore, MD 21203

Don Stickles
Nabisco, Inc.
E. Hanover, NJ 07936

Public Relations Dept.
J.C. Penney Co., Inc.
1301 Avenue of the Americas
New York, NY 10019

Mario Chavez
Metro Water District
Box 54153
Los Angeles, CA 90054

Tim O'Connor
Deere & Company
John Deere Road
Moline, IL 61265

Chuck Gillies
Peter Parsons
Ceco Publishing Co.
30400 Van Dyke Avenue
Warren, MI 48093

Wayne Burkart
Deere & Company
John Deere Road
Moline, IL 61265

Lon Busch
Ralston Purina Company
Checkerboard Square
St. Louis, MO 63188

Bob Humbert
AT&T Long Lines
Room 3B232
Bedminster, NJ 07921

TEMPO
Touche Ross & Company
1633 Broadway
New York, NY 10019

John Richards
Pennzoil Company
Box 2967
Houston, TX 77001

Rick Anwyl, for
Coyle Publications, Inc.
2 Park Central, Suite 740
1515 Arapahoe
Denver, CO 80202

John Gerstner
Deere & Company
John Deere Road
Moline, IL 61265

Ron Panfilio
Georgia-Pacific Corp.
900 SW Fifth Avenue
Portland, OR 97204

Frank Farah
Georgia-Pacific Corp.
900 SW Fifth Avenue
Portland, OR 97204

John Pilgreen
AT&T Long Lines
Room 3B232
Bedminster, NJ 07921

David Thompson
Crown Zellerbach
One Bush Street
San Francisco, CA 94119

Patrick McCabe
US Postal Service
475 L'Enfant Plaza, SW
Washington, DC 20260

Harriet Blickenstaff
Ralston Purina Company
Checkerboard Square
St. Louis, MO 63188

Wendell Metzen
Exxon Company, USA
Box 2180
Houston, TX 77001

C. Bryan Jones
Pennzoil Company
Box 2967
Houston, TX 77001

Robert Kollar
Tennessee Valley Authority
400 Commerce Avenue
Knoxville, TN 37902

Margie Roe, for Southwest
   Bancshares
4130 Southwest Freeway, Suite
   202
Houston, TX 77027

Ellie Childers
Smith Tool
Box C-19511
Irvine, CA 92713

Marvin J. Wolf
Transamerica Financial Corporation
1150 South Olive Street
Los Angeles, CA 90015

Index